The Passionate Advocate

Anthony Gifford

Wildy, Simmonds & Hill Publishing

The Passionate Advocate

British Library Cataloguing-in-Publication Data:
A catalogue record for this book is available from The British Library

Front cover: Author, Lord Anthony Gifford, with President Joaquim Chissano of Mozambique, addressing 5th FRELIMO Congress, Mozambique, 1989
Permission to reproduce by courtesy of publisher and author(s) passages
i) from Hazel Bennett and Philip Sherlock, *The Story of the Jamaican People* (Kingston: Ian Randle Publishers, 1998)
ii) from Ben Okri, *In Arcadia* (London: Weidenfeld & Nicholson, an imprint of The Orion Publishing Group, 2002)

ISBN 1 898029 88 1

First published in 2007 by

Wildy, Simmonds & Hill Publishing
58 Carey Street, London WC2A 2JF
England

Printed in Singapore

To Tina

and

To the Memory of Ian Ramsay QC

Contents

Part One

Barrister-at-law: England and Northern Ireland

1

BREAKING
the SHELL

How did you become what you are? What led you, son of a Lord, educated at a top British school and university, to be a radical human rights lawyer, citizen and resident of Jamaica, committed to justice for the underdog? People often ask me such questions, for they find my story unusual. I live in the middle of a Black culture and find it the most natural thing in the world. I feel more integrated in Jamaica than in Britain, where for most of my life I have been a rebel. 'The left wing peer' was the usual description of me in the British press, when it was not being openly insulting. I have been called 'Lord Potty' by the *Sun* newspaper and 'Lord Splifford' when I campaigned for the liberalisation of the laws against cannabis. I received hate mail when I led campaigns for African freedom, and when I exposed racism in the British police. 'A traitor to his class' was one description which I adopted with pride.

In Jamaica it is not considered crazy or extreme to stand up for human rights, or to advocate the legalisation of ganja. Jamaicans have been in the forefront of campaigns against apartheid in South Africa and against racism in Britain. In a country which has been painfully shaped by British imperialism, it is something of a badge of honour to have been a rebel against the British ruling class. After a journey which has lasted 66 years so far, I have reached a place where I can be at home. My travels may have been unusual, but they have had a logical direction, and they have been hugely enjoyable.

Any review of a journey through life should begin with parents. Mine were not typical of the class into which they were born. My father had been a naval cadet sent out at the age of sixteen to fight in the First World War at Gallipoli. On his return he went to Cambridge University, where he could not stand the conceited young men who had missed out on the war, for whom life was a privileged party. He had a deep sense of duty and service to others. He always tried to help people solve their problems, and he was adored by his staff at the travel agency and theatre ticket business which he ran. He never expected to be a Lord, inheriting the title from a distant uncle. He was a staunch member of the Conservative party, in the tradition of conservatives who believe that privilege entails responsibilities to those who are worse off than you.

Above all he had a wonderful ability to laugh. Our house resounded with the peals of his laughter at anything which he had found funny during the day. "I got this letter today from a bank", he said one day. "It offered me a loan to be repaid with interest at five per cent per anum." Pause while he repeated "PER A.N.U.M" with the giggles starting to bubble. "I wrote back saying thank you very much for the offer, but I would prefer to pay through the nose." Guffaws followed, which I loved for the joy of seeing him happy as much as for the brilliance of the joke.

My mother had lived the first forty-three years of her life in Australia as one of the daughters of the Allen family, part of Sydney's social elite. She was an expert photographer, a pioneer of ski-ing, a horsewoman and polo player, a breeder of Dalmatians, and a dressmaker, but she did none of these – or anything else – for a living. She met my father when he served as aide de camp to the Governor of New South Wales, but when he left Sydney at the end of his posting she was nearly forty and resigned to being single and childless. Three years later he proposed to her by telephone from London, flew across the world and married her on the day of his arrival. It was a love match and I was the unexpected issue. My mother had to leave her beloved Australia, and she never adjusted happily to being a Lady in London. She found the snobbery of the English intolerable.

So while my parents lived a conventionally privileged life in a comfortable house in the Surrey countryside, they were two unique individuals with core values of decency and kindness, and an unusual sense of boldness and adventure. My father valued his many friends, and my mother kept a vast Christmas card list. We would often be travelling in some remote part of England and my father would say, "let's call on so-and-so", and a link with an old acquaintance would be renewed.

Their ideas on a good education for me were orthodox. Five years at a boarding preparatory school, so that from the age of eight I only saw them on the occasional weekend visits and in the holidays. Five more years at an elite 'public school', Winchester College, where I specialised in Latin and Greek and was cocooned from most aspects of life in the outside world. Six months working as a 'jackaroo', or farm hand, on a cattle station in Australia. Three years at Kings College, Cambridge, one of the most beautiful environments for learning in the world, where I got a first in Classics and switched to a final year studying law. A year at Bar School, cramming the rudiments of English law. At the end of all this, I emerged as a barrister at the age of twenty-two, supposedly well educated, member of a noble profession, qualified to start on a glittering career in law, but in reality feeling deeply ignorant of the wider world.

In retrospect I see it as a pernicious form of education, created for and by the ruling class, designed to produce the arrogant British empire builders who have caused such havoc in the world. When children are at boarding school, the influence of the parents is minimised and the values of the educators hold sway. My mother would complain that she was made to feel like an alien intruder when she visited. The parents cannot deal with the problems of their child, as they may never know what the problems are. Whether it is bullying, or sexual advances from older boys, part of the code is that you do not sneak. You are enclosed in a world in which prefects are given the power to give orders to the younger boys and to beat them if they disobey. You are expected to grin and bear it, and to wait for the day in which you can give orders and administer beatings in your turn.

For thirty years after I left, I never visited Winchester College or any other public school, until in 1988 I accepted an invitation to give a lecture on law reform to the Political Society of Radley School, a boarding school in the Oxfordshire countryside. I gave an analysis of how the legal system failed in many ways to produce justice. The sixteen-year-old president of the Society proposed a vote of thanks at the end. "We who are the inheritors of power in the next generation should take careful note of what Lord Gifford had to say", he said. Such is the elitism which is still to be found at the British public school.

I was not unhappy with my lot, far from it. I was brainy and got good marks, and in the end I enjoyed the poetry of Homer and Virgil, the philosophy of Plato, and the history of Greece and Rome. I kept a cool head and avoided most of the bullying. I had an English teacher who filled me with a passion for Shakespeare. My housemaster had a grass tennis court in his garden and a collection of classical music records in his living room, and he allowed us to take full advantage of both.

Holidays were exciting. Every winter my father through his travel company organised a group skiing holiday in the Swiss Alps. I learned to ski when I was eight years old. To glide at speed over crisp snow, on a sunny day with mountains all around you, still ranks as one of one of my life's most exciting pleasures. In the summer my father loved to tour around Europe, and I learned map-reading skills which have never left me. He had some exciting friends, of whom my favourite was Zlatko Balokovic, a concert violinist from Yugoslavia. When he was to play at the Dubrovnik festival we rented a villa next to his, and the holiday was a heady mixture of exploring the walled city, listening to Mendelssohn's *Violin Concerto* in rehearsal next door, and swimming in the beautiful Adriatic Sea.

In April 1961, just before my twenty-first birthday, I was a witness to two unexpected deaths. I went on a skiing trip with friends to Saas Fee in Switzerland, and for the first time in my life I went on a skiing tour. Normally skiers go uphill in cable cars or ski lifts, but on a ski tour you climb uphill, using seal skins attached to the skis which grip the snow and stop you sliding backwards. Five of us climbed the Alphubel, a 14,000 foot mountain, starting soon after dawn on a glorious day. It was hard going, but at the top we looked over at the Matterhorn on the opposite side of a valley, and at other peaks stretching for miles, and felt the exhilaration of being alive in the midst of such grandeur. Then we took off the seal skins and started the long descent. Five minutes off the top of the mountain I skied across a crusty surface and stopped to wait for the others in the group. Following me was my friend Nicholas, and Robin who I had met on the trip.

There was a sudden "boom!" and a flurry of snow beside me. The crusty surface was the roof of a hidden crevasse, and both Nicholas and Robin had fallen into it and disappeared from view. Nicholas cried out to say that he had landed on a ledge and was not hurt. Robin's voice was never heard again. Guides quickly organised a rescue ladder, and Nicholas was pulled out after an hour, cold but intact. Robin's body was recovered from deep inside the crevasse, and it had to be left on the mountain until next day when a plane could retrieve it. We skied down what would otherwise have been a glorious descent, in total shock and despair.

A week after my return home from Saas Fee I woke one morning to learn that my father had had a sudden coronary during the night, and was dead. He was only 61, and I have missed him ever since, often wondering what he would think of me. But at the time my sense of grief was blunted by the shock of the death of Robin at the start of his adult life. I felt responsible for that death. I had led him across the crevasse, when I should have waited for a guide to show us the way. My father had led a full life and died without pain, and I found it difficult to grieve for him.

My mother showed her indomitable spirit by thanking God for twenty-two years of loving marriage, which she had never expected to have, and she put a serene face to the world. She went on to enjoy over thirty more years of life, and she published her autobiography in Australia at the age of eighty-six.

The Nicholas who so nearly died in the crevasse was Nicholas Phillips, who went on to become Lord Phillips of Worth Matravers, Master of the Rolls and Lord Chief Justice, and a leading exemplar of the progressive tendency in the modern British judiciary.

Before my father died he had enrolled me as a student of the Middle Temple. I cannot claim to have had a burning ambition to be a barrister; I had no idea of what I wanted to do in life, and went along with his wish that I should get a legal qualification. He chose the Middle Temple because his ancestor, the first Lord Gifford, who had been Attorney General and Master of the Rolls in the early nineteenth century, had been a member there.

In 1962 when I was called to the English Bar, I knew that I was not ready to be a barrister. The European Common Market was in its infancy, and I had an urge to spend some time in Europe, whose beauty spots I had visited but whose people I did not know. I spoke reasonably good French, so I enrolled in a summer course in international law in Luxembourg, to be followed by a *stage*, or pupillage, in a law office in Paris.

The course in Luxembourg, attended by students from across Europe and beyond, was a mind-opening experience which revealed for me something of the glorious kaleidoscope of peoples who inhabit this earth. I made friends with Nena from Athens, who remains a close friend to this day. I remember Jef from Belgium who invited us to drive up to meet his family. And I fell seriously in love for the first time, with Khursheed, a law student from Bombay. I owned a two-seater convertible MG Midget, and Khursheed and I had a romantic holiday when we raced down the German autobahns to visit Salzburg and Vienna in Austria.

We returned to England together, as Khursheed was booked on a steamship which would take her back to Bombay. We stayed a few days at my home. My mother greeted Khursheed with her usual graciousness, and when we were alone whispered "Anthony, isn't she a little dark?" I was naively amazed at her comment. I realised that my dear mother had been totally unprepared for her son bringing a dark-brown-skinned girlfriend home. Maybe she had envisioned a pale Anglo-Indian. If I have to explain why the whole concept of labelling and judging people by race and colour has appeared to me to be laughable, contemptible and absurd, the starting point would be my love affair with Khursheed.

We parted on the Liverpool quayside, where we held two ends of a paper streamer which broke as the ship pulled away. It was one of those goodbyes which leave lumps in a young man's throat. She did not quite go out of my life, since unwittingly she played a part in my losing my inheritance. While I was still dreaming about seeing her again, I was introduced to a man called John Marshall. He claimed to have the film rights to Lionel Davidson's *The Rose of Tibet*, which was going to be filmed in the Himalayas. He needed some finance to put the production together and, of course, when that was organised I would have a free trip to India to see the filming. I was the classic sucker, longing to visit my beloved, seduced by the offer of a piece of the action, ready to part with the money which my father had left me. I was almost broke by the time I realised that the film rights contract was bogus and my money had been wasted on women and gambling by a consummate con man.

After three months I had to give up the pupillage in Paris and get a properly paid job. I advertised in the *International Herald Tribune*: "Bilingual barrister seeks employment". I got a job offer from WASIM S.A., a company based in Geneva, owned by a Brazilian, and dealing in coffee and real estate in various parts of the world. I was its legal associate, liaising with its lawyers in Geneva, Rome, London and New York. The work was not that absorbing, and it even landed me in jail for 24 hours, as a punishment for contempt of court in telling a Swiss judge that my boss was out of the country when he was not. I have never lied to a court since then. But working in Geneva was a delight. I took a room in a student lodging in a house across the border in France, and lived a cosmopolitan life for a year and a half. I had friends from France and Switzerland, and (intimately and deliciously) Germany. I acted in performances staged by the Geneva Amateur Dramatic Society. I took trips in my sports car into the mountains and over to Milan and Marseilles. And when a high society American friend of my father came to visit, I met Grace Kelly and David Niven in their villas in the Alps.

The Anthony Gifford who returned to London in the autumn of 1964 was a changed man. I was still undecided about what I wanted to do in life, but I saw my country with new eyes. Just before my return, on a visit to England I had been invited by a friend to see Mozart's *Magic Flute* at Glyndebourne Opera House. The theatre is set in the rolling hills of Sussex, and walking through its gardens during the interval on a summer evening was a dreamy experience – and more than that, for my friend had invited a sparkling, vivacious, dark-haired girl called Kate to be my partner for the evening.

Kate Mundy and I were engaged by Christmas and married in April 1965, with Nicholas Phillips as my best man. Our favourite restaurant was Mon Plaisir in Covent Garden, a little piece of Paris in London. One night in Mon Plaisir Kate said, solemnly, that there was something serious that she had to tell me. All kinds of dreadful possibilities crossed my mind as I asked her what it was. "I'm Jewish," she said with a deep sigh. I was as amazed as when my mother had measured the shade of Khursheed's skin. "So what difference does that make?" I said in bewilderment.

In the first years of our marriage Kate and I pushed each other rapidly leftwards. We moved from being non-political to being staunch activists on the left wing of the Labour Party. I was reacting against Winchester and Cambridge, and the elitism which I had never questioned before. She was reacting against parents who had pushed her into a 'good' school where Jewish girls were excluded from the singing of carols. After working for a time as personal assistant to David Frost, she was already a rebel. Once together as a couple, we ditched most of our old friends, and our rebellion became focused on social change and political action.

During our first year together I still rejected the idea of being a barrister. The Bar looked stuffy and unattractive, the very embodiment of the attitudes which we were busy rejecting. I got a job with my father's travel company, which was pioneering luxury package tours. Kate and I spent a working honeymoon in the Caribbean, prospecting hotels in Antigua, Tobago and Jamaica. The company was also involved in pioneering something called a credit card. If I had any head for business I could have stayed with credit cards and become a millionaire.

In the spring of 1966 I realised that a career in business was not for me, and the profession which my father had pushed me to enter began to look attractive. Law and justice were at the heart of the new politics that Kate and I were learning, and we both decided that I had hesitated about being a barrister for too long. One of my new friends, Robert Swann, had become director of Amnesty International, and Amnesty had supporters among barristers. Robert introduced me to Anthony Lincoln, who specialised in commercial law and libel. He offered me a year's pupillage in his chambers at 2 Hare Court in the Middle Temple. It was the key for me to enter the profession which has become my passion.

My father's death in 1961 had made me a Lord and 6th Baron Gifford of St. Leonard's, in the County of Devon. He was the 5th Baron Gifford. Robert Gifford, the 1st Baron, was the son of a poor Devonshire draper, who got a scholarship to read law at the Middle Temple. He became Solicitor General in 1818, Attorney General in 1820, and Master of the Rolls in 1824, before dying at the age of 47. He served the reactionary government of Lord Liverpool. He prosecuted the Cato Street Conspirators, who attempted to blow up the whole cabinet while they were dining, and Queen Caroline, the persecuted wife of King George IV. Robert Francis Gifford, the 2nd Baron, was only memorable for being a Master of Fox Hounds. Edric Frederick Gifford, the 3rd Baron, fought for the expansion of the British Empire as a Lieutenant in the Ashanti Campaign in Ghana. He was awarded the Victoria Cross for his exploits in subduing the Ashanti people. Edgar Berkeley Gifford, the 4th Baron, was a colonial administrator in Western Australia. Maurice Gifford, his brother and my father's father, was a close associate of Cecil Rhodes and lost his arm in the war against the Matabele in South Africa.

They were all the product of the imperialist Britain which I was coming to hate. I would have been happy to have defended Queen Caroline and the Cato Street conspirators, especially as one of them, William Davidson, was a Black Jamaican who challenged the court to put aside its prejudice. Later in my life I was to visit Ghana and South Africa to show solidarity with the very people whom my ancestors had tried to oppress. The very idea of a hereditary title derived from these forebears was offensive to the socialist ideas which I came to adopt, but I was lumbered with it.

One of the oddities about a hereditary peerage was that peers could not stand for election to the House of Commons, or even vote in general elections. The theory was that since they were already members of the Upper House of Parliament, they did not need to be represented. In 1963 Tony Benn fought a famous legal battle to remain a member of the House of Commons after his father died and he inherited the title of Lord Stansgate. He lost the case but won the cause, since Parliament passed a law which allowed peers to renounce their title if they wished to. Those like me who were already Lords had a year in which to decide; if they did not renounce within the year, they were stuck with it for life.

At the time I was having fun in Geneva, but I paused to reflect on whether I wanted to renounce the title. My instinct then was to keep it and try to use it for good purposes. In later years, when I was fascinated by politics and longed to be able to stand for the House of Commons, I sometimes got annoyed with the immature young man who lost the chance to be rid of the title. But on the whole I have stood by the decision, and I have tried to use the title as a weapon to be used for the benefit of oppressed people. As a member of the House of Lords I had influence which could be used for good. I had a ready-made public platform. I could ask questions in the House, or introduce debates, or propose amendments to Bills, or get access to ministers. Being a Lord carried a cachet, so that my support for a cause indicated that a person of substance was involved in that cause.

Yet I refused to make a career out of membership of the Lords. I could not afford to spend all my days there, and once I had children I was not prepared to spend endless evenings listening to boring debates. My real career was that of a barrister. My membership of the House of Lords was a weapon which I unsheathed on occasions, usually when I felt sufficiently angry to use the platform and denounce some outrage which was going on.

My maiden speech in the House of Lords was delivered on 12th April 1965. I was then an independent, speaking from the cross-benches. I had started as a Conservative, dutifully following in my father's footsteps, and I was soon to join the Labour Party. I spoke in a debate about the reform of the House of Lords. I said that "I abominate the House and I am ashamed that it should be part of the British Parliament." A disgruntled Lord asked, "Why does the noble Lord come here?" (in the House of Lords everyone has to call you a noble Lord, whatever they really think of you). I replied, "Because I hope I can take some part in improving it." I said that I would happily give up my place to see a dynamic modern body in place of this "quaint and slightly ridiculous chamber".

Thirty-four years later my wish was realised. When the House of Lords Act 1999 was passed, by which hereditary peers were excluded from automatic membership, I entered the House for the last time and happily voted myself out of parliamentary existence. By then I was so well known as Lord Gifford (in Britain) or Lord Anthony Gifford (in Jamaica) that it seemed foolish to try and excise it from my identity. I remain a people's Lord, content now that if my clients and those whose causes I support see the title as an advantage, I will use it. I am just as happy to be called Mr Gifford, and I often am. I have tried to carry the name well, and to lend it to causes which my forbears would have shuddered at. I am glad that the flummery of hereditary entitlement has now disappeared from the British political system.

2

PEOPLE'S LAWYERS

For my first three years as a barrister, 1967-70, I shared a room with Anthony Lester, now Lord Lester of Herne Hill and one of the pioneers of the Human Rights Act in Britain. I was rather in awe of him as his credentials as a progressive lawyer seemed so perfect. He had recently returned from being a volunteer with the Civil Rights Movement in Mississippi. He was one of the leaders of the Campaign Against Racial Discrimination (CARD), the first national organisation set up to fight racism in Britain. He was writing a book about racial discrimination and the law, and later became an adviser to the Home Secretary, Roy Jenkins, on race relations legislation. But he was not easy to get close to. My boyish enthusiasm for good causes did not fit easily with his analytical mind. We never became close friends, but I respect him to this day for being among the first lawyers to deal with the racism which then, as now, made a mockery of Britain's claim to be a tolerant nation.

I became a member of CARD, and helped to organise experiments in which Black and White volunteers answered advertisements for jobs. The Black applicant would write in with better qualifications than the White. When the time came for them to be interviewed, it nearly always turned out that the Black applicant would be told that the job was filled, and the White applicant would come later and be offered the job. The experiments revealed the tip of an iceberg of discrimination which was encountered by Black people in housing, in employment, and in the enforcement of the law by the police.

It was the time when community relations councils were being set up around the country to represent the grievances of Black and Asian people.

Kate and I were living in Kensington, one of the most divided boroughs in the country. South Kensington was rich and privileged, while a few blocks away North Kensington was a near ghetto, with substandard housing, high unemployment, poor facilities, and a police force notorious for its abuse of Blacks. Kate and I started married life in the South but moved to the North in a deliberate effort to be closer to the people with whom we felt committed to work. We were founder members of the Kensington Inter-Racial Council.

We were both in an exciting turmoil of self-education. We were learning about racism, learning about colonialism, learning about the war in Vietnam. We were fascinated by the protest movements which sprang up around Europe in the late sixties. We were in many ways appallingly ignorant. We had no basis of theoretical study, unlike many of our friends who were steeped in the writings of Marx and Lenin. But we had enormous enthusiasm, a desire to help wherever we could, and an instinct for justice which helped us to focus on practical remedies. In the autumn of 1966 I went to the Conference of the Labour Party, and was thrilled to find people in the left wing of the party who articulated what I was groping to express. I joined the Labour Party and remained a member until Tony Blair sent British troops into Iraq in defiance of international law.

At first my law practice was a dull mixture of commercial law and road accidents. But it changed when I started to get involved with life in North Kensington. I gave free advice in the evenings at the offices of the local Labour Party. Another free clinic was operated by a solicitor, Peter Kandler, at a local Community Centre. I soon realised that we were living in the midst of massive injustice. It was the era of 'Rachmanism': the word was coined from the name of Peter Rachman, a notorious enforcer who was used by landlords to terrify tenants, persuading them to give up tenancies which were protected by law. The eviction of the tenants would greatly increase the value of the property. Black youth who walked around the streets were commonly arrested on a charge of 'being a suspected person loitering with intent', or 'sus' as it was called. Racial discrimination, domestic violence, unfair dismissals from jobs, sub-standard council housing, were all common themes brought to us 'poor man's lawyers', and we could do little to help.

For although these injustices could in theory be remedied by legal action, there were no lawyers prepared to take the cases. There was a legal aid scheme which allowed people without means to be advised and represented by solicitors, but in North Kensington only one solicitor offered to take cases on legal aid, and she specialised in family law. The other solicitors in the area worked for the businesses and property owners, and considered legal aid cases to be to unprofitable, or too low-class. The Labour Government which had been in power since 1964, had passed a number of laws to protect the weak. The Rent Act gave protection to tenants who were illegally evicted. The Industrial Relations Act gave remedies to those who were dismissed from their employment without good cause. But laws are useless when there are no lawyers who are prepared to stand up for those who need the protection of the law. In North Kensington, landlords and employers could break the law with impunity. The local police stations at Harrow Road and Notting Hill became notorious for the activities of racist officers who planted drugs and harassed young people. The situation was a mockery of justice.

In 1968 a committee of the Society of Labour Lawyers published a pamphlet entitled "Justice For All". Anthony Lester was one of its authors. Drawing on the experience of the neighbourhood law firms which had been created in the United States as part of President Johnson's anti-poverty programme, the authors proposed that a network of neighbourhood law centres be set up in Britain to deal with the unmet need for legal services. Ministers in the Labour Government promised to study the proposal.

Peter Kandler and I decided that we were not prepared to wait for the Government to solve the problems which we saw around us. We decided to start a law centre in North Kensington. It would serve the community by taking on the cases which local solicitors refused. Its priorities would be set by local people. We formed a steering committee of people who represented the main local community organisations. We invited Muir Hunter, a leading Queen's Counsel who lived in the smart part of Kensington, to be Chairman. Charles Wegg-Prosser, a local solicitor who had a keen social conscience, helped us to sell the idea to the Law Society. I was the secretary of the steering committee.

For two years we wrote to every charity we could think of. I well remember Kate, pregnant with our second child, typing up letter after letter appealing for funds. At last two foundations responded, the City Parochial Foundation and the Pilgrim Trust. Between them they offered a grant of £4,000 per year for a three-year pilot programme. This was just enough, and in May 1970 the North Kensington Neighbourhood Law Centre was launched. Muir Hunter secured the blessing of Lord Hailsham, who was Lord Chancellor in the recently elected Conservative Government. Peter Kandler was the Centre's solicitor, armed with a special waiver from the Law Society allowing him to advertise in the community for business. I was Honorary Secretary to a Management Committee representing local interests. It was Britain's first Law Centre, and I am proud to have been a part of its creation. I know that my father would have been proud of me too – his example had always been to find practical ways of solving a problem.

The impact of the Law Centre was immediate. It got the law working in the interests of those whom the law was supposed to protect. Landlords who evicted their tenants in the morning were faced with a court injunction in the afternoon, ordering them to reinstate the tenants by the end of the day, on pain of being committed to prison for contempt of court. The Centre organised a 24-hour service with the help of a panel of volunteer solicitors, so that police officers who arrested a youth at midnight were amazed to receive a visit within the hour from a solicitor who would demand the right to see his or her client, and if appropriate would arrange for bail. The local council, which was landlord to thousands of tenants, was another target. The Centre had the capacity to organise groups of tenants who had a common problem such as disrepair or insanitary conditions. It would commission an expert report from a public health inspector, and threaten to bring a test case if the defects were not put right. The Centre gave meaning to the cliché that no one is above the law.

For three years ours was the only Law Centre, the pioneer, and then the idea caught on. Law Centres were founded in London in Brent, Paddington, Islington, Camden, Stepney and Lambeth, and outside London in Liverpool, Birmingham, Cardiff and Belfast. Today there are 65 centres in Britain, and the idea spread overseas. I have direct knowledge of the Central Australian Aboriginal Law Centre in Alice Springs, and the Kingston Legal Aid Clinic in Jamaica. They are all based on the philosophy that the practice of law involves a responsibility to confront the injustices which are suffered by the poorest in our society.

The experience of founding and helping to organise a Law Centre taught me that radical change in the lives of apparently powerless individuals can be achieved through the intervention of the law. The theory of the law is that all citizens have equal rights and equal access to the courts. In practice those who have money are often greedy, and those who have power are often arrogant. They abuse their dominant position, and they hire expensive lawyers to represent them. They think that they can get away with it. But whether it is a violent husband in the home, or a policeman who frames a suspect, or an employer who exploits his staff, or a 'Rachmanite' landlord who evicts his tenants, the law is capable of reaching them. What is required is that lawyers be willing and able to take these cases.

Just as the practice of medicine should be directed towards the prevention and cure of disease, so the practice of law should be directed towards the prevention and remedying of injustice. This has become a tenet of my work. But my work is not a selfless dedication to duty. I am not a Puritan. Rather I celebrate the excitement, the challenge, the joy when you win, the satisfaction of using your skills to transform someone's life, the human interaction with clients whose rights need to be defended. Being a 'people's lawyer' rather than a business lawyer presents both an intense intellectual challenge – how to find and secure a legal remedy for a human problem – and a learning experience. A human rights lawyer is always learning something new about the human condition.

My new focus on community legal issues clashed with the values of the law chambers in which I continued my practice. I began to get briefs in cases of confrontation between the police and left wing demonstrators, the police and smokers of cannabis, the police and Black youths. One day in 1970, after a particularly idle month when few briefs had come in, I met a solicitor from the progressive firm founded by Benedict Birnberg, who used to brief me a lot. He complained that I was so busy that I was turning away his briefs. I could not believe it. I went straight to the senior clerk in my chambers, the man who was supposed to be nurturing my legal practice. I asked him if he had been turning Birnberg's work away. "Oh yes sir, we felt that you should be doing a better class of work," he said without a hint of apology for not even consulting me before rejecting my briefs. It was time to move on.

By now I had links with the small group of socialists who were then at the English Bar. Many of them were in 'Cloisters', the chambers led by John Platts-Mills QC. John was unique: he had all the appearance of being an English gent, complete with rolled umbrella and bowler hat, but in reality he was a dissident from New Zealand who had been a Member of Parliament in the 1940s on an Independent Labour ticket. He was totally fearless in confronting authority when justice demanded it. He presided over a chambers where radicals were welcomed, and he agreed to take me on as a member of Cloisters.

For four exciting years I was in Cloisters, sharing a room with Stephen Sedley, a supporter of the Communist Party and a barrister with extraordinary legal talent. He had the ability to remould legal norms to meet new situations of injustice. He was supreme in cases about education.

He won cases for pupils, students, teachers and lecturers who had been unfairly expelled or dismissed. I admired him for being both highly principled and intellectually brilliant. He was a mentor to me as no other English lawyer has been. His outstanding merit has been recognised by his appointments - despite his known left-wing views – as High Court judge and Lord Justice of Appeal.

Soon after joining Cloisters I started to take pupils. A pupil is a newly called barrister who for six months may not appear in court but must study with a pupil master or mistress, to whom in those days the pupil had to pay one hundred guineas. It has been a joy to me, and continues to be, to influence the mind of a keen student and to show him or her how I see the vocation of barrister. My first pupil was Dorothy Lightbourne from Jamaica, who is now a Senator in the Jamaican Parliament. My second was Sibghat Kadri from Pakistan, who on his first day after the six months were over was briefed to defend a client accused in the Central Criminal Court (the 'Old Bailey') of conspiracy to smuggle illegal immigrants. I would have been quaking at such a daunting first case. Sibghat was unperturbed and secured an acquittal for his client. He is one of many of my ex-pupils who is now a Queen's Counsel.

My pupils and ex-pupils began to complain that, unless they were able to get a place in Cloisters, they had nowhere to go. In 1974 the Bar remained stultifyingly traditional, not just in social class, with White male Oxford and Cambridge graduates forming the overwhelming majority of barristers, but also in attitude. If you did not fit the traditional mould, your chances of obtaining a seat in chambers were slim. Places in chambers were not advertised, nor obtained through any competitive process. They were given to those who were considered to be congenial by the other members, and to be promising material in the eyes of the clerks. Radicals and idealists were not likely to be recommended, as my experience with my first senior clerk had shown. It was common for chambers of twenty or more males to boast that they had one or two women, as if that was quite enough, and to consider themselves most daring if they had a single Black member.

I said to my pupils that things will surely improve in time. One of them riposted that if people like me did not take a lead in organising things in a different way, how could anything change? One of my most promising pupils, Henry Spooner, had left the Bar and become a probation officer, but promised to return if I started a new chambers. A group of us started to make plans. I was excited at the idea of breaking out of the mould into which barristers were cast. I was convinced that many people who were not toffs in pin-striped suits could be brilliant barristers if they were given the chance. So in 1974 six of us set up chambers outside the Inns of Court in a small office across the river in Lambeth. Three of my ex-pupils – David Watkinson, Andrew Arden and Henry Spooner – were founding members, along with Joanna Dodson and Maggie Rae. Our clerk was Mary Hickson, who had worked in the North Kensington Law Centre. She shared our values and in the way she clerked the chambers she was appreciated as being the very opposite of the traditional Temple clerk.

The essential objective of the new chambers was that we would provide a first class barristers' service, especially to those who were not well represented by the conventional Bar. We let it be known that we would not want to prosecute cases for the police, nor would we act for landlords against tenants or for employers against employees. At one point we were threatened with a disciplinary charge of breaching the 'cab-rank rule'. This is a rule of the Bar which states that a barrister must not refuse a brief in a field in which he or she is competent, provided that a proper professional fee is paid. In its origins the rule derives from a time in which barristers were criticised for defending unpopular clients, and it is an honourable rule which ensures that no person will be left undefended. Now it was being used to prevent us from directing our services towards those who most needed them. It was said that if we were experts in, say, housing law, we should not refuse a brief to appear for a landlord.

We prepared a careful line of defence. We had not refused any brief, but had merely made it known that we would prefer not to be offered certain types of case. We drew attention to the fact that the barristers who acted for the rich were entitled to refuse to act for the poor on legal aid because legal aid was not considered to be 'a proper professional fee' by the Bar at that time (a position which has now been reversed). How then was it right to discipline us, who were seeking to act for the very people whom the Bar had left undefended? After a letter written by me along these lines, the threat of disciplinary action never materialised.

We operated the chambers, which became known as the Wellington Street chambers, as a fee-sharing co-operative. Some fields of work were more profitable than others, or were paid more quickly. We felt it wrong that members who worked equally hard should be unequally rewarded. We also wanted to build up a surplus which could be used to pay a decent salary to pupils and new members. We wanted to be no part of a system which made pupils pay a hundred guineas for their training, and which forced them to be penniless for a year or more until their first fees were paid. The surplus also allowed us to pay for maternity and paternity leave for members who had children. We skated close to breaking another rule of the Bar, which is that partnerships are not allowed. If we had been challenged on this, which we were not, we would have argued that a co-operative is a different kind of organisation from a partnership. All barristers' chambers have systems for paying for their overheads. Our system was more equitable, as the fees of the high earners were used to subsidise the pupils and young barristers as they struggled to build a practice.

The fee-sharing system had its problems. There were endless discussions as to what differences in earnings should be permitted. At first we only allowed increments for members who had children. Later we introduced income bands based on experience. Inevitably as the chambers grew, the reality became clear that some members were more talented or more hard-working than others, and were consistently contributing a greater proportion of their earnings to the communal pool. It began to rankle with the more successful members that they had to share equally with those who were failing. In retrospect, I think those of us who were high earners were more idealistic than wise, as there was a strong tendency not to save any money at all during the years of the Wellington Street chambers. The fee-sharing system was never adopted by other chambers, but it was right for its time and it helped a number of members who had no private means to get started at the Bar.

By contrast, our decision to pay a living wage to pupils proved to be brilliantly successful and has always been a source of pride to me. Our first pupil was Barry Macdonald, now a Queen's Counsel in Northern Ireland. Two others, Fara Brown and Carol Davis, now have successful legal careers in Jamaica. James Wood, Adrian Fulford and Ben Emmerson were all Wellington Street pupils who became QCs in England. Adrian, who from the start of his career has been openly gay, is now a judge of the High Court and has been appointed one of the founding judges at the International Criminal Court. Ben is recognised as one of the leading advocates in cases under the Human Rights Act. Today the whole pupillage system has changed, and it is mandatory for all chambers who take pupils to pay them a minimum award of £10,000 per year. Some chambers pay awards of £30,000 or £40,000. The Bar has come a long way from the days of the hundred-guinea pupillage system .

Wellington Street was not the only radical chambers. A group of four young barristers, including my pupil Owen Davies, started a chambers which burgeoned into what is now Garden Court Chambers, with over 100 barristers including some of the best human rights lawyers in the country. Michael Mansfield started Tooks Court Chambers which now has over 60 members. Helena Kennedy and Geoffrey Robertson founded the Doughty Street Chambers. Sibghat Kadri led his own chambers from an early stage. Len Woodley became head of chambers at 8 Kings Bench Walk and moulded it into a significant multiracial team. We were part of a tide of change which swept over the Bar in the 1970s and 1980s, turning it from a stuffy and arrogant elite into a broad-based profession which now includes hundreds of barristers who are ready and able to fight for the under-privileged.

Our new chambers was also the first to be set up outside the Inns of Court. The Inns are a series of ancient courtyards and squares, lit by gas lamps, interspersed with gardens, containing the offices (chambers) of barristers. Each of the four Inns has an imposing dining hall and a fine legal library. The atmosphere is like an Oxford college, beautiful, exclusive and intimidating to the outsider. For us it was an important statement of our difference that we should set up our chambers in a normal street. We checked the rules and found that there was nothing to prevent a group of barristers from setting up chambers outside the Inns. I wrote to the Chairman of the Bar to ask for his support for the venture, arguing that the Inns were overcrowded and chambers in new areas should be encouraged. His reply was not encouraging: "There is no rule to prevent you, but the Bar Council intends to consider whether to make one." We went ahead, and today there are dozens of chambers in London outside the precincts of the Inns.

For two years we were in Lambeth. We worked closely with the local law centre, and had plans to be a neighbourhood chambers for the people of South London. But that did not work. Our skills were in demand from solicitors' firms and law centres all over London and beyond, and we decided that we ought to be in a central location – but not in the Inns. The Chairman of the Bar tried again to discourage what he must have felt to be a worrying precedent. He asked whether I would accept chambers in the Inns if some rooms were offered to me. I thanked him and declined. In 1976 we moved to Wellington Street, Covent Garden, reasonably close to the main law courts but in delightfully un-Temple-like surroundings. It was just after the flower and fruit markets had moved away, but before Covent Garden became trendy. Our numbers grew from the founding six to a high point of 25 in the mid-eighties.

My own work ranged over housing, employment, criminal law and administrative law, and occasionally immigration and family law. My colleagues were working with law centres and community solicitors in all these fields, and they specialised more than I did. My original pupillage in commercial chambers had encouraged me to believe that nothing was too complex or difficult. If advocacy was needed, we were there to provide it. Our members were frequent contributors to the *Legal Action Bulletin*, which was required reading for the growing numbers of solicitors working in law centres and legal aid firms. Andrew Arden became a leading expert in housing law within a few years of our founding. Joanna Dodson led a team which specialised in family law and children in care. Robin Allen was strong in employment and discrimination law. All are now leading Queen's Counsel in these fields.

The fifteen years of the Wellington Street chambers were exhilarating. We knew that we would be viewed as subversives by many in the Bar and in the judiciary. The only way for us to succeed was to be excellent at the job. We had to understand the facts of our clients' cases more deeply, and know the law more thoroughly than the opposition. The test of our effectiveness would not be the colour of our politics but the quality of our arguments and the number of our victories.

Part of our success lay in the simple fact that we took our clients seriously. We checked out what they said to us and found out that they were generally speaking the truth. If a client complained of living in an insanitary tenement with a leaking roof, we not only visited ourselves but asked the judge to view it. I remember appearing in the Bloomsbury and Marylebone County Court against a landlord's barrister who arrogantly scoffed at the allegations of disrepair which I had made against his client. The presiding judge gently rebuked him, saying: "I think you will find that if Lord Gifford has signed this pleading it is likely to be accurate" – a clear signal that lawyers who committed themselves to truth could achieve justice.

One of the chambers' best team efforts happened in 1983 when the Greater London Council led by Ken Livingstone briefed me to advise the Council on the legality of its proposed budget. The Council was planning a massive increase in the rates (local taxes) in order to fund a large number of projects designed to improve the quality of the lives of Londoners. There were projects for abused women, for gay and lesbian organisations, for community theatre and arts, for housing advice, and much more. It was a bold programme which was certain to be opposed bitterly by the Conservatives and probably challenged in the courts. Ken Livingstone had lost one legal battle when his plan to subsidise the underground fares ad been declared illegal, and he did not want to lose again.

I told Ken that he could only succeed if he could show that every individual project had been studied and costed. The Council's committees would have to have evidence of the need for each project, and to balance the importance of meeting the need against the cost which the ratepayers would have to pay. I assigned one barrister to each committee which was considering controversial projects. I chose barristers for each committee who had knowledge of the needs in question – a women's rights expert for the women's committee, and so on. For about a month they worked almost full time with the Council officers, advising on the drafting of the reports which the committees were to approve. Because they understood the aspects of poverty in London which the Council was trying to relieve, their advice was very thorough. At the end I was able to write a legal opinion, saying that although the costs of the programme were high, the needs had been so well articulated that the Council would be legally entitled to vote for the budget. It did so, and there was no legal challenge.

The Wellington Street Chambers was dissolved in 1989 when I decided that I would be practising mainly in Jamaica. The other members did not feel confident of sustaining the chambers in my absence, and they joined other chambers where they continue to excel. Its early demise might indicate that it was a brilliant failure. But by the time it ended, it had helped to change the legal scene out of all recognition. It was no longer unique. It had blazed a trail which others followed, building more permanent structures as they went.

The North Kensington Law Centre and the Wellington Street Chambers were institutions which shaped my growth as a lawyer. They were my personal response to the unjust world which I found around me as a young lawyer. The personal journey merged into a collective journey undertaken by thousands of British lawyers. Some worked in law centres. Some left the law centres and set up private solicitors' practices dedicated to people's rights. The solicitors briefed the growing number of barristers who joined the radical chambers. A trickle of pure water can become a stream, and many streams make a mighty river. British legal practice today has benefited immeasurably from those small but bold steps which a few of us took over 30 years ago.

3

INTO *the* CLIENT'S SKIN

dvocates undertake an awesome responsibility when they
accept a brief to represent a client. They are the champions of
their clients. They are the channel through which their clients'
case is presented to the court. Whether it is civil litigation or
a criminal trial, the clients themselves only speak to the court if they are
called by their advocate to give evidence on oath. (I use the word 'advocate'
to describe any lawyer, whether barrister, solicitor or attorney, who speaks
for his or her client in the courtroom.)

In a civil case it is the advocate who pleads the case in a written claim
or defence, so that it is the advocate's words which are read by the judge
before the case begins. It is the advocate who introduces the case and
explains to the judge what it is all about. It is the advocate who drafts
the written arguments which are increasingly fundamental to the effective
presentation of a case. It is the advocate who challenges the witnesses for
the opposing side and makes the closing speech to the judge.

In civil litigation, the advocate will have been retained because the
client claims to have suffered an injustice which the court should remedy, or
because the client believes that a claim made by someone else is unfounded.
At stake may be the client's job, or the client's home, or the client's right to
be a parent to his or her children. The injustice may be a personal injury
which has scarred the client for life; or a beating which has traumatised the
client's psyche; or an act of racial or gender discrimination which has caused
humiliation or loss of self-respect. Or the client may have been cheated out
of money which is due. Whatever the basis of the claim, the client cries out
for justice. To the client it is so simple. Surely the judge must understand.

The system virtually demands that an aggrieved person must seek justice through the medium of an advocate. The litigant conducting his or her case in person usually loses. Although most judges are courteous and patient with litigants who represent themselves, there is a gap of language and understanding which the litigant in person can rarely cross. The courtroom is like a foreign land. Time and again the litigant in person will say things which the judge will consider to be irrelevant. The litigant in person, when asked to cross-examine a witness for the other party, will start to explain his or her side of the case instead of asking questions, and will be told to stop. It can be a sad spectacle to see a litigant in person floundering before the judge.

In a criminal case the responsibility resting on the advocate is even more awesome. The clients sit in the dock, exposed and often terrified, while people dressed in a strange garb and speaking a strange jargon argue about their case. In Britain it is still obligatory for judges and barristers to wear wigs. In Jamaica the judges wear wigs and red robes, and the attorneys are in black robes with white collar-tabs, like mediaeval clerics. It all adds to the alienation of the client from the proceedings. If the client has said the word 'guilty' when the charge is read out, then that is the only word which he or she will utter. Everything which the client might want to say – why the crime was committed, whether there is any remorse or apology, why there should not be a prison sentence – will usually be said by the advocate. The outcome may affect the client's life for years to come, but the client must remain silent.

I have been in court when two young men pleaded guilty to the same crime. One man's barrister spoke for five minutes, and his client was sent to prison. I spoke for twenty minutes and my client was put on probation. I had tried to find words to describe my client's background, his reasons for the offence, his remorse, and his hopes for the future. I had helped the judge to look beyond the offence and to see the human potential of the criminal. My colleague had treated the case as a routine guilty plea.

If the client pleads not guilty, he or she will have to sit in the dock while the prosecutor explains the facts of the case to the jury (from the prosecution point of view of course), and while a series of witnesses are called. It may be days before the client steps into the witness box, and by then many things will have happened to influence the minds of the jurors. Counsel for the defence will have cross-examined the witnesses, and in doing so will have made known to the jury what the essence of the defence case will be. A cross-examination can be passionate, incisive and compelling, or it can be perfunctory, vague and half-hearted. The burden rests on the advocate. By the time the client reaches the witness box, the case may be half won, or half lost.

It may seem obvious to say that a good advocate must know and understand the client's case in depth. The advocate does not know what happened. The client knows, or at least claims to know. The client has suffered, but the advocate has to explain the suffering to the court. The client may assert that the police were lying, but the advocate has to persuade the jury that they were. The client knows the conditions of his or her life – the poverty, or the bad housing, or the provocation – which may be relevant to the case. The advocate has to make those conditions real to the judge or jury.

In preparing to do that job the advocate faces huge disadvantages. Most times the advocate will not have suffered anything comparable to the suffering of the client. I have spent my whole professional life defending people who are not like me. I am not black, or gay, or female, and I have not been poor. That is not a barrier to my defending those who have been oppressed because of their race, or their sexuality, or their gender, or their poverty. But it does place a heavy burden on me to open my ears and my mind to be educated by my clients about the details of what happened to them and why. For unless I know their reality, I will not be able to represent it to the court.

The decision makers before whom I am appearing, the judges and juries, will often have even less experience than I do of the realities of my client's life. An all-White jury trying a Black defendant may share a number of assumptions and stereotypical ideas about Black people. But these will vary from juror to juror, and will usually not be so ingrained as to be unshakeable. Most people also bring into the jury box a basic sense of decency and fair play. It is the advocate's task not only to have a deep understanding of the client's case, but to be able to put it across to the jury, so that they will move from a prejudiced position ("this looks like another Black mugger") to an open-minded position ("this is a human being who may be innocent"), and finally to the verdict which you want ("I don't think he did it"). This involves a process of humanising the defendant, giving him or her the dignity of really being innocent until proved guilty.

This process of dignification must take place within the advocate's own consciousness before it can possibly be put over to the jury. I recall a superb example of the process in a trial of Asians in Newham in East London, the 'Newham Eight', who were accused of acting as vigilante groups and taking the law into their own hands. Asian children had been attacked by racists on their way from school, and when their elder brothers confronted the racists, they were arrested, not the racists. Helena Kennedy was defending a young Sikh who, after his arrest, had had his turban removed and used as a football by police officers. To convey the humiliation which her client had felt, Helena appealed to the women on the jury to imagine a sexual violation, an assault on a most private part of oneself. She had both understood the depth of the outrage on her client, and found words to give it meaning to the jury.

In 1995 I addressed a conference of the Criminal Lawyers Association of Ontario in Canada. They had invited me to speak on miscarriages of justice, and in particular the Birmingham Six case. The six Irishmen, who had been wrongly convicted of planting bombs in public houses in Birmingham, had recently been released after their third appeal. I had represented Gerry Hunter, one of the six, at the second and third appeals. In order to get the flavour of the conference I sat in on a session which was about dealing with clients. A questioner asked the speaker: "How do you deal with those clients who are real donkeys?" Everyone fell about laughing, and the speaker gave a frivolous answer. Later, when I made my presentation about the Birmingham Six case, I thought about the defence lawyers who had represented them at their first trial. They had done a technically competent job. The transcript showed that they had brought up every allegation which the six had made against the police who forced them to sign confessions. But the six had got the distinct impression that the barristers had not really believed that their clients might be innocent. I wondered aloud in my speech whether those barristers, when they came back to their chambers after meeting their clients, might have said to each other, "How do we deal with these donkeys?" The audience was not amused, but I hope the point was made that you must never stereotype a client.

Many cases are lost because the advocates have simply not reached the point of being able to believe that their clients' instructions might be true. When I was a young barrister I remember sitting in the Birmingham Assize Court and seeing a senior barrister saying to a police officer, rather apologetically, "It is my duty to suggest to you that you beat this man up, did you not?" When the officer denied it, the barrister quickly moved on to another point. The effect on the jury was clear. If the barrister did not believe the client, why should they? One of the achievements of the radical chambers which grew through the 1970s and 1980s was to produce a cadre of barristers who rejected this apologetic approach to police malpractice. It is quite simply unprofessional for a barrister whose client says that he was beaten up by the police, not to put forward those instructions, if they are relevant to the case, with all the conviction of which he or she is capable.

In 1988 the Liverpool 8 Law Centre, which served the Black community of Toxteth, wrote to me and other heads of chambers in London, asking for help. Young people were being convicted and sentenced to prison in large numbers for vague crimes such as 'violent disorder' and 'affray'. The charges were laid after confrontations on street corners between the police and Black youths, in which the police had been at least as violent and as disorderly as the youths. We arranged for two Black barristers, Nigel Fraser from my chambers and Peter Herbert, a leading member of the Society of Black Lawyers, to be briefed in the next trial of this kind. Their impact on the court was electric. They had the knowledge, the ability and the courage to tell the story as their clients had seen it. The White Liverpool jury did not need much persuading that the police could be brutal, once the facts were laid before them with conviction, and the defendants were acquitted.

Months later, when I was chairing an Inquiry into Race Relations in Liverpool, I went to Doncaster prison to interview a man who had been a defendant in two trials on 'violent disorder' charges. The facts of each case were similar. In the first trial, where he was represented by a Liverpool barrister, he was convicted and sentenced to three years imprisonment. In the second, when Fraser and Herbert were the defence barristers, he had been acquitted. He said to me:

> White barristers don't want to go in on racism. They didn't go deep into the truth. They don't know what goes on between police and community. They don't want to believe you. I had witnesses in the first trial, but because of their criminal record I was advised not to have them called. I have never had decent representation in Liverpool – until the other two [Fraser and Herbert]. They went the whole way.

If the advocate has not mastered all the details of the case, the consequences can be serious. In a civil claim, the facts of the case are set down in the particulars of claim, which is drafted by the advocate. Months or years later, the case comes to trial and the client gives evidence. If he or she says something different, or additional, to what was written in the particulars of claim, the other party's advocate will seize on it in cross-examination, and will argue that the client must be embroidering the story. So the advocate has to get the full details on record from the beginning.

Different problems arise in a criminal trial. When the witnesses for the prosecution are cross-examined, the defence advocate has a duty to confront the witness with any points on which the defendant and the witness may disagree. If your client is going to say that the witness did X or said Y, then the advocate must ask the witness: did you do X? Did you say Y? I suggest that you did? The witness then has the chance to agree with the suggestion or deny it. It is called 'putting' the client's case. If your client then gives evidence, and says something different from what you have 'put', or makes an allegation against the witness which you have not 'put', the inevitable comment from the prosecutor and often from the judge is: "Why was that not put?" The jury will then be invited to conclude that the defendant has been making up his story in the witness box. Often the true answer to the question 'Why was that not put?' is that the advocate did not spend enough time with the client to find out what the full story was. In the English system, where a solicitor's clerk may have taken the client's statement, and a barrister appears at trial who may not have met the client before, this happens all too often.

How then can the advocate make sure that he or she has grasped the full reality of the client's case so as to be able to put it across fully and convincingly in court? The answer is that the advocate needs to develop a deep empathy with the client. This means spending time with the client, listening to the client, checking every detail of the client's story, and learning it almost as an actor learns a part. If the matter in issue is a fight, I often re-enact the scene with my client, understanding how each blow was struck and the physical positions which each of the participants assumed. Then in the courtroom I can reproduce with gestures and bodily contortions, if necessary, the scene which my client has described so that it becomes real and believable.

In many cases the issue is not so much what was done but why and with what intention it was done. A judge or jury is often asked to judge what was in a person's mind. Did he intend to cause serious bodily harm? Did he believe that his own life was threatened? If he went along with a group, and one of the group committed the crime, did the client know that the crime was intended? In a case of conspiracy, did he agree to the commission of the crime? These issues of intention, knowledge, and agreement require even more empathy and understanding than simple issues of disputed fact. The answer to the question: 'Did he intend to commit the crime?' often depends on a deeper question: 'What sort of a person is he?'

In 1985 I represented Parmatma Singh Marwaha, the treasurer of the Sikh Youth Association in Leicester. He was accused with two others, Jarnail Singh Ranuana and Sukhwinder Singh Gill, of conspiracy to murder Rajiv Gandhi, the Prime Minister of India. The main evidence for the prosecution was that the three men had been present in a room with two police officers who were pretending to be IRA hit men. The whole conversation was secretly tape-recorded. On the tape the voice of Mr Marwaha could be heard agreeing to a plan whereby the hit men would assassinate Gandhi on a forthcoming visit to London in exchange for a payment of £60,000.

The whole case was based on a deliberate provocation by the British authorities, who were under pressure from the Indian government to do something about Sikh militants in Britain, who were agitating for a separate Sikh state. The Leicester police recruited an Irish informer to tempt Mr Ranuana, a Sikh businessman, by offering to set up a meeting with his 'IRA friends'. Mr Ranuana fell into the trap, and after a first meeting with the 'hit men', he was asked to bring two other community leaders to confirm the deal. That led to the tape-recorded meeting. There was, of course, no danger at any stage to Rajiv Gandhi, and Mr Ranuana would never have got involved with a plot to kill him if he had not been entrapped by the police. But under the law conspiracy – an agreement to commit a crime – can be punished almost as severely as the crime itself. In most conspiracies the agreement has to be inferred from the circumstances. In this one, the agreement was recorded on tape. Shortly before Rajiv Gandhi arrived in Britain, all the 'conspirators' were arrested, and Mrs Thatcher was able to tell Rajiv Gandhi that the British police had foiled a plot to kill him. Good relations between Britain and India were restored.

When I first met Mr Marwaha in Leicester prison, I found a distinguished looking, grey-bearded elder wearing a black turban, in the depths of despair. My instinct was to ask him about himself rather than discuss the details of his case. He began slowly to give me a remarkable history. He came to Britain in the 1960s and worked in the Leicester textile factories. He had joined the Indian Workers Association, which was affiliated to the Transport and General Workers Union. He had organised a number of strikes against the deplorable working conditions in the factories. Eventually he was blacklisted by all the Leicester employers, and had started his own business making jeans. He built up a successful small business. He was active in the Sikh community, but he was not a militant and did not believe in violence.

In a later meeting, when we began to discuss the case, he said that Mr Ranuana had told him about these 'IRA men' who had offered to kill Mr Gandhi, and who wanted to meet the treasurer of the association. Mr Marwaha thought that the men must be confidence tricksters. They were even prepared to do the job on credit, so they could not be serious. But when he reached the meeting, the officers were so convincing that he decided that they must really be the IRA. He was frightened, and decided to pretend to agree to the plan.

In these meetings two vital things had been achieved. First, I had learned that Mr Marwaha had a defence to the charge. To be guilty of conspiracy you have to genuinely agree to commit the crime. If you are only pretending to agree you are not guilty. Secondly, I had learned about Mr Marwaha's background and character. He had been a leader in trade union struggles, and then he had become a successful entrepreneur. To me, and later to the jury, he became an interesting and believable individual, rather than a man with a strange religion and strange headgear who could easily be classified as a fanatic.

When it came to the trial, the defence barristers tried to have the case thrown out as being an abuse of the process of the court. The evidence had been secured as part of an elaborate trick. We were able to expose the deliberate planning of the operation by the authorities, and their motive in wanting to impress Mr Gandhi. But it was then no defence in English law that a crime was procured by an agent provocateur. The judge ruled that the trial should proceed.

Mr Marwaha was a most impressive witness. I made sure that he told the jury all about his background. They acquitted Mr Marwaha and convicted Mr Ranuana and Mr Gill, who received prison sentences of 16 and 14 years. I have no doubt that if I had not been able to clothe Mr Marwaha with dignity and individuality, showing him to be a real person with an admirable history, he too would have been convicted.

Much earlier in my career, a similar approach to a case involving six defendants had cost me dearly. I was defending Aston Bingham-Walker, a young member of a Rastafarian group called the Universal Black People's Improvement Organisation. He had gone to visit another youth group called the Dashiki Organisation, which had a centre near Marylebone railway station in London. While he was there, someone rushed in to say that there was a fight going on at the station. Half a dozen people rushed to see what was going on. The fight turned out to be between a ticket collector and a Black youth who was a member of the Dashiki Organisation. The police came on the scene soon afterwards, and they testified that they saw a crowd of Black youths attacking the ticket collector, and arrested them all.

Mr Bingham-Walker's defence was that he had just arrived on the scene and was merely observing what was happening, and was not part of any attack on the ticket collector. It could well be true; I knew his organisation and I had helped it in its work, and I knew it to be a peaceful group. The difficulty was that the other men who were charged were also saying that they were the last to arrive. There was a real danger that the jury would say that everyone was in it together. So I stressed to the jury that my client was a member of a completely different organisation. He was a peaceful Rastafarian who had merely come to visit. Why should he get involved in this fight? The defence was most successful. My client was acquitted, but all the others were sentenced to three years' imprisonment. They and their friends blamed me for having run a 'divisive' defence. For some years after I was not briefed in a number of important Black community trials, and was told it was because of that case. I maintain that it was my professional duty to Mr Bingham-Walker to present him to the jury as the individual that he was.

As a barrister in the English system, I have deplored the common practice of last minute delivering of briefs. Solicitors often deliver a brief in a serious case to a barrister on the evening before the trial, or the barristers' clerk switches the brief from one barrister to another. It happens because solicitors think that once they have taken a statement from a client and any witnesses, the barrister will read up the case and does not need to see the client ahead of the trial. Or because barristers get double-booked by their clerks, so that often the barrister who was briefed in advance is not free to appear at the trial. From the client's point of view, it must be an agony to meet a strange lawyer for the first time on the day of the trial, and to know that this stranger is going to have to speak in your defence. From the point of view of the barrister, the system encourages him or her to think of the client as 'just another case', rather than as a person with feelings and experiences which may or may not be fully or accurately recorded in the written brief.

My way of dealing with this problem was first, to make a careful note of all the questions which I needed to ask the client before the case started; and secondly, to insist on a period of quiet time in which I could sit with my client and get the answers to the questions, as well as establish some kind of rapport with the person whom I was to represent.

To have an empathy or rapport with a client is not the same as to be a friend. Few of my clients have become my friends. There is always a kind of professional separateness. The client needs you to be excellent at your job, and you are being paid for that purpose. It does not matter whether you like the client. Some clients are intensely dislikeable. What the advocate needs are qualities which are deeper than friendship or liking. They include a deep respect for the human being with whose destiny the advocate becomes engaged; a belief in the potential goodness of every human soul; and an ability to listen to the experiences of others and take them seriously.

The requirement of empathy is hardest to achieve when your client has admitted committing a horrible crime, but it is still essential. I remember a boy of 14 who had battered an elderly woman in the course of robbing her, and left her to die in a closet. He admitted the crime. My task as his advocate was to advise him what he should plead – guilty to manslaughter – and to address the court on the issue of sentence. But there was nothing to be said which would mitigate the crime. The only hope for him would be if he had begun to understand the awfulness of what he had done, and if he could show some resolve to redirect his life and make use of the opportunity for education which he would get in the secure children's home where he would be sent. So the process of representing him turned into a kind of therapy session. After several interviews with him, he had changed from being an angry, closed-up, frightened boy into a young person who had some insight into what he had done and what he could become – for good and for bad.

Priests say that they hate the sin and love the sinner. It is not a cliché, and advocates should practice it also. Nothing which I have said requires the advocate to tolerate criminality or deal in lies. On the contrary, an advocate must be a champion of what is true and right. By listening, understanding, empathising with, learning from and sometimes teaching your clients, you can be a faithful interpreter of their true reality to the judges and juries who have to make decisions about them. If you do it properly, you will be bringing out the best in them in words which are more eloquent than the words which they would use. You will, literally and metaphorically, be doing them justice.

4

JUSTICE *and* TRUTH

In the Jamaican National Anthem there is a line 'Justice, truth be ours forever'. It suggests that justice and truth are linked ideals. I believe that they are. Yet many people are surprised that a lawyer can have a commitment to the truth. In Jamaica the word 'lawyer' is often deliberately pronounced 'liar'. Jokes about grasping and crooked lawyers are common. The most frequently asked question to any lawyer who practises in the criminal courts is: 'How can you defend someone who you know to be guilty?' The unspoken assumption behind the question is that lawyers knowingly deal in lies. People assume that if an advocate is committed to the interests of the client, and if the client has committed the crime, the advocate must become a confidence trickster in order to deceive the jury into believing that the client is innocent. Or they assume that even if the client claims to be innocent, the advocate must somehow 'know' that the client is guilty. These assumptions are wrong.

Let me face the familiar question, 'How can you defend someone who you know to be guilty?' The answer is that I do not. If I know someone to be guilty, I am prevented by the canons of ethics of my profession, and by my conscience, from asserting that he or she is innocent. An advocate has an absolute and solemn duty not to deceive the court. If a client were to tell me that he committed the crime, deliberately and without any excuse, and he wants me to get him off by putting forward a false defence, I must and will refuse. Indeed this happened to me quite recently, when a police officer told me that he had falsified the scene of a crime. He wanted my advice in drafting a statement which would exonerate him. I was unable to help him.

In practice, the issues which face the advocate are far more complex than the familiar question supposes. We need to examine further the assumption that the advocate 'knows' whether the client is guilty or innocent.

Imagine that an advocate is meeting a client for the first time. The client claims to know nothing about the crime. The advocate may have read the evidence which the prosecution intends to rely on. It may be that an eye-witness has claimed to have seen the client commit the crime. But the client says that the eye-witness is lying or mistaken. It may be that the client has signed a written confession. But the client says that he was forced to sign after being threatened or beaten by the police. What is the truth?

The advocate is entitled to press the client hard on the weak points of the case. If the prosecution case is strong, and the client's explanations are weak, the advocate may advise the client that his defence is likely to be rejected by the jury. Faced with that advice the client may change his story. The new story may be much more believable. But it must be the client's story, not a story which the lawyer has told him to tell. Many clients in Jamaica start off by saying that they know nothing about the crime, and then admit that they did strike the victim, but only after they were attacked. The advocate can then work on a plea of self-defence.

I had an experience in England of a client changing his story when I probed him in a prison consultation. He was accused of murdering his brother-in-law. The body had been washed up on the coast, naked and bound in chains. The pathologist who performed the first post-mortem examination had reported that it was the body of a female who had had a hysterectomy. The police checked the fingerprints, and found that they matched the prints of the brother-in-law, who had undergone a complete surgical sex change, including the feminine features which had deceived an experienced pathologist.

The last people to see the brother-in-law alive were my client and his sister. My client had visited his sister and brother-in-law to talk about their daughter, whom my client had virtually adopted. The sister claimed that after my client left, her husband had gone out and never returned. Painstaking detective work by the police revealed that flecks of paint found in my client's car were a scientific match with the paint from the chains. The detectives had located the shop where the chains had been bought, which was close to a mobile phone site, which had transmitted calls from my client's phone shortly after the time of the purchase. Grains of sand from the same car matched the sand from a beach five miles north of where the body was found, and an expert in tidal currents said that the body would have been carried from that beach to the place where the body was found.

My client had for months been denying any knowledge of his brother-in-law's death. I told him that the prosecution had presented a powerful case to show that at least he helped to dispose of the body. He asked me the question which many lawyers dread: "do you want to know the truth?" "Yes," I said. The truth turned out to be that the brother-in-law was an insufferable character who had been aggressive and provocative. He had neglected the little girl, but quarrelled about my client looking after her. He had run at my client, who had pushed him hard against a door. He had fallen violently against a table, fracturing his skull. My client, desperate to cover up what had happened for the sake of his niece, hid the body. The next night he weighted it down with chains, put it on an airbed, and swam with it out to sea, nearly drowning as he tipped it into the depths from which he hoped it would never emerge.

I then knew that he was not guilty of murder, but of manslaughter and illegally disposing of a body. I could see that there was a dramatic family history which provided a lot of mitigating factors in relation to the death. Hiding the body was impossible to justify, and my client felt thoroughly ashamed of it. He pleaded guilty and was sentenced to one year for the manslaughter, and three years for illegally disposing of the body. He was happy with the outcome which he felt to be just. If he had persisted in denying everything he would probably have got life imprisonment for murder.

This was a case of a client owning up to the truth. But what if your client, in spite of overwhelming evidence, insists that he is innocent? Then you have to believe that what he is saying might be true, and try your utmost to persuade the jury to agree. It is not a question of what you personally think about your client's innocence. It is not your business to judge him, and if you did you could be wrong. You simply do not know. All you know is that he claims to be innocent, and he could be right. There have been many well-known cases of people who have appeared to be guilty when they were not, so you cannot dismiss his pleas of innocence as nonsense. Equally there have been many defendants in the criminal courts who have lied to their lawyers, so you cannot assume clients to be innocent just because they say so.

Once you accept the possibility of your client's innocence, you can and must defend him or her with all the passion and skill of which you are capable. You should test the weak spots in the prosecution case; seek out points of doubt and contradiction; and look for objective evidence which supports the case which you are defending. Sometimes as you dig deeper into the case things emerge which point strongly to innocence. Sometimes the opposite happens and it seems increasingly likely that your client may be guilty. Either way, you should express your belief in the possibility of your client's innocence as eloquently as you can. If you do your work well, your client and those who are listening (including the jury) may think that you believe that he or she is in fact innocent. Only you, as a professional, know that you do not know. If you forget that there is also a possibility that your client may be guilty, you may ask rash questions and the whole defence will collapse.

So I recognise that the 'truth' that the client tells me may not be the real truth. Why then do I maintain that I bring to my work a passion for the truth? Because in the end you cannot separate truth and justice. For every client who may have told me lies, there have been many whose honesty has been vindicated by the evidence. A lawyer who has a reputation for integrity may attract some clients who are crooked. He or she will also be retained by innocent people who want the lawyer to get justice done in an honest cause.

In Jamaica it is particularly difficult to 'know' whether a client is innocent or guilty. The resources of the police are overstretched, so that their detective work is often limited and perfunctory. Often there is no forensic evidence apart from a post-mortem examination. The case may depend on a single eye-witness or a confession to the police, and nothing else. Since witnesses do lie, and policemen do use violence to get confessions, in Jamaica as anywhere else, you simply do not know who is right and who is wrong. You just have to take your client's plea of innocence and run with it, and try to validate it with any evidence that is available.

In those circumstances, when you fight a man's case you do not know where your efforts may lead. I did a murder case in Jamaica where the prosecution relied on a thumb print, said to be a perfect match with the accused man's thumb, found on a TV set in a house which had been broken into. The set had been lifted off its stand onto the floor. The householder had disturbed the burglars and had been fatally shot. There was no innocent reason why the client should ever have touched the TV set. The case looked hard to win. The client was poor, and we could not afford to retain a finger print expert for the defence. He swore that he had never been to the house or taken part in any crime there.

I studied the negative with a magnifying glass. I saw that the thumb print had been photographed against the background of a grainy wood surface. I demanded the production of the TV set in court. I noticed that if you lifted up the set, using the handholds on the side, your thumbs would press against the grainy wood surface on the top of the set, in just the position where the print was said to have been located – and your thumbs would then be aligned with the line of the grain. But in the negative the thumb print was at right angles to the grain. Try as I might, I could not lift the TV set in any way which could bring my thumb into the alignment shown in the negative.

I looked again at the negative. I saw that there were uneven angles at the corners, as if someone had been snipping with scissors. When the negative was developed and enlarged, the slivers in the corners became more pronounced. By the time of the trial I felt confident enough to suggest that the negative was taken from a photograph of a thumb print, laid on the surface of the TV and re-photographed. Neither the police photographer nor the fingerprint expert could explain the odd features of the photograph. The jury acquitted the client. They simply could not be sure that he had not been framed by a concocted piece of evidence. Nor could I.

Of course it is possible that my meticulous efforts with the thumbprint helped to get a guilty man acquitted. The family of the victim must have hated me for getting him off. But this is the perpetual conundrum of the criminal justice system. Some who are innocent have been convicted, and some who are guilty have been acquitted. I know of no better way to resolve it other than by the fundamental requirements which the law lays down: that an accused person is presumed to be innocent until proven guilty, and that guilt can only be established if a jury, after a fair trial, is sure of guilt on the basis of reliable evidence put before it. There have been many trials in which I have strained to show that a client is innocent, and I have failed, and in most of those cases I have been ready to accept that the jury got it right.

Many cases do not involve the simple issue 'did he do it?', but complex psychological questions where it is necessary to search for a deeper truth. Take the case of a woman who admits that she struck a blow against a man who was abusing her. He died as a result of the blow, and she has been charged with murder. There are at least six possible outcomes of her case: (1) guilty of murder (she deliberately killed the man without any legal excuse); (2) guilty of manslaughter by reason of provocation (she lost her self-control after he provoked her); (3) guilty of manslaughter by reason of diminished responsibility (she did it, but was suffering from a mental condition, which could be the 'battered woman syndrome', which reduced her responsibility for her acts); (4) guilty of involuntary manslaughter (she meant to hit him but not to do him any serious harm); (5) not guilty because she was acting in self-defence (he attacked her and she acted reasonably to defend herself); (6) not guilty because it was an accident. To do justice to the woman's case may involve the advocate taking a detailed history of all that led to the fatal action; gaining a deep insight into the mind of a person who may have been responding to intolerable pressure; taking advice from a specialist in mental health; and researching the cases decided by the courts, whose judges are constantly developing and refining the law relating to homicide. The practice of law involves unending study, covering both the intellectual content of the law and the psychological make-up of human beings.

Sometimes the search for truth reaches an almost philosophical level, requiring the lawyer to consider whether what was done by the client was a crime at all. In Britain, the Human Rights Act requires that every Act of Parliament must be interpreted in a way which conforms with the fundamental human rights laid down in the European Convention on Human Rights. The Constitutions of Jamaica and other Caribbean countries contain charters of fundamental rights which override any law which Parliament may enact. The rights contained in these documents are not absolute. For example the rights to freedom of speech, freedom of association, freedom of religion, and privacy of the home are all protected; but they may be curtailed to the extent which is prescribed by law and necessary in a democratic society, in the interests of (for example) public health or public order, or to protect the rights of others. But if the law which the client appears to have broken is a law which contravenes a fundamental right, and is not justified in a democratic society, your defence may involve challenging the constitutionality of the law itself, or arguing that it must be re-interpreted so as to conform with fundamental rights. So the simplest case may raise complex and fascinating issues.

In the Supreme Court of Antigua and Barbuda I represented a Rastafarian who was charged with possession of a small amount of ganja (cannabis). He had been on his way to a gathering at which the ganja would be used as a religious sacrament. He argued that the arrest was an unjustifiable restriction on his right to freedom of religious observance. The case raised many questions. Was Rastafari a religion? Was the use of ganja an integral part of religious observance of Rastafari? Were the laws against ganja necessary for the protection of health? Did the use of ganja by Rastafarians interfere with the rights of anyone else? Expert evidence was called by both sides, and I cited cases from Zimbabwe, Canada and the United States. The judge found that Rastafari was a religion, but he was not prepared to say that the law against ganja was unconstitutional. The case showed how a lawyer may have to consider the fundamental values which the law is supposed to uphold; to look beyond the literal truth to find the moral truth of the client's situation.

So far I have considered issues of truth and justice in the criminal law, where truth can be elusive. More than half my practice has been in various fields of civil law, where the search for the truth is more straightforward. A family law case may involve a dispute as to whether children should live with their mother or their father. The advocate will need to go into the family history to discover the truth of the relationship of the children with each parent. In employment cases, where the issue may be whether the dismissal of an employee was fair and reasonable, the full history of the employment relationship and the behaviour of each side may be relevant.

The pursuit of truth sometimes requires that the judge or jury visit, or 'view', the scene of the crime or the place which is at the centre of the dispute. As a young lawyer I would insist on judges viewing the slum properties which my clients were claiming to be insanitary. Once I went on such a view with a judge who used to travel from his mansion in Hampshire to administer justice in the Clerkenwell County Court in north London. We drove through the streets of Islington, passing through depressed areas full of Black people. The judge was wide-eyed. "Are we in Brixton?" he asked, unaware that Brixton was miles away on the other side of the River Thames. When we reached the slum dwelling his eyes were opened still further.

The most remarkable example of a 'view' is to be found in the reports of a case called *Tito v. Waddell*. Tito was one of the leaders of the people of Banaba Island, who had been driven from their homes in the South Pacific and relocated 1600 miles away in Fiji because their island was wanted for the mining of phosphate. The mining operations had reduced the islands to an uninhabitable outcrop of rock, and the islanders sought compensation and the replanting of trees. The plaintiffs argued that the judge had to see the island in order to understand the case, and the judge, Sir Robert Megarry, agreed. The journey from London to the South Pacific and back took eleven days, including two nights on aircraft and two more on boats.

In the quest for the truth, advocates should remember that the evidence of eye-witnesses is highly fallible. Not only do witnesses tell lies, but honest witnesses make mistakes. Human error, coupled with instinctive bias, can cause two or more witnesses who are trying to recall the truth as they saw it, to be in complete contradiction with each other and with the real facts.

The danger of mistake has been recognised in cases of identification, but it is still difficult to persuade a court that witnesses have pointed out the wrong person. In 1987 I handled the appeal of David Avondale, who had been convicted of armed robbery of a bank and sentenced to fifteen years. Two police officers had chased the actual robbers, who were Black, and were asked to look at photographs of known criminals in the police records. "That's him", they cried when they saw the picture of Mr Avondale, who had a minor police record. The jury, having been duly warned by the judge of the danger of mistake, found Mr Avondale guilty.

I was asked to represent Mr. Avondale on his appeal by John Roberts, a Black barrister who founded the first multi-racial chambers in London. John was tall, dark in complexion, and wore distinctive rimless glasses. He acted as my junior counsel. We appeared before Lord Lane, the Lord Chief Justice, and it looked as if we were losing the appeal. I was trying to argue that identification was even more dangerous when people of one race were trying to identify a suspect of another race. The judges were not impressed. Then something which John had told me as we were preparing the case came into my mind. "Indeed my Lords," I said, "my learned junior Mr John Roberts has told me that he has often been mistaken for Clive Lloyd." There was an instant reaction. Lord Lane, who was a keen cricket fan, peered down at John as he sat behind me in his wig. He got the point, and Mr Avondale was set free that day.

I had an experience early in my career of the fallibility of eye-witnesses in recounting not just who did something, but what it was which they did. It was 1968, the year of student protest in many countries. Britain had experienced less upheaval than other countries, until an eruption of student anger broke out at Essex University. It began when the University's Chemistry Society invited a scientist called Dr Inch to give a lecture. Dr Inch worked at a research establishment at Porton Down, which was believed to supply chemical warfare materials to the United States for use in Vietnam. The anti-war protestors at the University, who were numerous, decided to attend the lecture to pose a number of questions to Dr Inch. When he arrived, their attempts to 'ask questions' resulted in pandemonium. Blows were exchanged, and Dr Inch had to be escorted from the room through a milling crowd.

The University authorities were angry that the liberal principles of the University had been violated. They insisted that all views, however unpopular, were entitled to be heard at an institution of learning. So they expelled the three students who they considered to be the ringleaders of the demonstration. This caused an even greater reaction, with students of many political views united in outrage at the victimisation of the three. The University was in a state of rebellion, and the authorities decided to resolve the conflict by setting up an inquiry, before a panel of two members of staff and two students, with an independent lawyer - me - as chairman.

At the first hearing of the inquiry we invited all who had witnessed the scene at the lecture hall to submit written statements. About 70 witnesses responded. Some were demonstrators, some were chemistry students, some were college servants who had been called in to keep order. What the different witnesses claimed to have seen correlated precisely with their views about the demonstration. The demonstrators saw a scene in which the organisers of the meeting had aborted a useful exchange of views. The chemistry students saw threatening behaviour and acts of violence from the demonstrators. The college servants saw a disgraceful scene of indiscipline. They not only had different views, but they 'saw' different things. Everyone interpreted what they saw, and selected what they remembered, according to their attitude to the event.

We handed down a judgment of Solomon, finding that the demonstrators had (contrary to their argument) intended to wreck the meeting, but that (contrary to the authorities' view) there had been no ringleaders. The three students were able to complete their studies. One of them became Lord Triesman, General Secretary of the Labour Party and a Government Minister. Ever since that experience I have tried to look beyond the bias which inevitably affects the evidence of witnesses, to reach nearer to the real truth.

I love to examine pieces of physical evidence such as documents, photographs, forensic evidence and tangible exhibits. This is contemporaneous evidence which does not change with time, like the wood grain on the TV set. I recall doing a case in Birmingham, where the officers of the Serious Crime Squad had a reputation for shady behaviour, which was eventually exposed by an official investigation. The charge was of conspiracy to rob a bank. The main evidence against my client was a confession which he was said to have made to the police in an interview. One officer had asked the questions and another claimed to have written down the answers. The client agreed that he had been questioned, but said that he had answered "no comment" throughout and signed the paper at the end. The document put forward to the jury contained incriminating answers, and no signature. The police said that he had confessed but refused to sign the confession.

The more I looked at the document the more suspicious it appeared. The handwriting was very neat, whereas in an interview of another defendant, recorded by the same officer, his handwriting was scrawled across the page. The text included an answer preceded by the words '(interrupting him)', which read more like the script of a play than a genuine record. If the client had interrupted the interviewer, the recording officer would have hastened to record the words, without pausing to write '(interrupting him)'. I found about ten oddities of this kind in the document, which the officers could not explain. The jury found that the 'confession' was bogus and the client was acquitted. If I had merely asked the jury to believe the client and not the police, the result might have been different. A document can lead you to a truth more accurate than memory could ever recall.

What if there are no documents to help you, and the evidence of your client is in flat contradiction to the evidence led by the prosecution? Then the only way to persuade the judge or jury that your client is telling the truth is to appeal, if you can, to basic common sense and human experience. Time and again in Britain I have defended people who have been the victims of an abuse of power by the police. I have defended protestors who have been hauled into a police van for no good reason. I have defended Black families who have been arrested after an argument in the street. I have defended young men who have been beaten by the police, and then were charged with assaulting the police. In case after case I have heard evidence from police officers to the effect that "the defendant went berserk and jumped on me", or "the defendant struggled violently and I had to restrain him".

It is easy in such cases to believe that your client may well be telling you the truth. Most sensible people do not jump on the police. The police in Britain have been notorious for their prejudice against Black people and left-wing demonstrators. This kind of evidence bears all the hallmarks of a trumped up attempt to justify a wrongful arrest. But how do you get that across to a case-hardened magistrate or an all-White jury?

Sometimes you will win cases like this, and you will feel really elated. Maybe you will have found a fatal contradiction between the evidence of two different officers. Maybe there will be a photograph which supports your client's case, or an injury to your client which the police can not explain. Or you will have an understanding judge or jury who realise that you were talking sense. Sometimes you will lose, and to lose cases like this can be really depressing. But provided you have been faithful to the truth as your client saw it, it will not be your fault. You will have had the courage to speak a truth which the court was not prepared to accept. Win or lose, you will have served the cause of truth and justice.

POLITICAL
Trials

5

In theory the criminal law is divorced from politics. Crimes are committed and the police investigate them as neutral agents of society. Once there is evidence which indicates that a suspect has committed the crime, he or she is charged and brought to trial, where the judge, as an impartial referee, presides fairly over the hearing and testing of the evidence. The jurors convict the accused person if they are sure, on the basis of the evidence, that he or she committed the crime. They are directed to exclude from their minds any prejudice, sympathy or political opinion. It is all meant to be rational and fair, and it often is. To take part in a well conducted trial in front of a decent and reasonable judge and an alert jury can be a joy.

But throughout history, and in my life as a barrister, political considerations and motivations have been introduced into the criminal law system, and often they have poisoned the fountain of justice. When the law is used as a tool of state policy, the system of justice falls into disrepute and people come to disrespect the law. The law must be a bulwark to protect the rights of the people, if necessary against the state, not a tool to be used for the oppression of the people by the state.

The state retains an armoury of laws which it can use to suppress unwelcome views. The crime of 'sedition' is committed when acts are done, or words are spoken or written, which have 'a seditious intent'. The leading criminal law book *Archbold* says that a seditious intent may include

> an intention or tendency to bring into hatred or contempt, or to excite disaffection against the person of, Her Majesty, her heirs or successors, or the government and constitution of the United Kingdom, as by law established,

or either House of Parliament, or the administration of justice, or to excite Her Majesty's subjects to attempt, other then by lawful means, the alteration of any matter in Church or State by law established, or to raise discontent or disaffection among her Majesty's subjects, or to promote feelings of ill-will or hostility between different classes of such subjects.

With the aid of these grandiose words a multitude of subversive activities can be presented as being seditious. It has been said that 'lawful criticism' does not amount to sedition, but one can see how blurred the line might be between what is lawful criticism and what is not. Charges of sedition were often used against radicals in the 19th century, and although there have been no recent cases, the crime has not been abolished.

'Libel' is not only a matter which the individual who is libelled can sue for, but also a crime for which the state can prosecute. It means a statement which is calculated to expose a person to public hatred, contempt or ridicule. 'Blasphemous libel' and 'blasphemy' are indictable offences at common law. They are not relics of history; the magazine *Gay News* and its editor were prosecuted successfully for blasphemous libel in 1977, when the magazine published a poem which was said to impute homosexual feelings to Jesus Christ. 'Incitement to disaffection' is another offence which can threaten free speech. Under the Incitement to Disaffection Act 1934 it is committed by any person who "maliciously and advisedly endeavours to seduce any member of Her Majesty's forces from his duty or allegiance to Her Majesty".

I was involved in the defence of fourteen pacifists who were prosecuted for 'incitement to disaffection' in 1975. They were all members of the British Withdrawal from Northern Ireland Campaign. Their offence had been to hand out a leaflet entitled "Some Information for Discontented Soldiers". The leaflet argued that the British Army's role in Northern Ireland was repressive and immoral, and if soldiers thought so too, they should consider ways of avoiding service there. After sections on conscientious objection, buying oneself out, and discharge on grounds of health, the leaflet invited the soldiers to consider desertion. It was a difficult option and entailed imprisonment or exile; but if a soldier decided to desert, the leaflet provided addresses of supportive organizations in Sweden where he would be given help. The pacifists handed out the leaflets outside military bases and military shows.

The authorities reacted furiously to this campaign. Pat Arrowsmith, one of its prominent members, was jailed for 18 months for distributing the offending document. The sentence did not deter the supporters of the campaign, who continued to distribute the leaflets and were duly arrested and charged. Some defended themselves and some had barristers, including Louis Blom-Cooper and myself.

Our clients showed a spirit of independence and originality which can be very useful in a political trial. At a pretrial meeting in Louis' home in Islington, they asked us if it was really necessary for them to stand up when the judge came into Court. After all, they said, why was he so much more important than anyone else? We urged them not to create a scene. It would be seen as disrespectful if they did not stand when the judge entered and left the court. The clients agreed to think about it.

On the first day of the trial, the judge came in. The fourteen men and women in the dock stood solemnly and bowed to him. An hour later, after the jurors were empanelled, they had to leave the court so that a point of law could be argued in their absence. As soon as the jurors got up to leave, the fourteen stood solemnly and bowed. When the jurors returned, the fourteen stood solemnly and bowed. At the end of a session, when the judge got up to leave, the fourteen stood solemnly and bowed. And so it continued every day, whenever the judge or the jury came in or went out of the court. Judge Neil McKinnon was red-faced and angry, but there was nothing he could do. The principle behind every trial before a jury is that the judge is judge of the law and the jury are the judges of the facts. The same respect was due to both. Our clients had thought about the ceremony of the courtroom and had found in it a deeper truth.

The judge clearly considered that the fourteen had no defence. Our clients had indeed handed out the leaflets, and they did encourage soldiers to consider desertion in certain circumstances. But we looked at the language of the offence, and particularly at the word 'seduce'. We argued that seduction implied the use of underhand and deceitful methods, and that our clients had been open and honest in their leaflet. It was for the jury to decide whether we were right.

The prosecution was led by Michael Coombe, who clearly thought that our clients were public enemies. The defendants included Gwyn Williams, a social worker who ran a legal advice clinic for soldiers, who defended herself brilliantly. She was able in cross-examining the army witnesses to establish that soldiers were woefully ignorant of their rights. I represented Albert Beale, editor of the magazine *Peace News* and a very serious and intellectual pacifist. Also in the dock was a gay poet who had assumed the name 'Tenebris Light', who when asked "how do you plead" said "I plead for peace in a world of war". In addressing the jury he said, in his most camp voice, "I have never tried to seduce a soldier in my life."

After the prosecution had closed its case, Gwyn Williams stood in the dock to introduce her defence. "Members of the jury," she said, "it is my pleasure to tell you that from this point on you are entitled to acquit us at any time if you think that we are not guilty." The judge interrupted: "Miss Williams, you are not allowed to say that." "But isn't what I have said correct?" asked Gwyn. "Yes, but you may not say so," replied the judge. "Oh," said Gwyn, looking directly at the jury, "yet another example of people not being allowed to know their rights." Gwyn Williams faced down Michael Coombe magnificently in cross-examination, and the jury acquitted all fourteen defendants, taking only half an hour to decide after a three month trial. "A sad day for British justice," Michael Coombe was heard to say.

The case illustrates some of the truths about political trials, the most important of which is that only the jury can pronounce a verdict, no matter how guilty the authorities believe the defendants to be. So it has been throughout the history of political trials. Edward Thompson, in his classic history of dissent and resistance in England, *The Making of the English Working Class* (1964), records case after case in which leaders of political movements were prosecuted for sedition and libel and blasphemy, and often acquitted by juries. The great judge Lord Devlin was right in commenting that the first act which a tyrant would perform would be to abolish the right to trial by jury. It is truly, as he said, "the lamp which shows that freedom lives".

It is a privilege for an advocate to be briefed for the defence in a political trial. He or she needs to absorb the outrage of the client at being charged for doing acts which are not morally wrong but which are said to offend against a repressive law. At the same time the arguments which the advocate can use must, if possible, be legally justifiable – like our argument in the pacifists' case about the meaning of 'seduction'.

My next experience of a political trial was as a junior barrister in the 'ABC' trial in 1978, so called after the initials of the defendants Crispin Aubrey, John Berry and Duncan Campbell. I was junior counsel for Crispin Aubrey. Berry was a soldier in the Signals Corps who was concerned about the spying operations of the Government Communications Headquarters (GCHQ). Campbell and Aubrey were journalists who had met Berry and taped an interview with him. They had been followed, and were arrested before anything could be published. They were prosecuted under the Official Secrets Act, under which it was an offence to impart, and to receive, information from a servant of the Crown.

The defence was led by Jeremy Hutchinson QC, a passionate and subtle advocate for human rights. What outraged him was that the three men were being prosecuted under section 1 of the Official Secrets Act, which concerned information useful to an enemy, and allowed for punishment of up to life imprisonment. His client Duncan Campbell, who was a specialist in investigative journalism about security matters, was further charged with an offence of keeping material which might be useful to an enemy. Campbell's defence was that all the information was available to anyone who did some basic research, and it was almost certainly in the possession of any potential enemy already. It was the British public which was kept in the dark. Hutchinson deployed this defence with such brilliance that in the end the charges under Section 1 were dropped, and the three were convicted under a lesser charge and were not imprisoned.

The Official Secrets Act is a law which is necessary in some contexts, as when an agent is leaking information to a hostile country. It can be abused by a secretive state, when it wants to punish those whose conscience moves them to leak information about Government actions which they believe the public ought to know about. In 1984, Foreign Office clerical officer Sarah Tisdall leaked news to the *Guardian* newspaper about the deployment of US Cruise missiles at Greenham Common air base. She pleaded guilty to a breach of the Official Secrets Act and was sentenced to six months imprisonment. A year later Clive Ponting, an assistant secretary at the Ministry of Defence, informed Member of Parliament Tam Dalyell about the deployment of the British navy at the time of the sinking of the Argentinian battleship *General Belgrano* during the Falkland Islands war in 1983. His information tended to show that the battleship was sailing away from the war zone, presenting no danger to the British navy, at the time it was sunk. Ponting's legal team, headed by Bruce Laughland QC, ran the defence that a disclosure to a Member of Parliament could not be an unauthorized disclosure. The judge told the jury that Ponting had no defence in law, but the jury acquitted him. It was another case of the good sense of a jury of twelve people selected at random being stronger than the might of the state.

The Official Secrets Act was revamped in 1989, so that the objectionable section 2 of the old Act, which prohibited disclosure of any information at all, has been repealed. The new provisions still make it an offence for any information relating to security and intelligence to be disclosed. In relation to information about the armed forces or international relations, the disclosure must be 'damaging', a word which is vaguely defined as a disclosure which, among other things, 'endangers the interests of the United Kingdom abroad'. The Act remains a potent weapon for the punishment of those who leak information which the government finds embarrassing.

In combating the use of laws which suppress freedom of speech and other basic rights, defence lawyers now have the weapon of the Human Rights Act. This Act provided that for the first time the European Convention on Human Rights would be directly applicable to cases in the British Courts. Previously, the clear words of a statute, and the decisions of British Courts, took precedence over the Convention, and people had to go to the European Court of Human Rights in Strasbourg to get justice. Under the Human Rights Act, every Act of Parliament ever passed has to be read and given effect to in a way which is compatible with the rights contained in the Convention. The decisions of the European Court have to be followed. Every rule of the old common law, every precedent laid down by judges in the past, has to be modified and if necessary disregarded, if it violates the fundamental rights contained in the Convention.

The Human Rights Act was in my view the most progressive and far-reaching piece of legislation passed by Tony Blair's government. It is right to congratulate Blair, while also recognizing the role of those who campaigned over decades for this legislation, especially my old room-mate Anthony Lester, who as Lord Lester of Herne Hill QC helped in its drafting and pressed for it year after year in the House of Lords. I pay tribute also to the Lord Chancellor, Lord Irvine of Lairg, who in the years before the Act came into force insisted that every judge, from the Lords of Appeal to the lowest magistrate, should be educated about the European Convention and the ways in which it would impinge on their role as judges. My former pupil Ben Emmerson QC played a leading role in the education process.

The effect of the Human Rights Act is felt every day in the British Courts. Articles of the Convention are cited at all levels of the legal system. Article 5 on the right to liberty and security; article 6 on the right to a fair trial; article 8 on the right to respect for private and family life; article 9 on freedom of thought, conscience and religion; article 10 on freedom of expression; and article 11 on freedom of association, have all been relevant in shaping the criminal law in the years since the Act came into force. The Human Rights Act has made it more difficult today for the state to succeed in staging a political trial of the kind described above.

Another kind of political trial occurs when the state is confronted with demonstrations against its policies, and it tries to use the criminal law to punish and deter the protestors. In the course of political protest, clashes with the police can frequently happen. Sometimes clashes are provoked by over-aggressive policing, and sometimes by over-militant protesting. Usually when demonstrators are arrested they are charged with low level offences before the magistrates' court, such as assault, criminal damage, and threatening behaviour. I have taken part in many bitter encounters in court over such cases, sometimes winning and sometimes losing.

There is another level of public order offence to which the authorities sometimes resort. The definition of the offence of 'riot' is that 'wherever twelve or more persons who are present together use or threaten unlawful violence for a common purpose and the conduct of them (taken together) is such as would cause a person of reasonable firmness to fear for his personal safety, each of the persons using unlawful violence for the common purpose is guilty of riot'. The maximum sentence for riot is ten years. The offence of 'violent disorder' is exactly the same, except that it can be charged wherever three or more persons are present, instead of twelve. The maximum sentence for violent disorder is five years. The offence of 'affray' is similar, but it does not require a minimum number of persons to be present. The maximum sentence for affray is three years. Thus if an incident of violence occurs at a demonstration of more than twelve people, the police can lay charges or riot, or violent disorder, or affray, against anyone who they allege took part in the violence. Or they can simply bring a charge of threatening behaviour, for which the maximum sentence is six months. The choice of charge depends not so much on the seriousness of the violence but on the desire of the authorities to crack down on the demonstrators.

My first exposure to a riot trial was in 1970 when students of Cambridge University were charged with 'riot' and 'unlawful assembly' after demonstrating against a dinner hosted by the Garden House Hotel to celebrate a 'Greek Week', at which the Greek Ambassador was guest of honour. It was during the rule of the Greek fascist colonels, and the students were outraged that the University should be honouring their representative. The students chanted slogans outside and at one point entered the hotel. No one was hurt but the dinner was disrupted. The trial was held before Mr Justice Melford Stevenson, a legendary judge of the hard old school. A Cambridge jury, clearly antagonistic to these privileged left wing activists, convicted four of them for riot and three for unlawful assembly, and prison sentences of up to eighteen months were passed. The sentences were upheld on appeal. The authorities in that case were successful in teaching a lesson to the rebels. The words of one of the judges of appeal emphasized the collective guilt attributed by the law to everyone who takes part in a disorderly demonstration:

> On these confused and tumultuous occasions each individual who takes an active part by deed or encouragement is guilty of a really grave offence by being one of the numbers engaged in a crime against the peace.

The same tactics were tried in 1971 against Black community leaders in the 'Mangrove' trial. A demonstration was held in Notting Hill to protest against the harassment by the police of Frank Crichlow, owner of the Mangrove Restaurant. The police considered it to be a Black Power gathering and drafted hundreds of officers to guard the Notting Hill Police Station. Scuffles broke out between some of the demonstrators and the police, and arrests were made for minor offences. Six weeks later, nine activists including writer Darcus Howe were arrested in dawn raids and charged with a panoply of offences including riot and incitement to murder (some home made placards at the demonstration had said 'kill the pigs').

The Mangrove trial lasted for 55 days at the Old Bailey. Darcus Howe wrote later that his solicitor had advised him that if he pleaded guilty he would 'only' get a five year jail sentence. He and others decided to defend themselves. Some barristers, including Len Woodley, were prepared to run a strong defence, arguing in the face of hostility from the judge that this was not a riot but a political prosecution of Black dissenters. The jury acquitted the defendants of all the serious charges, and no one was sent to prison. The Mangrove trial was an inspiration to young lawyers, and to political activists. The courage of the Mangrove Nine and their lawyers taught us that if you can expose the real truth behind an oppressive prosecution, the jury will listen and understand, and you will win.

In 1984 the miners' strike erupted in every coalmining area of Britain, in protest against the closure of mines by the National Coal Board. Prime Minister Margaret Thatcher saw the National Union of Mineworkers as 'the enemy within'. The police were mobilized on a national level to break the picket lines which were set up every day by the striking miners to persuade non-strikers, or 'scabs', not to go to work. Dozens of arrests were made every day in Yorkshire and Nottinghamshire. At first the arrested miners were charged with low level offences such as threatening behaviour. But after several months of the strike, there was a change of policy. Many of those who were arrested found themselves charged with riot and facing the possibility of many years imprisonment.

The first two trials of miners for rioting took place in Sheffield in Yorkshire, the 'Orgreave trial' and the 'Coal House trial'. Fifteen miners were on trial in each case. The Orgreave trial arose out of the demonstration at the Orgreave coking plant, where there had been a massive confrontation between miners and police. It was a high profile trial, as the 'Battle of Orgreave' had been one of the most dramatic events of the year-long strike, with hundreds of mounted and foot police being used to make charges into the crowds of demonstrating miners, in scenes reminiscent of a mediaeval battle. Michael Mansfield was leading the defence team, and he did a magnificent job in exposing the truth that it was the police, overwhelmingly, who had staged a riot.

The Coal House trial arose out of a demonstration at the Yorkshire Headquarters of the National Coal Board, the 'Coal House'. There had been a picket of the building aimed at asking the employees of the Coal Board not to go into work. The employees included a number of women secretaries, who testified that they were put in fear because of the pickets. But the picketing had been peaceful, and the only clashes had occurred when the police tried to break up the picket line.

I had been briefed to defend the fifteen miners accused of rioting at the Coal House. I had picked a team of five junior barristers, and we divided up the work. Over the three months of the trial we developed a deep respect for our clients, and understood the depth of feeling which had motivated them to support the strike. One of them, Terry Lynskey, was a former miner who worked at the Coal House. He has since become a firm friend. He composed a poem about the trial which he presented to the legal team; in the last line of one stanza he managed to work in a translation of the Gifford family motto, *non sine numine.*

> The 'A' team comprises Lord Gifford & Co.,
> They fight for a principle, not just the dough.
> They all like a laugh and a jolly good drink,
> "Not Without God's Assistance" they'll save us from clink!

There was some personal rivalry involved. We heard that Michael Mansfield's team was expecting success for the miners in their case but defeat in ours. But ours was the first to go to the jury, and our jury pronounced fifteen not guilty verdicts. The sound of a not guilty verdict after a long battle in a good cause is one of the sweetest that a passionate advocate can hear. The next day, the prosecution in the Orgreave trial announced that they were giving up, so all the miners went free. It was a deeply satisfying result. We had worked as a team. We had defeated an oppressive prosecution, and we had saved fifteen decent men, who were in no sense criminals, from the jail sentences which the State had wished to see them serve.

So far I have been describing political trials where there has been no crime, at least in a moral sense, committed at all. The law has been used to attempt to criminalize conduct which fellow-citizens, as represented by the jury, have not found to be criminal. There is another kind of political trial, in which a crime has undoubtedly been committed, but the authorities are hell-bent on convicting the wrong people for it. Trials of this nature often occur when society faces some kind of crisis. Norms of justice are swept away because of the eagerness of the authorities to see someone pay for crimes which have outraged the community. One would hope that the justice system would be able to maintain its integrity at times of social and political turbulence, but it does not. Some of Britain's most notorious crimes have led to notorious miscarriages of justice. It is no coincidence that Irish and Black people, the two most generally abused minorities in Britain, have been the main victims.

In November 1974 21 people were killed when bombs were detonated inside public houses in Birmingham. The 'Birmingham Six' were convicted of their murders. It took 17 years, and three appeals, before it was acknowledged that they were wrongly convicted. Later in the same month five people were killed by a pub bombing in Guildford, and two in Woolwich. The Guildford Four were convicted and served 15 years, even though the real bombers were later arrested and confessed to the crimes in graphic detail. In 1985, a police officer was brutally murdered at Broadwater Farm in North London while a 'race riot' was in progress, and he was escorting a unit of the Fire Brigade. Three men were convicted for his murder, but the convictions were overturned four years later. In all of these cases the police officers who investigated the crimes were found, years later, to have forged their police notebooks, so as to invent 'contemporaneous' records of 'confessions' which were never uttered. In all the cases, the conduct of the police during the questioning of the suspected criminals was oppressive, and in the Irish cases brutally violent. I fear, although I am not directly involved, that the current hysteria over Islamic terrorists will lead to similar miscarriages of justice.

My experiences with the Birmingham Six taught me how dedicated and persistent a lawyer may have to be in order to obtain justice for an innocent client in a politically charged case. The Birmingham Six were six Irish men who were travelling from Birmingham to Belfast on the day after the bombings. They were arrested at the port of Heysham, and taken to Morecambe Police Station, where forensic scientist Dr Skuse carried out tests which, he claimed, showed that four of them had recently handled nitro-glycerine. The Birmingham police had then arrived, and subjected the six to prolonged interrogation, in Morecambe and Birmingham, during which it was claimed that all had made oral or written confessions. The six all claimed to have been beaten hard and continuously. Four of them had signed whatever was put in front of them. The other two had signed nothing, but the police in their 'contemporaneous' notes had recorded verbal admissions to the crime. The combination of scientific evidence and the confessions, in the atmosphere of anti-Irish feeling generated by the bombings, had meant that their defence stood little chance before the jury. They were convicted and sentenced to life imprisonment in August 1975. Mr Justice Bridge in passing life sentences said that the six had been convicted "on the clearest and most convincing evidence I have ever heard". If the death penalty had still been lawful in Britain, they would undoubtedly have been hanged within months of their conviction.

My client was Gerry Hunter, and I was briefed to represent him by Ivan Geffen, an indomitable fighter for justice in the West Midlands. Neither of us took part in his original trial or in the first appeal which followed. I was briefed in 1978 by Geffen to bring an action for assault, claiming damages for the injuries which had been inflicted by the police during their 'interrogation'. The lawyers for the West Midlands police argued that it would be an abuse of the process of the court for the action to be allowed to go ahead.

The case came before Lord Denning in the Court of Appeal, who upheld the police's argument. He said:

> If the six men win, it will mean that the police were guilty of perjury, that they were guilty of violence and threats, that the confessions were involuntary and were improperly admitted in evidence and that the convictions were erroneous. That would meant the Home Secretary would either have to recommend they be pardoned, or he would have to remit the case to the Court of Appeal. This is such an appalling vista that every sensible person in the land would say "It cannot be right these actions should go any further." They should be struck out.

In spite of the certainty of the judges, the campaign to free the Birmingham Six continued. Tremendous credit is due to those who refused to forget them, such as solicitors Gareth Pierce and Ivan Geffen, and Member of Parliament Chris Mullin, who actually tracked down and interviewed the two men who had really planted the bombs. The media are a key part of any campaign to remedy a miscarriage of justice, and a team from the *World in Action* television programme put out two films in which they succeeded in debunking the scientific tests which had played such an important role in the convictions. The programme showed that the positive results relied on by Dr Skuse could be obtained after shuffling a pack of cards. The six men had been playing cards for hours on the train to Heysham.

In January 1987 the Home Secretary referred the case back to the Court of Appeal for that court to consider the new material which had come to light. Two former police officers had come forward to testify that they had witnessed assaults on the six at Birmingham. Scientific evidence was called to cast doubt on the findings of Dr Skuse. Most telling of all, a document had been discovered in the handwriting of Superintendent Reade, who had been in charge of the investigation. It was a schedule of the interviews which the police had claimed to have had with the suspects, with a note of what had been 'revealed' at each interview, and a column headed 'knowledge of' which recited what each officer must have known at the time of each interview. One interview had been scrubbed out and marked 'OUT', and it never featured in the evidence at the trial. The only explanation of the schedule which made any sense was that Reade had devised it as a scenario for the guidance of the interviewing officers, to assist them to make false entries in their notebooks, in order to concoct the evidence of multiple confessions. Reade himself was quite unable to offer any explanation for the schedule.

The appeal lasted for 32 days, and was one of my most depressing courtroom experiences. The Lord Chief Justice, Lord Lane, presided over the court, and it was clear from an early stage that he was treating the evidence with scorn. He openly sneered at the suggestions made by Michael Mansfield, who cross-examined Superintendent Reade about the schedule, refusing to accept that it could possibly be a blueprint for a false case. The court disbelieved the police officers who had witnessed assaults, and believed Dr Skuse. We knew we had lost long before the day of judgment. Lord Lane ended his judgment by saying: "The longer this hearing has gone on, the more convinced this court has become that the verdict of the jury was correct."

The campaign to free the Six continued. It crossed the Atlantic to the United States, where the Human Rights Caucus of the US Congress held a full day's hearing into the case. A new police investigation was ordered. Scientific tests were done on the notebooks of the police, which showed that they had been written up months after the event, not contemporaneously as the police had claimed. So the police were proved to have been dishonest after all. As for the scientific tests, it had been shown that positive results could have been obtained by using Dr Skuse's test on the constituents of soap. The case had rested all along on two pillars – scientific accuracy and police integrity. By March 1991, both pillars had crumbled to the ground, and a third Court of Appeal declared that: "We have heard enough. In the light of fresh evidence which has become available since the last hearing in this court, your appeal will be allowed and you will be free to go."

A year later Gerry Hunter and I went on a joint lecture tour to Toronto, Boston and New York. It was humbling to share a platform with a man who had fought from jail for seventeen years to establish his innocence. For the credit for the victory of the Birmingham Six goes first and foremost to the Six themselves. When they were convicted they were hated throughout Britain. They were the Birmingham Bombers. Now they are free and respected citizens. One of them, Paddy Hill, has started an organization for the support of victims of miscarriages of justice. It was their refusal to give up which inspired the politicians and journalists and ordinary citizens who supported them, and the lawyers who were proud to have known them.

6

THE CALL
from AFRICA

B efore I had even accepted my first brief as a barrister, I had started on a journey which took me to Africa, and taught me the meaning of solidarity between peoples of different colours and cultures. For many years I worked for my clients in the courts by day, and I worked for the liberation of Africa in my spare time. I still feel drawn by the magnetism of Africa.

The journey began with Amnesty International. Amnesty had been founded in the early 1960s by Peter Benenson. His vision was that prisoners of conscience in countries suffering under repression could be freed by the peaceful intervention of concerned people around the world. Amnesty encouraged the formation of groups in different communities in many different countries. Each group would be assigned three prisoners, one from a country aligned with the west, one from a communist country and one from the third world. Their task was to write letters of protest to the authorities of the imprisoning country. They also wrote to their assigned prisoners, whose spirits would be lifted by knowing that they were not alone and forgotten. The criterion for the choice of prisoners was that they had been imprisoned because of their non-violent opposition to the regime in power. Each month Amnesty highlighted three 'prisoners of the month'.

My friend Robert Swann took over as Director from Peter Benenson, and I soon became fascinated by Amnesty's work and eager to help. I was intrigued by the idea that ordinary people could play a part in freeing prisoners in far-off countries. People did not have to watch and wait for their government to make a protest, which it often didn't. They could be participants in the movement for justice and human rights. For two years I was Treasurer of Amnesty, and in 1966 Amnesty sent me on two missions, the first to communist Hungary and the second to fascist Portugal.

The purpose of the Hungary visit was to make contact with the Hungarian authorities, inform them about Amnesty's mission, and open channels of communication so that they would supply information about cases of concern and allow observers to attend trials. I was politely received by the Ministry of Justice and the Hungarian Lawyers' Association, and met a number of ex-prisoners and dissidents. I was assured by the authorities that the courts behaved with absolute legality and that there were no prisoners who had been convicted for their ideas alone. I did not believe them. My report to Amnesty concluded that a few doors had been opened but they could well be closed again. I wondered whether I had achieved anything worthwhile. I had not yet learnt the lesson that the value of a human rights mission rarely becomes manifest at the time when it is undertaken.

The mission brought me into contact with former political prisoners, the first of many experiences I have had of meeting people who have suffered imprisonment and torture for the simple act of speaking or writing or organising against a repressive regime. It is humbling and inspiring to meet such people. Before going to Hungary I was briefed by the writer Paul Ignotus. Both he and his wife had been imprisoned by the Hungarian regime for many years. He had met her in prison in the strangest of ways. In the isolation of the prison where he had been in solitary confinement, the only means of contact with other inmates was to tap against the bars, one tap for A, ten taps for J, and so on, which a few prisoners in the same block could hear and respond to. When a new inmate was moved in, and Paul began his tapping, an unexpected answer came back: I—W—O—M—A—N. Over weeks and months of tapping he began to court her, and after years when they were released he saw her for the first time, proposed to her and married her.

My second mission was to Portugal, which had been ruled by the fascist dictatorship of Antonio Salazar since 1926. Salazar operated a highly efficient political police unit known as the PIDE, which had informants deep within the opposition groups. Political prisoners could be sentenced by the courts to 'security measures', which meant that after their official sentence was over they could be further detained by order of a government minister for as long as they were thought to be dangerous to the security of the state.

I was sent by Amnesty to be an observer at the trial in Lisbon of Pedro Vieira de Almeida, an architect whose crime was to have given shelter to an escaped communist prisoner. He had been accused in the government controlled media of being a notorious communist, and it was feared that he would be sentenced to security measures. His lawyer was Mario Soares, a defender in political cases who had himself served terms in prison and who was later to be President of Portugal.

The trial was to last a day. As with many trials in the civil law system, much of the evidence had been sifted by the examining magistrate, and the proceedings in court were largely theatrical, a public airing of the issues. At the end of the day the three-man court adjourned. They were to give judgment in two days time. In the free day I composed a letter to the court, thanking the judges for allowing me to observe and making it clear, in respectful terms, that British people would be most interested in hearing how justice was done in Portugal.

On the third day, we assembled to hear the verdict. In a fast monotone the President of the Court rattled off the decision. Mario Soares nudged me and said, "We've won." Pedro Viera de Almeida had been found guilty as charged and sentenced to six months imprisonment, with no security measures. Since he had been in custody for more than six months awaiting trial, this was in effect an acquittal.

But there was more to come. The President of the Court put aside his files, reached into his lap and brought out a pile of letters which spilled over his desk. Hundreds of letters written by Amnesty members. In a voice cracking with stress and emotion, he declared:

> I have received these letters from all over the world. I did not show them to my fellow judges in case they might be influenced. I wish to make it clear that the Court has NOT BEEN AFFECTED IN ANY WAY by these letters. Foreign observers should go to communist countries where human rights are being abused. Portuguese justice is independent. It has integrity.

In that speech the glory of the Amnesty mission and the vision which inspired it were revealed. Here was a man, a judge serving a repressive regime, driven by the impact of the pressure on his conscience to do the right thing, pleading with the outside world to leave him in peace. Many times since then I have been asked, what difference can it make to write to the judge, or the minister, in some faraway country? It makes a difference. Each letter is another drop of pure moral decency which can become a torrent which sweeps away repression.

Mario Soares was a social democrat, but he took the trouble during my stay to introduce me to many strands of opposition to the Salazar regime: Christian Democrats, liberals and communists. He briefed me about the abuses of the dictatorship and about its colonial grip on its overseas 'provinces'. He was the first of many lawyers whom I have met on human rights missions, who risk their lives and their liberty for the cause of justice and human rights. It is inspiring to meet them. You come away from such a visit, and return to your country, where standing up for justice may at worst bring you a little scorn, and you say to yourself, "What more can I do?"

What I did was to speak on public platforms about the Portuguese regime and the support it received from Britain. I had become an activist in the Movement for Colonial Freedom, an organisation which had been the friend and supporter of countless freedom fighters in Asia, Africa and the Caribbean. Its founder and president was Lord Fenner Brockway, a gentle, passionate anticolonialist, who often spoke as a lone voice in Parliament on issues of racism and imperialism. He was my mentor in the House of Lords over many years. Its secretary was Tony Gilbert, a tireless veteran of the Spanish Civil War. Tony and I would put up a soap-box in the Charing Cross Road in the evening rush hour and declaim against colonialism to whoever wanted to listen. It was a good lesson in public speaking.

My theme was that it was a scandal that a European country, Portugal, had been ruled by a dictator for nearly 40 years, yet was treated by the British government as a respected NATO ally. Portugal boasted that it was Britain's oldest ally, in an unbroken alliance since 1373. British people were largely ignorant regarding the dictatorship of Salazar. Portugal was known mostly as a nice place to take a holiday.

The Portuguese regime was not only responsible for the repression of its own people, but also for the subjugation of its colonies: Mozambique in the east of Africa, Angola in the south-west, little Guiné-Bissau in the far west between Senegal and Guinea, as well as the islands of Cape Verde and São Tomé and Príncipe off the West African coast, East Timor in the East Indies and Macao in China. It called them its 'overseas provinces'. It claimed that its rule in Africa was benevolent and not racist. Its apologists said that there was no apartheid in Mozambique and Angola. They pointed to the mixed marriages which were allowed in the Portuguese colonies but forbidden in South Africa, and to the system of 'assimilation' whereby Africans who met certain educational standards could become 'asimilados' and be citizens of Portugal. This policy was a sham, since less than half of one per cent of the inhabitants of the African colonies had succeeded in obtaining 'asimilado' status after 500 years of Portuguese rule.

The reality for the inhabitants of 'Portuguese' Africa was wretched. Portugal was poor compared to the rest of Western Europe, so that its capacity to develop its colonies was limited. Education and health facilities were rudimentary. A system of forced labour was widespread. Local government was in the hands of chiefs known as 'regulos', appointed by the regime, whose job was to ensure that taxes were collected and order maintained. Any expression of dissent was ruthlessly crushed. Most people know about the massacre of civilians at Sharpeville in South Africa. Not many know of Mueda, in northern Mozambique, where in June 1960 the Portuguese army opened fire on a peaceful demonstration, killing 500 people and rounding up the rest for punishment. A survivor, Teresinha Mbala, said: "Our people were empty handed when they began to shoot. To defend ourselves we picked up sticks and stones. We had gone to ask for liberty, for elections."

In 1956 the People's Movement for the Liberation of Angola (MPLA) was founded. It was led by Agostinho Neto, who later became the first President of Angola. In 1962 a number of freedom groups in Mozambique were united in the Mozambique Liberation Front (FRELIMO), whose leader was Eduardo Mondlane. A movement had also been launched to claim freedom for Guiné-Bissau and the Cape Verde Islands, the African Party for the Independence of Guiné and Cape Verde (PAIGC) led by Amilcar Cabral. The leaders of the movements, who were necessarily living in exile, formed a close collaboration. After the experiences of seeking change by peaceful means, they realised that they would have to be freedom fighters, using whatever arms and tactics were available to them to confront the violence of the dictatorship. In 1964 FRELIMO sent small detachments of guerrilla forces, trained in Algeria and operating from bases in Tanzania, into the two northern provinces of Mozambique, Niassa and Cabo Delgado. Guerrilla actions had already been started in Angola in 1961 and in Guiné-Bissau in 1963.

The Portuguese regime had no intention of decolonising. It saw itself as part of a front of white supremacy in Africa, along with the illegal Smith regime in Rhodesia and the apartheid government of South Africa. It pushed for the recognition of a 'southern flank' of NATO, in which these white-ruled countries would be a bastion against the spread of communism. The NATO governments, while formally advocating decolonisation, supplied Portugal with all the support and weapons it needed.

This was the grim situation about which I spoke on platforms organised by the Movement for Colonial Freedom. The case against Portugal was easy enough to articulate. It was an obvious disgrace for Britain to be allied to a fascist and racist regime which was ruthlessly suppressing independence movements in its colonies. An advocate looks for good quotations to illustrate the force of his or her case, and the Portuguese leaders were crass in the explanations which they gave of the benefits of their civilising mission. I often used the words of the Bishop of Beira about the need for education: "Schools are necessary, yes; but they must be schools which teach the native about the grandeur of the nation which protects him."

Our eloquence did not have much effect on the government of Harold Wilson, which had been unable, or unwilling, to put down the rebellion of Ian Smith in Rhodesia, and showed even less interest in confronting Portugal within the councils of NATO. My interest in Portugal might have been nothing more than a short-lived and not very effectual effort to speak out about a people in distress, if it were not for an extraordinary initiative which came out of Africa.

In February 1968 the President of FRELIMO, Eduardo Mondlane, was invited to give a lecture to a students' group in Oxford headed by the Jamaican Trevor Munroe. During his visit he also addressed a meeting organised by the Movement for Colonial Freedom, which I chaired. After the meeting he introduced me to Polly Gaster, a British woman who had been working for the Mozambique Institute, the cultural and educational arm of FRELIMO based in Dar-es-Salaam in Tanzania.

Mondlane had been the first Mozambican African to graduate from the University of Lourenço Marques, the capital of Mozambique. After further study in the United States, he joined the staff of the United Nations, and was sent back to Mozambique to make a study for the UN of the living conditions of the people. His experiences on that visit moved him to realise that his true mission was to be involved in their liberation. He quit the UN and was instrumental in the formation of FRELIMO in 1962. He was a man of great intelligence, humanity and vision. When he spoke of the aims of FRELIMO; of the need to create a new society free of racism and exploitation; of the hideous injustices and cruelties of the Portuguese colonial system; of the achievements of FRELIMO in setting up liberated areas in the northern provinces of Mozambique; and of his certainty that his people's cause was not only just but would inevitably succeed, however long it might take, I was totally won over, and eager to do what I could to help.

Mondlane was shocked at the level of ignorance in Britain about the struggle of FRELIMO, which had by then been inside Mozambique for four years and had freed huge areas from Portuguese control. The Portuguese were penned in their urban garrisons, while vast areas of bush, well covered with trees, were liberated territory in which a new society was slowly being built. Because of the hugeness of the country – which I used to illustrate by saying that the distance from the north to the south of Mozambique was the same as the distance from London to Morocco – the

Portuguese army could rarely find the liberated villages, and if they did their locations could quickly be moved.

In Britain the Anti-Apartheid Movement was beginning to be effective, but its focus was on South Africa and Rhodesia, and in any case Mondlane's vision was not of a movement *against* colonialism so much as a movement of *solidarity with* the liberation movement. He foresaw that if a fifth column of support could be created inside one of Portugal's strongest allies, it would erode and ultimately destroy the support on which Portugal depended. Polly Gaster and I were among the few people in Britain who had any depth of knowledge of FRELIMO's history. Another was the historian Basil Davidson, who had written sympathetically about the evolving struggle against Portugal. By the time Mondlane left Britain, we had agreed to form the Committee for Freedom in Mozambique. I was its Chairman and Polly its Organiser and Secretary, and Basil was our most erudite expert.

Within a few months we appreciated that it would be sensible to broaden the scope of the committee to include support for the MPLA in Angola and the PAIGC in Guiné and Cape Verde. The three movements were fighting a common enemy with similar tactics and principles. We obtained the consent of all three movements to change the name to Committee for Freedom in Mozambique, Angola and Guiné. But our closest bonds were always with Mozambique. Mondlane had taught his leading cadres to understand that visits to conferences and speaking tours in Britain, however cold and dispiriting they might appear, were a necessary part of FRELIMO's struggle. They could not defeat Portugal by military means alone. They could not organise within the Portuguese dictatorship, since any support for 'terrorists', as the movements were labelled, would be instantly suppressed. So diplomacy and solidarity in Britain and other European countries – Holland and Sweden had particularly active committees – was a front which they never neglected.

Another element of Mondlane's strategy was the need to be non-aligned between the protagonists of the cold war. Inevitably most of FRELIMO's arms and financing came from the socialist bloc. African nations also helped, but the Soviet Union, East Germany and Bulgaria were strong in their support. While the support from the East was appreciated, it would be the kiss of death for FRELIMO to be identified as pro-communist. Seeking support in Western nations made it clear that an independent Mozambique would be nobody's pawn. It was a further sign of the wisdom of Mondlane. It is no coincidence that Mozambique today is the only member of the Commonwealth which is not a former colony of Britain. Former President Chissano, who negotiated Mozambique's accession to the Commonwealth, was one of Mondlane's young cadres whom we used to drive from meeting to meeting in the early 70s to spread FRELIMO's message. The links which we forged were strong and enduring.

The committee which we set up included Members of Parliament (Joan Lestor and Frank Judd) and student activists who organised meetings in their universities. It was slow going. Few newspapers were interested in giving coverage to a series of bush wars in little known parts of Africa. The worst moment came less than a year after we had started. On 3rd February 1969 we got the news that Eduardo Mondlane had been assassinated by means of a parcel bomb sent to his headquarters in Dar-es-Salaam. We mourned him angrily in a demonstration outside the Portuguese Embassy in Grosvenor Square, London.

This was the first man whom I had met who had inspired me with his vision, and then been killed because of the very qualities which had inspired me – the commitment to the freedom of his people. It was a deeply personal loss. It also showed the depths of evil to which tyranny can sink. It made us all determined to carry on and do what we could to further his vision and so avenge his death.

The committee continued the activities which are the unrecognised but indispensable work of all such committees. It published a journal. It spoke to those who would listen: Black groups, trade union groups, Labour Party groups, church groups, student groups. It studied the situation in the three territories and in Portugal. In 1970 Salazar died and Marcelo Caetano took over the leadership of Portugal. While he claimed to be a modernist, he made no change to the structures of the dictatorship in Portugal, and prosecuted the colonial wars in Africa with increased military aggression.

In 1971 we organised a speaking tour for Amilcar Cabral, the President of the PAIGC and the most articulate exponent of the values and principles for which the liberation movements were fighting. By October 1971 the PAIGC controlled two-thirds of the territory of Guiné-Bissau. Basil Davidson had made a journey inside PAIGC-held areas and had written a book about his experiences. We felt that it was time for British supporters to hear directly from an African leader. We booked the Central Hall in London, which can hold over 2000 people, and other venues in London, Manchester and Dublin.

Amilcar Cabral was modest, charming and intellectually brilliant. The Central Hall was packed with supporters. The meeting got off to a bad start when our first speaker, Joan Lestor MP, tried to justify the policy of the previous Labour Government on Africa. Since the policy had been weak and ineffectual in dealing with the illegal regime in Rhodesia, and had done little to challenge apartheid in South Africa, the meeting reacted with angry heckling. Cabral calmed the audience with a friendly rebuke to two of the speakers who had introduced him:

> Tony Gifford told you that I'm a great revolutionary. It's not true. I am a simple African man, doing my duty in my own country in the context of our time. My comrade Ron Phillips said that I am his hero. We have no heroes in our country – the only heroes there are the African people.

He went on to speak of the life of the people in the liberated areas, where "the people rule the people", and ended with a definition of liberation which has lost none of its resonance today:

> We have to ask what does 'liberation of the people' mean? It is the liberation of the productive forces of our country, the liquidation of all kinds of imperialist or colonial domination in our country, and the taking of every measure to avoid any new exploitation of our people. We don't confuse exploitation with the colour of one's skin. We want equality, social justice and freedom. I don't need to remind you that the problem of liberation is also one of culture. In the beginning it's culture, and in the end it's also culture. The colonialists have a habit of telling us that when they arrived in Africa they put us into history. You are well aware that it's the contrary – when they arrived they took us out of our history. Liberation for us is to take back our destiny and our history.

Cabral's visit was an inspiration to us and to many who heard him. It vindicated the trust which we had placed in the liberation movements, and also the trust which they had placed in us. We had boldly said that we supported these movements not only for the justice of their cause but also for the integrity of their principles. Amilcar Cabral was the embodiment of those principles, a leader who could, had he lived, have stood out against the corrupt and self-seeking leaders who have given Africa a bad name. But he did not live to see his country's independence. A Portuguese raiding party entered Conakry by sea in the night of 20th January 1972, attacked Cabral's house and murdered him. Once again a man whom I could genuinely call a hero had been brutally assassinated.

The successor to Eduardo Mondlane was Samora Machel, who emerged after a protracted argument within FRELIMO between two factions within the movement: those whose motivation was purely nationalist, to replace Portuguese rule with African rule as soon as possible, and those who aimed to transform society, empowering the people and ending all forms of exploitation. Samora Machel was a transformer par excellence. He was ebullient, charismatic, with an infectious laughing energy which inspired loyalty to the point of adoration among Mozambicans. He lifted the FRELI-MO forces after the death of Mondlane, so that they were able to withstand a major Portuguese counter-offensive in the two northern provinces.

In 1971, FRELIMO opened a new front in Tete province. If you look at a map of southern Africa, Tete province is that tongue of Mozambique which sticks out to the west, bordering Zambia to the north and Rhodesia, now Zimbabwe, to the south. The Zambezi river runs through it. Strategically, the Tete front was crucial; if FRELIMO could cross the Zambezi, they could penetrate towards the populous centre of Mozambique. Until then, their activities had been confined to remote northern areas bordering Tanzania. Tete province was also the location of the Cabora Bassa Dam, which the Portuguese were building with South African assistance, aiming to create a massive hydro-electric network which would serve South Africa and Mozambique and thereby create stronger bonds of mutual interest between the two racist regimes. I had been involved in denouncing the dam in a debate in the House of Lords at a time when a British company was planning to join the consortium which was to build it.

I first met Samora Machel in Dar-es-Salaam in August 1972. He had invited a delegation from our Committee to visit the liberated areas and see for ourselves what FRELIMO was doing. I went with Polly Gaster and Pam Logie, an active member of the committee who was engaged to, and later married, one of FRELIMO's leaders Jorge Rebelo. We had been preparing ourselves by long walks over the Sussex Downs, and I had been cycling to court every day, as we knew that the only means of movement inside liberated Mozambique would be on foot.

I had never met a man with such energy and charisma. At our first meeting he was so full of bubbling laughter that I could not believe I was meeting a revolutionary leader. The next day he became serious as he presented the options for our visit. He had decided that we should not go to the northern provinces, where there had been many visitors already, but to Tete. He suggested that we could either go all the way to the river Zambezi, so that we could report that FRELIMO had not only reached it but crossed it. But this would involve a march of about 100 miles each way, and the walking would take up most of the two weeks which we had to spare. Or we could go about half way to the Zambezi and visit a series of settlements which FRELIMO had set up, which would give us more time to study the way in which their administration was working. We chose the second option. We flew to Lusaka, the capital of Zambia, and then went concealed in a lorry, as the Zambian police were not considered reliable, to the Mozambican border.

For the next two weeks we were the guests of, or rather under the command of, a detachment of about fifty FRELIMO guerrillas. We marched for three days through the bush to the district of Fingoe, where liberated villages had been set up less than a year before. We spent over a week in the district. We visited makeshift health posts and schools, held many interviews and took photographs. Each time we arrived at a settlement we would be greeted by singing children and led to the centre of the village for a ceremony of welcome. Our commander, Sebastiao Mabote, would explain who we were and why we had come. He used us to illustrate FRELIMO's policy that they were not fighting against White people but against an evil system. Here were White people who were their friends. Look at the clothes on your back, Mabote said. We have no factories for making clothes. Your clothes have been sent by friends like these. One of us would reply to the welcome and give an account of our work.

I felt utterly secure during the whole visit. Occasionally we were told to stay still, while an aircraft (which I had not heard) passed high overhead. Often along the path we saw children in trees, who were part of a network of lookouts. In each village, old men with ancient rifles patrolled the surrounding area. Mabote told us that the enemy might well know that a foreign delegation was in the district, but they would never know how to find us. Only on the last day, as we were on our way home, did he get a bit concerned. He felt that we had stayed too long and that the enemy was not far off. He sent a detachment to investigate, and an hour later we heard the distant sound of gunfire. That was as close as I got to being in a war.

The experience was mind-blowing on many levels. In terms of the committee's work, we were now able to speak with authority. We had photographed the health posts and school huts, including their pitifully inadequate supplies of materials. We had seen women in the guerrilla army. We had seen girls being educated on an equal footing with boys. We had talked to the elders who were acting as a people's tribunal to settle disputes. We had understood the incredible effort which FRELIMO put in to explain their ideas to their people and seek their consent, to debate with them and not dictate to them.

Beyond that I had learnt that trust and collaboration, on a footing of total equality and mutual respect, was possible between Africans and Europeans. Indeed it was natural, since we shared the same ideals and goals. I had educated and I had been educated. I returned as a better advocate for the freedom struggle. I had acquired, indelibly, a deep love and respect for Africa and its people.

Viva
FRELIMO!

ollowing our visit to the liberated areas of Mozambique, I
was invited to testify to the United Nations Committee on
Decolonisation in New York. The Committee was chaired by
Salim Ahmed Salim, Foreign Minister of Tanzania, who later was
Secretary General of the Organisation of African Unity. The Portuguese
colonies were now the biggest item on its agenda. Appearing before a
United Nations body, I realised that much of what I stood for, which was
regarded as left wing and even extremist in Britain, was accepted as normal
by the vast majority of the nations of the world. I have never thought of
myself as being radical for speaking against racism and apartheid. Any
person with a conscience would do the same. It was the right wing mindset
of the British establishment, articulated by many of its newspapers, which
tried to place me on the fringe. In reality, to champion the right of people
to be free from oppression is to align yourself with the world's majority.

In 1973 the Portuguese and British governments decided to celebrate
the 600th anniversary of the Anglo-Portuguese alliance. The highlights of
the celebrations were to be a visit by the Duke of Edinburgh to Lisbon,
and a state visit by Marcello Caetano to Britain. From the point of view
of Portugal, this was a bold attempt to win respectability within Europe.
Neither Salazar nor Caetano had ever visited any of Portugal's European
allies. We thought that it was outrageous that the British government,
led by Edward Heath, should so blatantly embrace an evil regime which
continued to repress its own people and to stamp on the just claims of its
African subjects. Our committee formed the 'End the Alliance Campaign',
which was a coalition of organisations representing a wide spectrum of

opinion. It included church groups, communists, liberals, trade unionists, Portuguese exiles, anti-racist organisations, and the Anti-Apartheid Movement.

We first tried to picket the Duke of Edinburgh, but this proved difficult. We could not keep track of his engagements, and when we did find him and staged a protest, people found it hard to understand why we were protesting. He went to Lisbon unmolested and no doubt was received with great ceremony. Our efforts concentrated on planning an effective response to the visit of the Portuguese dictator. We had a meeting with Harold Wilson, the Leader of the Opposition, and asked him to boycott the official banquet to be held at Buckingham Palace. He said that he agreed with our objectives and was opposed implacably to colonialism, but this was an invitation from the Queen and he could not properly refuse it.

An amusing sideshow happened a few weeks before the Caetano visit. A high-powered Portuguese trade mission was visiting London, and was to be received by the London Chamber of Commerce at the Ritz Hotel. The committee considered picketing the hotel, but we feared that we would be kept well away by the police. So Kate and I volunteered for a piece of direct action. We dressed up in our best clothes and took tea at the Ritz, sitting close to the room which was booked for the reception. At first everyone was formally announced, but after a while the room was filled and we slipped in and mingled with the guests. The British host then prayed for silence and introduced the leader of the Portuguese delegation. Before another word could be said, Kate jumped on a table and said "First you should realise that Portugal is a brutal colonial regime which…", at which point she was hauled down by irate businessmen. As she spoke I was handing out leaflets which explained why we had interrupted the party. We were quickly expelled from the room. As we sat outside, a number of Portuguese people came up to us whispering, "Well done, we agree with you." They were the little people, the journalists and interpreters who were against the regime.

Caetano was due to arrive on Monday, 18th July 1973. For the Sunday before we had planned a march through London and a rally in Hyde Park. After that we would demonstrate against Caetano wherever we could find him, but we did not know the complete programme. The End the Alliance Campaign had received a lot of support, but we were concerned that the protest would not make much of an impact.

On 11th July, the *Times* printed as its front page lead the story of the massacre of Wiriamu. Wiriamu was a village in Tete province which had supported the FRELIMO guerrillas. The Portuguese army had decided to teach them a brutal lesson. On 16th December 1972, troops entered the village by helicopter, rounded up the villagers in a central place, and gunned them to death. Several hundred men, women and children had been killed. News of the massacre had been brought out by a network of priests and had reached Father Adrian Hastings, a priest of the White Fathers order. He had contacts with the *Times*, which had checked the story and, to its great credit, gave it maximum prominence.

Opposition to the Caetano visit was galvanised. Harold Wilson denounced the Portuguese government in the House of Commons, and declared that the Labour Party would take no part in the celebrations, including the banquet. The numbers on the march on the eve of the visit were far greater than we had expected. The rally was to have been addressed by Gil Fernandes, a representative of the PAIGC in Guiné, but British immigration officers refused to let him in when he arrived on Saturday night. I had been allowed to see him at the airport and read his speech to the rally. This spiteful action of the government only served to increase the anger that the visit was generating.

A friendly journalist had leaked to us the full timetable of Caetano's engagements. In five days he was to attend fifteen functions, including the banquet at Buckingham Palace, a reception at the Naval College in Greenwich, and visits to the City of London and the British Museum. We staged fifteen demonstrations, some of them large, some small but vocal. In Greenwich a large contingent of dock workers joined in, and mounted policemen had to clear the road for the guests to pass through. The Portuguese exiles set up a chant of "Caetano Asesino" (Caetano the Murderer) which was taken up by everyone. By the end of the week it was clear that the visit had brought shame on Portugal rather than respectability. Portuguese friends told me later that the reports which reached them said more about our protests than about the official business of the visit.

Eight months later the regime of Marcello Caetano was overthrown by the 'Rose Revolution' of April 1974. Its fall marked the beginning of a rapid end to Portuguese colonialism. Guiné, then Mozambique, then Angola all celebrated their independence during the course of 1975. Far sooner than any of us had thought, the dream of freedom was realised. The whole edifice of white supremacy in Southern Africa had been fatally weakened. African rule had reached the borders of South Africa itself. The capital of independent Mozambique, formerly Lourenço Marques and renamed Maputo, was a mere 50 miles from the South African border.

The downfall of the Portuguese colonial dictatorship had many causes. The most important was the determined struggle of the liberation movements, which had caused the Portuguese treasury to be depleted by the need to deploy military forces in three parts of Africa. The armed forces themselves were sick of defending a colonial rule which most of them did not believe in, and they took a leading part in the revolution. But I have no doubt that the fiasco of the Caetano visit played a part in his downfall. It demonstrated that Portugal was a pariah within Europe, and it gave great encouragement to those in Portugal who were working for change.

If our committee could claim some credit for the part which we played, we must remember that the credit for that credit lay in the foresight of Eduardo Mondlane in getting us going, and in the efforts of Samora Machel, Amilcar Cabral and their colleagues who made sure that we understood the meaning of their people's struggle. It was a magnificent example of that solidarity which can arise, when those who are suffering injustice join together with those who can be their advocates, each respecting the part the others can play in securing the just outcome which they all desire.

For some years after the defeat of Portuguese colonialism I switched my main focus away from African solidarity to the newly-formed Wellington Street chambers. The committee changed from being a Committee for Freedom (CFMAG) to an Information Centre (MAGIC), which assisted the new states by putting out information and by organising the recruitment of skilled workers, or 'co-operantes', as they were called. For many doctors, agronomists, teachers and other experts, being a 'co-operante' in the early years of Mozambique's independence meant the start of a life-long association with that country. Polly Gaster, who had been the hard-working organiser of CFMAG, continued as the Director of MAGIC, until she moved to Mozambique where she now lives and works.

In 1980 I was drawn back to Mozambique by an invitation from President Samora Machel to Kate and myself. "Gifford," he said when we arrived, "you know more about our liberation struggle than most of our people. Go and tell them about it." Kate and I then went on a journey by plane and jeep for three weeks through most of Mozambique's provinces. We were guests of the FRELIMO provincial governors, one of whom, Armando Panguene, was a good friend from the pre-independence days. We were privileged visitors, and we were inspired by the opportunity of seeing at first hand the new society which FRELIMO under Samora Machel's leadership was building.

In Tete province we were taken to Wiriamu. The villagers who had survived the massacre gathered to welcome us in front of a memorial, a stone pillar with a glass window revealing a pile of skulls. They told the story of the massacre, pointing to where the helicopters had landed, where the soldiers had herded the people and killed them, and where the dead were buried. I then told them the story, which they did not know, of the survivors who told the missionaries, who told the English priest, who told the editor of the most famous newspaper in London. I told them that the story had led to the protests, which brought disgrace to the Portuguese dictator, who was then overthrown, leading to the independence of Mozambique. We wept together. I felt that death and life, despair and hope, had been intertwined across continents, linking with each other because of the desire of good people to make known the truth and to act upon that knowledge, in order to end evil and promote justice.

It was a heady time for Mozambique. The illegal regime in Rhodesia, which had bombed parts of Mozambique, had just ended, and we were all celebrating the independence of Zimbabwe. FRELIMO's network of cadres, which had been so effective in the liberation struggle, had become the FRELIMO party, a formidable organisation with members working to build a new society nationwide. Before we arrived, the government was congratulating itself on a successful change of the national currency from the Portuguese escudo to the Mozambican metical. The change had to be kept secret in order to prevent people from transferring their money out of the country. The change had been carried out by FRELIMO cadres in the course of a weekend, without a hitch.

Mozambique was beginning to pull round from the aftermath of independence, when most of the skilled Portuguese had abandoned the country, unable to accept a multiracial government. Many of them sabotaged the plant and equipment which they had owned. The new government, building on the experience of the liberated areas, had set up a network of communal villages, each with its own school and basic health facilities. Foreign aid was coming in from a variety of sources, reflecting FRELIMO's determination to be non-aligned. We visited projects funded by East Germany, China and Sweden. The Mozambican government had declared the decade of the 1980s to be 'the decade of ending underdevelopment'. Samora Machel said that by this they meant that by 1990 every Mozambican should have access to the basic essentials of a decent life: education, shelter, work and health facilities. We felt that they were capable of doing it.

I paid particular attention to institutions in the field of justice. At the time of independence there was only one qualified attorney left in Mozambique, Luis Sacramento, a White lawyer who had secretly supported FRELIMO during the liberation war. He became Mozambique's first judge. One of his first tasks was to organise a system of people's tribunals. Respected local people were appointed to do justice and resolve disputes. The law students at Eduardo Mondlane University in Maputo had volunteered to train the first tribunal judges.

Judge Sacramento met us in Nampula, in central Mozambique, and took us to a session of the local tribunal. The dispute was between a husband and a wife. The husband complained that the wife had deserted him. Under probing questions from the five members of the tribunal, it soon became clear that the husband had taken a second wife, but he expected the first wife to keep house for him. The tribunal ended up by giving the first wife a divorce, which was not what the husband had come for at all. The hearing was attended by about a hundred villagers. Judge Sacramento had not intervened, but at the end he made a short speech in which he emphasised that FRELIMO was committed to the emancipation of women. The government had not abolished polygamy which was the custom in parts of Mozambique, but it tried to ensure that a wife would not be an economic prisoner of her husband. The case had been a good example of this policy.

One day we were passing through Nampula and had a couple of hours to wait before our next plane. Judge Sacramento said that there was time to fit in a visit to one of Mozambique's new 'penal centres'. A few years earlier, Samora Machel had visited one of the old dungeon-style prisons which had been inherited from Portuguese rule. He was appalled at what he saw. The conditions were crowded and filthy, typical of many post-colonial prisons. He said that such a prison could only create more criminals, and he called for an overhaul of the whole penal system. The penal centres were the result of the new policy for dealing with crime.

We visited the Nampula centre and later another centre outside Maputo. They were the most remarkable penal institutions that I have ever seen. They were farms managed by committees of prisoners. The state could not afford to pay for many warders; at the Nampula centre there were 2 warders and 150 prisoners. At the Maputo centre one of the prisoners on the managing committee was so keen on the work he was doing, that he intended to enlist as a warder when his sentence ended, so that he could continue doing the same job.

We entered the Nampula centre through a makeshift barrier manned by a prisoner. A thin wire fence surrounded the compound. We were told that the centre was run by ten committees, and the secretary of each committee gave an account of his committee's work. A former teacher, jailed for sex offences with pupils, was in charge of the education committee, organising literacy classes for the illiterate and advanced education for others. An ex-accountant who had embezzled millions from the government was in charge of the prison finances, and he proudly told us how the prison had made a profit of a few hundred meticals from a recent cultural show. There were committees for agriculture, animal husbandry, construction and culture. There was a security committee, run like all the others by a prisoner. We asked him if there were problems with prisoners escaping. At the beginning, he said, a few escaped, but they were soon caught and sent to the old-style lock-up. After that everyone realised that they were better off in the centre. The security committee's problem was not with prisoners breaking out, but with people from outside trying to break in.

There was a committee for the welfare of prisoners. Its secretary asked us to walk over to a corner of the compound where there were about a dozen huts. Women and children were going in and out of the huts. Proudly he explained that the welfare committee had negotiated this as a family area. Wives of the prisoners were able to stay there for periods of time, and their husbands could live with them during their stay. I know of no prison in the civilised West which so effectively enabled family ties to be maintained during a prisoner's sentence.

Judge Sacramento told us that so far no prisoner who had been through a penal centre had re-offended, and I could understand why. So often prisons foster the very factors which drive a man to crime. They strip away dignity and self-respect. They prevent any possibility of worthwhile work. They allow for no sense of responsibility for a person's own destiny. These Mozambican prisoners were proud of what they were achieving. They had a sense of their own self-worth.

Back in Maputo we met up with a number of friends who had come to work in Mozambique. Albie Sachs, law professor and former political prisoner in South Africa, whom I had first met on a mission to Northern Ireland, was now teaching law at the University in Maputo. Ruth First, the South African journalist and activist who had also been jailed and exiled, was working as a consultant to the Mozambican government. They were such a contrast. Albie was bubbling with excitement about building a new system of justice in a multiracial country. He was enthusiastic to a fault – a fault which I also share, and which leads us sometimes to overlook the weaknesses of a situation. Ruth judged everything through her own hypercritical standards. When we met her in Maputo, we waxed lyrical about the communal villages, which had seemed to be a triumph of sensible organisation. "The communal villages are an economic disaster," she said, and proceeded to prove her point with statistics of agricultural production.

Before we left, we talked with Samora Machel and his wife Graca about the cloud which we could see threatening the growth of Mozambique. The Rhodesian army had financed a dissident group called Mozambique National Resistance (RENAMO), which had been infiltrated into the country and carried out acts of sabotage. There were signs that South Africa would take over the sponsorship of the group. The independence of Mozambique had already been an inspiration to South Africans fighting apartheid. Would the White South African regime allow a successful Black government to thrive on its borders, giving the lie to the propaganda that Blacks were not able to govern? Samora Machel believed that it would be possible for South Africa and Mozambique to be good neighbours and agree not to attack each other. He was wrong.

My last meeting with President Samora Machel took place during an official visit which he made to London in the early 1980s. We had organised a demonstration of welcome at Claridges Hotel, where he was to stay. About 100 supporters waited on the pavement opposite to the hotel, in one of London's smartest areas, waving Mozambican flags. As the line of limousines and police escorts drew up, I raised the cry of "Viva FRELIMO! Viva Mozambique! Viva Presidente Samora Machel!" The President stepped out, looked across, and gave me a beaming smile. Before the bodyguards could hustle him into the hotel, he beckoned me to cross the road, and embraced me with a warm and comradely hug. The gesture was typical of his open and loving personality. We talked later of the worsening situation in Mozambique.

The decade of the 1980s, instead of being the decade to end underdevelopment, became the decade of the ruin of Mozambique. The South African security forces not only took over the direction of RENAMO but vastly increased its capacity. They financed, armed, trained, and transported into Mozambique squads of 'bandits', as FRELIMO called them, whose sole aim and tactic was to destroy the infrastructure which the independent government had set up. They ransacked schools and health posts, mined the roads, blew up electricity pylons, and murdered teachers and government officials. They kidnapped children, as young as ten years old, and forced them to be killers of their own people, sometimes of their own parents. By the end of the 1980s Mozambique, which could have been a showpiece of self-reliance and people-centred development, had become another African disaster, one of the world's poorest countries, propped up by foreign aid, ravaged by drought and floods, as well as by the civil war.

South Africa not only attacked Mozambique through RENAMO, but directly with its own special forces. In January 1981 South African commandos attacked the houses of members of the African National Congress in Matola, near Maputo. Thirteen ANC cadres were murdered and three were abducted. In August 1982 Ruth First was killed by a parcel bomb sent to her office in Maputo, assassinated because as a White anti-apartheid activist she had chosen to work for a non-racial African government. In April 1988 South African agents planted a bomb under the car of Albie Sachs in Maputo. It exploded as he got in to drive to the beach, blowing off one of his arms and narrowly failing to kill him. He survived to become one of the founding judges of the South African Constitutional Court.

The worst direct attack occurred on the night of 19th October 1986, when the apartheid regime engineered the death of President Samora Machel and over thirty other Mozambicans, as he flew back to Maputo from a conference in Zambia. His plane crashed into a mountain inside South Africa, close to Mozambique. I have read the text of the voice recording from the plane's black box. The pilot believed that he was approaching the Maputo runway, but was surprised that he could not see it. He had been following a signal which he thought had come from the Maputo control tower, but was in fact a decoy signal put out by South African forces, who had been authorised to bring about the death of this great charismatic leader. Once again one of my heroes, the greatest of them all, had been assassinated. Other Mozambicans whom we knew well died with him. At such a time it is hard to go on hoping, to go on organising, but we did. We held a packed memorial meeting in London. Basil Davidson, Polly Gaster, and I and many others spoke, and the choir of the African National Congress sang, as we remembered the man whose charisma had touched us, educated us, and inspired us.

My next visit to Mozambique was to attend FRELIMO's party congress in 1989. In spite of the war, delegates had gathered from all parts of the country. It was the first congress held under the leadership of Joaquim Chissano, who succeeded Samora Machel as President. Chissano was a much quieter man, a skilled and capable leader who was to steer Mozambique to peace and multiparty democracy in the 1990s.

By the last evening of the Congress, which stretched well past midnight, it was evident that the delegates were exhausted and subdued. They were about to return to a war situation in which they could be targets of murder. The final speech was delivered by Chissano in Portuguese, which can be a very ponderous language, particularly when used for political speeches. The Congress seemed to be ending on a low note. Then at the close of the speech, President Chissano started a song which was also a dance. It was like a conga, with a haunting repetitive rhythm. He moved across the platform, signalling to the other leaders to join him. Then the leaders, still singing and moving to the rhythm of the dance, snaked down into the hall and moved through every row of seats, seeming to touch and recognise each one of the audience. I had known of other examples of the ability of Mozambicans to interlace culture and politics. I had seen speakers at the Congress being applauded by enthusiastic singing and dancing from their comrades, interrupting the proceedings for several minutes – which nobody had minded. Samora Machel himself had been known to sing during his speeches at rallies. Now his successor was again fusing culture and politics in a poignant way, which must have lifted the spirit of the delegates as they journeyed home to their communities.

Angola had suffered from South African aggression from the first day of its life as a nation. On Independence Day in November 1975, a column of invading South African troops was making its way towards the capital Luanda from the south, while a group of rebels backed by the United States and assisted by British mercenaries was causing havoc in the north. Angola's first act as a sovereign state was to invite assistance from Cuba, whose prompt dispatch of troops turned back the South African advance. Both South Africa and the United States sponsored UNITA, a movement led by Jonas Savimbi which, like RENAMO, used terror and intimidation in order to control a portion of the country. Angola has huge deposits of oil, diamonds and other minerals, but it never had the chance to develop in peace.

I made one visit to Angola in 1981. My main memory is of a trip to the camps of displaced persons in the south of the country. Thousands of Angolans had been driven from their homes by South African forces invading from neighbouring South West Africa (now Namibia, then a South African dependency). Our plane was met by a jovial cigar-smoking Cuban officer, who drove us to one of the camps. Everywhere we walked there seemed to be a school in progress, some with children and some with adults. Under ragged tarpaulins stretched across the branches of trees, the education system was alive. The camp director explained that his purpose was to maintain as much normality as possible in these abnormal conditions. The visit gave me a glimpse of the Angola which might have been.

The hopes of Mozambicans and Angolans were dashed by the apartheid regime of South Africa. What an abomination that regime was! What a disgrace it was that Britain and other Western governments would parley and trade with South Africa as a friendly state, a brother in capitalism! Here was a government which alone in the world restricted the right to vote to people who were white in colour. The very existence of the apartheid regime was a comfort and encouragement to racists everywhere. Indeed one of the reasons why the regime had the support of many people in White countries was that it played on the racism within themselves.

In 1981 I was sent by the Defence and Aid Fund for Southern Africa on a lecture tour of Australia and New Zealand. I was keen to return to the country of my mother's birth. I spoke at public meetings in every major Australian city, and took part in countless radio interviews and phone-in programmes. In every city there were a few devoted souls who organised anti-apartheid activities, but it was an uphill task. Arguing to Australians the case for equal rights for Blacks and Whites in South Africa demanded all my advocacy skills. Not only were people desperately ill-informed, but their own dealings with Black people, if any, had been with Aborigines. White Australians have treated the aboriginal people as sub-human ever since they settled on their land and drove them out, often with extreme brutality. So people would phone in with comments like: "Well, I wouldn't like to be ruled by the Blacks, would I?"; and "I hear the Blacks in South Africa are much better off than in the countries where they rule themselves." These remarks had to be given a polite, firm and informed answer in the space of a few sentences.

When I arrived in New Zealand the reaction was entirely different. A coalition of Maoris and White activists had recently been very successful in disrupting a South African rugby tour. One man had been jailed for flying a small plane low over the rugby field and bombing the players with bags of flour. The people who phoned in were either passionately for or passionately against, but they knew what the argument was about.

I remained active in the Defence and Aid Fund during the 1980s. It had been founded by John Collins, a canon at St. Paul's Cathedral, and it made a precious contribution to the freedom struggle. Its objects were to defend those who were on trial for their activities against the apartheid system; to aid the families of political prisoners; and to awaken the conscience of the world to the issues at stake. It was banned in South Africa, so that any lawyer or prisoner's family who accepted its funds would be committing a crime. The Fund organised a network of channels, devious and totally secret, through which millions of pounds were sent for the defence of political prisoners and the aid of their families. The Fund was generously supported by the Governments of Sweden, Denmark and the Netherlands, and it had support groups in many countries. I served on the executive of the British support group, which was organised by Ethel de Keyser, a tireless fundraiser whose brilliance in organising auctions, dinners, lectures, receptions, shows, and anything else which could raise money was unsurpassed in my experience.

There were many heroes, known and unknown, who contributed to the downfall of apartheid. There were those thousands who gave up their lives or their freedom inside South Africa; the freedom fighters who trained in neighbouring states and penetrated back into the country clandestinely; the exiles who toured from meeting to meeting, conference to conference, spreading the news of their people's struggle; the many who worked in solidarity in anti-apartheid movements around the world; the activists of Transafrica in the United States, who successfully lobbied the United States Congress to introduce a bill imposing sanctions against South Africa; and the governments of the African states which gave shelter to the freedom fighters and exiles.

There were times when the might of the apartheid regime seemed to be so overwhelming that it could never be brought down. And yet it was. When a cause is just it will prevail in the end, because in the long run the desire of people to do what is right is greater than the capacity of governments to do what is wrong. In my life as a human rights activist, I have seen tyrannies overthrown in Spain, Portugal, Greece, Zimbabwe, Namibia, South Africa, Chile and a host of Central and South American states. I have seen the doctrinaire communism of the Soviet bloc crumble away like the Berlin wall which it erected. Today's tyrannies take different forms, and different strategies may be needed to defeat them. But the message for today's activists is the same. Everything which you can do in a just cause is worthwhile.

One of the most joyful experiences of my life was to attend the first democratic election in South Africa in April 1994. I was there as part of an observer team organised by the International Association of Democratic Lawyers. It was a mission of solidarity. All of us paid our own passage and were there because we had supported the freedom struggle. Ten of us were sent to Kwazulu-Natal. We accompanied the workers of the Independent Electoral Commission as they went into remote areas to explain the election procedures. We attended election meetings of all the main parties. On the four days of the election we watched as the queues stretched for hours of people waiting to cast their first ever vote. On the first day, which was reserved for the elderly and infirm, we saw voters being carried to the poll in carts and barrows.

After the election I went to Johannesburg to attend an ANC victory meeting, addressed by Nelson Mandela. His life's dream of a democratic, non-racial South Africa had been realised. The sabotaging of neighbouring states had been ended. The hatred shown by some of the South African Whites, while it had been vicious up to the eve of the election, had not prevailed. All of us observers were weeping with emotion, pinching ourselves to be sure that it was true that South Africa had held a fair and peaceful and democratic election.

You will see from these experiences that I have a view of Africa which is very positive. I have worked with African leaders whose aims and principles were selfless, uncorrupt, and centred on the needs of their people. I am aware that in many parts of Africa there have been leaders motivated by greed and self-aggrandisement. There has been massacre in Rwanda, civil war in Sudan and Sierra Leone and Liberia and Ivory Coast, and economic ruin over much of the continent. None of this lessens my belief that African peoples, given half a chance, could create a paradise of a continent. The devastating attacks on Angola and Mozambique were only the latest in a succession of assaults by people of the White race on the integrity of African society. Many of Africa's problems stem directly from Western intervention, and there is much that must still be redressed and compensated. My advocacy for Africa has not ended.

THE RACISM
of the BRITISH

I have lived through the decades of immigration and settlement of millions of people from the Caribbean, India, Pakistan and Africa. They came to Britain as citizens of the United Kingdom and Colonies. They were recruited into the health service, the transport services, the mills of the north and the factories of the Midlands. They worked at jobs which the British born in Britain did not want to do. They raised families in Britain, and sent remittances to the families whom they had left behind. Their children grew up with British accents and ambitions to do better than their parents. And from the arrival of the first postwar immigrants to the present day, they and their children and their children's children have had to deal with the racism of the British.

Face the facts. An alarmingly high proportion of the British people are infected with racial prejudice. Every week sees newspaper reports of racial harassment, racial attacks, studies of racial discrimination, analyses of institutional racism. A television programme broadcast in 2004 and called 'The Colour of Love' featured a survey showing that 50 per cent of White British people would not wish their child to marry a person of colour. Why not, for heaven's sake? Why is colour, rather than character, the defining feature in the minds of so many White British parents? In spite of the passing of Race Relations Acts, the election of Black and Asian members of parliament, the Stephen Lawrence Inquiry, and other notable landmarks in the relationship of Black and White in Britain, the picture remains bleak. People seem to be incapable of looking behind the colour to see the personality. Liberals who claim to be enlightened are sometimes the worst. For instance they often talk incessantly to Black people about race, as if race was the only important issue in their lives.

Ben Okri movingly described the daily experience of Black people in Britain in his book *In Arcadia* (2002):

> He had to cross a terrain in the minds of people. He had to submit to one of his life's endless trials – the trial of colour… He felt himself materialising from the realm of normal humanity into a state that Camus called 'humiliated consciousness': the consciousness of being automatically suspect, automatically distrusted, automatically dehumanised, less than humanised, because of colour differences, because of variety in nature's canvas, because of history, the eyes, what people read into the skin, illusions.

Previous waves of White European migration have engendered equally vicious reactions on the part of the British. Paul Foot, in his book *Immigration and Race in British Politics* (1965), quoted from the politicians and newspapers of the early 1900s who excoriated Jewish immigrants, who were thought to be introducing an alien way of life, in language which the National Front, and Enoch Powell, were to echo over 60 years later in their attacks on Blacks and Asians. But whereas the descendants of Jews, Italians, Poles and Cypriots can, if they wish, merge easily into the unity of whiteness, the descendants of Asians remain Asian, the descendants of Jamaicans and Nigerians remain Black, and thereby are thought to be different, in the mindset of great numbers of people. They bear the label 'ethnic minority', which may be necessary for statistical monitoring but is nonethelesss offensive, since it highlights the supposed separateness of people who should be no more separate than people with red hair.

I shall return to some of the reasons for this wretched prevalence of prejudice, to its roots in the practice of slavery and colonialism and the inculcation of white superiority in the minds of the youngest child. It is an issue which cannot be ignored by any barrister or solicitor who is concerned with human rights and justice. Racial prejudice is one of the two greatest causes of daily human rights violation in Britain today. The other is gender prejudice, the abuse of power by men over women, still occasioning cruelty and violence in thousands of homes across the land. Of the two I believe racial prejudice to be the most deep-seated and difficult to eradicate.

My commitment to oppose racism did not simply grow from an intellectual analysis of human rights issues. It was nurtured and strengthened by experiences which revealed to me, emotionally as well as intellectually, how ridiculous it is for people to think themselves better or more desirable than others because of their race or colour. Looking back to the young man of four decades ago it is hard to say what were the most formative events. Was it falling in love with an Indian student, and then having my dear mother say "but isn't she a little dark"? Was it joining the Campaign Against Racial Discrimination and taking part in experiments in which White and Black volunteers would apply for the same jobs, with the better qualified Black applicant invariably being turned down in favour of the worse qualified White? Was it the first cases on which I cut my teeth in the Marylebone Magistrates Court, which served the Notting Hill area, and hearing police officers telling blatant lies against Black defendants whom they had falsely arrested and charged? Or was it the experience of putting my life in the hands of the freedom fighters of FRELIMO?

Racism in the enforcement and practice of the law was plain for all who had eyes to see. As a barrister briefed by solicitors working in the multiracial communities of London, I became familiar with the armoury of offences which were regularly used against Black people. 'Being a suspected person loitering with intent' or 'sus' as it was known, was used especially against young people window-shopping in the West End. The offence arose not from in any actual criminal conduct, but from the policeman's interpretation of what the suspect was intending to do. 'Using threatening words or behaviour likely to cause a breach of the peace', was a charge which the police brought against Black people who raised their voices in the public street. 'Obstructing a constable in the execution of his duty' would be used to arrest anyone who protested against police misconduct, which they had witnessed. 'Assaulting a constable in the execution of his duty' was the charge of choice when police officers had beaten a suspect during an arrest or at the police station. "The defendant suddenly went berserk and we had to restrain him" – a theme I must have heard a dozen times, and on one which pandered to the subconscious racism of magistrates who were ready to believe that Black people were naturally prone to irrational violence.

Again and again I found that the clients whom I was representing were not criminals. The 'crimes' of which they had been accused would never have occurred if the police had not provoked them. A youth who was stopped and searched in the street, and complained about it vociferously, would be convicted of a crime (obstructing the police, using threatening behaviour) and could be sent to prison. The real crime was committed by the officer who had stopped and searched him, humiliating him in the process, for reasons which were dominated by prejudice. This sort of scenario is no fiction; when a team from the Policy Studies Institute spent two years with the Metropolitan Police in the 1980s, there were appalled by the extent of overtly racist attitudes. They described one chief inspector who 'worked himself up into a frenzy of hatred against Black people'. On stopping and searching, one officer told his colleagues, in the presence of the Institute's researchers: "How does an experienced policeman decide who to stop? Well, the one that you stop is often wearing a woolly hat, he is dark in complexion, he has thick lips and he usually has fuzzy hair."

Many of my cases involved the Special Patrol Group (SPG), a back-up squad of police who would be summoned when trouble broke out. They were deployed in mini-vans which held ten officers and riot gear, and they tended to create havoc wherever they went. I remember a case where a Black family was expostulating to the police in protest against the search of a youth in the street. The officers radioed for assistance. The SPG arrived, thinking that a riot was going on, and the whole family ended up under arrest, parents and sisters as well as the son who was first being targeted. Over the 1970s and 1980s, repeated incidents of this kind caused law-abiding people to hate and distrust the police.

The response of some barristers to these cases was to play down the accusations which their clients were making about police brutality. The attitude was: better not accuse the police of hitting you, or racially abusing you, because the judge or magistrate won't like it. If the beating had taken place at the police station, it would be considered irrelevant to the charges, and best not talked about. If it was necessary to make the allegation that the police officer was a liar and a racist, these barristers would put their client's case in apologetic terms.

Compared with the 1970s, there is now a huge movement of committed barristers and solicitors who are fully prepared to believe their clients' stories and present them to the court. But advocates can get tired and case-hardened, and you need constantly to listen to what your client is saying, especially if he is Black and you are White. The most enlightened of barristers can fall into the trap of thinking that 'he must be exaggerating', or of wondering 'did this urbane and polite sergeant really behave so badly?' My experience has been that people of good character, as many of those who complain of police abuses have been, do not invent the racist words and violent acts which they allege as part of their defence. A courageous and honest defence of Black people who have been brutalised by the police is not only your professional duty, but will secure the acquittal of your client more often than you may think.

A commitment to fighting racism is not only needed in the criminal courts. Cases of racial discrimination in employment or housing are now frequent under the Race Relations Act, which gives a remedy to the victim of discrimination. Proving racial discrimination is difficult. British employers do not usually say that they are passing you over because you are Black, but the Black victim can sense it easily enough. The law now provides techniques whereby the whole employment record of discriminating employers may be investigated. I am happy to see that Robin Allen QC, a product of the Wellington Street chambers, has become a leading expert in this field.

In my present chambers we have a brilliant team of young specialists in immigration and asylum law, who deal with clients who literally face life or death, depending on whether their case for asylum is upheld. These barristers themselves come from different parts of the world, and they defend the rights of people from different parts of the world. In my chambers' immigration team there is an Asian, a Ugandan, an Australian and a White Briton, and on a particular day they may be representing a Kosovan, a Somalian, an Afghan and a Kurd. These barristers have to explain the realities of people facing persecution in countries whose conditions may be totally unfamiliar, before tribunals whose members can often be sceptical and prejudiced. These barristers are upholding the rights of refugees in the midst of a wave of media hysteria over 'bogus asylum-seekers'. They have passed beyond being 'anti-racist'. They are part of the new movement of British lawyers, themselves composed of many races, who are committed to defend the rights of those who are persecuted, irrespective of colour or race. They give me a glimpse of how Britain could be.

As well as fighting cases from day to day, I have twice been asked to conduct public inquiries into situations where whole communities were affected by racism. The first was the Broadwater Farm Inquiry, which was set up by the Haringey Council in North London following riots which occurred in October 1985. The second was the Liverpool 8 Inquiry, set up by the Liverpool City Council in 1989, following seething discontent among Black people in Liverpool. Each inquiry was one of the most demanding assignments I have ever taken on as a barrister in Britain, and each assignment deepened my understanding of the unfairness and injustice of racial discrimination.

Broadwater Farm is a housing estate in Tottenham, an area of multiracial settlement. It had been built as a showpiece, with high-rise blocks connected by walkways. It was home to over 1,000 households, evenly divided between White and Black families. It had been neglected and run down, and had the reputation of being a place where 'problem' families were housed. It was regarded by the police as a haunt of criminals and drug dealers.

In the early 1980s some of the Black residents of Broadwater Farm, led by a remarkable Jamaican woman called Dolly Kiffin, formed the Broadwater Farm Youth Association. The young people set up services which benefited the whole estate, including meals and outings for the elderly White pensioners; a day nursery for young mothers; a play centre for children after school; and a number of co-operative shops and businesses. Every year they held a festival in a nearby recreation ground. The Haringey Council helped by providing services and improving the physical housing. The Council was led by Bernie Grant, who was later to be one of Britain's first Black Members of Parliament. He gave strong leadership at a time when it was needed. Broadwater Farm began to be recognised as a model, and in February 1985 it was visited by Princess Diana.

But the police viewed Broadwater Farm, in the words of the local commander, as "a haven for the wrongdoer". There were regular raids and clashes, with excessive numbers of police officers arriving after small incidents and angering the people of the Farm with their heavy-handed approach. One community leader, Clasford Sterling, who went to the local police station to seek information, was dragged backwards by the police, ending up with a broken nose and a charge of obstruction. While other agencies were building bridges with Broadwater Farm, the police viewed its residents with mistrust and even hatred, and over time the feeling became mutual.

On 5th October 1985 a party of police officers burst into the home of Cynthia Jarrett, a Jamaican mother who lived near Broadwater Farm. They had arrested her son for 'assaulting a police officer', and claimed to have a warrant to search her house. They pushed her aside, causing her to fall. The fall brought on a massive heart attack and she died instantly. She was a popular and respected woman, and the news of her death spread through the community within hours.

On the following day community leaders pleaded with senior police officers to defuse the growing tension by suspending the officers who were involved in the raid. The police refused, merely saying that the incident would be inquired into. At a time when great sensitivity was needed, none was shown. A meeting was held at the Broadwater Farm Youth Association, where the participants resolved to march to the local police station and hold a demonstration. In the evening as they attempted to leave the estate, they found that the police had forestalled them by blocking all the exits. From that moment, and all through the night, the police came under sustained attack from the young men penned inside the estate. Bricks and petrol bombs were thrown, cars were set on fire, and the police were unable to bring the riot under control. When one group of officers tried to escort the fire brigade into the estate, they were set upon by youths and one of them, Police Constable Keith Blakelock, fell and was stabbed to death.

In the aftermath of the riot, the death of Mrs Jarrett was forgotten and the death of P.C. Blakelock, who was known to be a gentle community policeman, was painted as the work of devils. Terms like hyenas, butchers and monsters were used in headlines. The popular press described Broadwater Farm in lurid terms. "White people living there feel they are living in an alien and terrifying land," said the *Daily Mail*. Bernie Grant was depicted by the *Sun* as "like the leader of a Black tribe - always looking for battles and shaking his spear". Nothing was said of the positive achievements which had attracted the notice of Princess 'Di'.

While this was going on, the police were arresting hundreds of youths in and around the Farm, holding them for days in secret locations, and extracting confessions to the murder of P.C. Blakelock which judges were later to rule to have been obtained by oppression. The police searched 271 homes and charged 167 people with various offences, including riot and affray, as well as six with murder.

In this situation, fraught with tensions, rumours and lies, the Haringey Council under Bernie Grant's leadership called for an independent public inquiry into the death of Mrs Jarrett and subsequent events and into the breakdown in police/community relations in Tottenham. When the Government refused to hold an official inquiry, the Council set up its own. Various liberal figures refused to act as chairman of the inquiry, fearing perhaps that it was too hot a potato. In February 1986 Bernie Grant asked me to be the chairman, and after being assured that I would have full independence and an adequate budget, I accepted without hesitation. I sat with five other members who had a range of skills and experience. They were Canon Sebastian Charles, the Asian Canon of Westminster Abbey, who had experience of prejudice in the Church of England; Dorothy Kuya, a veteran Black community leader from Liverpool; the Catholic Bishop

Philip Harvey; social scientist Paul Corrigan; and teacher Randolph Prime.

At our first public session on 21ˢᵗ February 1986 members of the community hid their faces behind sheets of paper, such was the climate of fear. In my opening words I expressed the reasons for the Inquiry in words which can be applied to many situations:

> Why have we taken on this task? Because we believe that an Inquiry is needed. We believe that you in this community want an independent and fair inquiry. Your presence here indicates that this is so.
>
> People do not attack the forces of the law out of mere wickedness or a sense of fun. As Lord Scarman said only last week, 'public disorder usually arises out of a sense of injustice.' There are causes to these events going back over many years. They must be recorded and made known.
>
> When there is conflict in society it is always the powerful institutions which find it easy to put out a version of events which - even if it is only based on hearsay - is reported by the mass media as if there were no other truth. Those without power have no such voice.
>
> Our task is to listen to the powerless as well as the powerful. To listen to the ordinary people of this community and the organisations which represent them. And having listened to everyone, to produce recommendations which can be used to bring about change.

The Inquiry involved public hearings, interviews, an opinion survey of the residents of the Farm, and research into social conditions and economic possibilities. It produced a report of 250 pages, in which we attempted to tell the full story of Broadwater Farm, and Mrs Jarrett's death, often using the words of those who had given evidence. We made comprehensive recommendations about policing, housing conditions, employment generation and education. The report was praised by local people as having told their story, and received a generally constructive response from the media and the Government. But there was another side to the reaction, in the form of dozens of anonymous letters, which reminded me of the extremes of racism in so many sick British minds. These are some of the more printable extracts:

> 'Can you wonder that the public wants to abolish the House of Lords if theres a lot of STINKERS LIKE YOU AND SCARMAN seems to me you and Scarman must have mixed blood (no Im not a Rascist)'
>
> 'Cowson's like you who condem the Police Force is nothing but a traitor to Britain. To think we lived in peace and solely relied on them until the Blacks came and needed control. While we have so called people like you

in office life is hell when you sympathise with the Blacks. This country will never be the same and will get worse thanks to your type.'

'You dirty cowardly homosexual looking filthy bastard I am getting on a bit but I am going to find out your private address and give you a dam good hiding.'

Two years later we were asked by the Haringey Council to return and report on how far the recommendations had been followed. The second report was positive in commending a number of changes in attitude and policy on the part of the police, and in praising new developments on the estate itself. By 1989 Broadwater Farm was graced with a memorial garden to honour both Mrs Jarrett and Mr Blakelock; a huge mosaic mural created by one of the Turkish residents representing symbols of harmony and unity; a painted mural with the faces of Martin Luther King, Mahatma Gandhi, Bob Marley and John Lennon set in a garden filled with children; and a system of internal phones which allowed safe access into the apartment blocks. It was a place transformed.

For me the experience of being chairman of the Broadwater Farm Inquiry brought many rewards. I was able to give leadership to the other five Inquiry members through a method of collective editing which gave full weight to their different views. We would have a discussion, then I would draft a chapter, then more discussion. I learned the benefits of using a computer when computers were still new toys. I developed a system of reading the huge volumes of evidence, noting every passage that I wanted to refer to, and at the same time inserting the notes into an outline on the computer, so that for each chapter the passages which were relevant to that chapter were noted in their right place. By this means, when it came to drafting the chapter, the framework was already in place. I have used the system many times since in handling complex cases.

We felt that we had done the job assigned to us. We were able to give a voice to people such as Dolly Kiffin, Clasford Sterling and others who in spite of their pioneering work had been derided and vilified. We had spoken up for a Black-led community which had begun to despair that anyone in the White ruling class would recognise their grievances. We had told the truth about the death of Mrs Jarrett. We had some impact on policing, for although the police did not officially take part, we learned later that our report had become required reading for police officers attending promotion interviews. For all who wanted to read, we had been uncompromising in setting out our conclusion that racism in the police force was rife, and that if not dealt with it would lead to further disasters. We called for a commitment to eradicate oppressive and racist policing.

Before 1985 the seminal inquiry into policing and race relations had been the Inquiry of Lord Scarman into the Brixton Disorders of 1981. He had shown that there was a connection between racial prejudice in the police and disorder in the Black community, but he had been cautious in his expression of the problem. His emphasis was on the perception of racism rather than its reality. He said: "Whether justified or not, many in Brixton believe that the police routinely abuse their powers and mistreat alleged offenders. The belief here is as important as the fact." Our report took the issue a stage further. We said that the fact of racism was crucial, not just the belief. Black people's beliefs were based on experience and not on fantasy. We said: "We have no doubt that the conclusions of Black people were deeply grounded on true experience of racially prejudiced police behaviour." In the next decade, Sir William McPherson in the Stephen Lawrence Inquiry took a further step, finding that racism in the police was institutional.

Another reward for me personally was that my work in Broadwater Farm led to an enduring friendship with Bernie Grant. Bernie had been an activist in Britain from the time he arrived from Guyana in the 1960s. From 1989 until his death in 2000 he was Member of Parliament for Tottenham. In a way he was MP for Black people everywhere in Britain. He forged links with many African leaders. He was not afraid to speak the truth about his people's sufferings, and he was hated and ridiculed for it by many in the British media. I loved and respected him deeply.

I have written earlier about the call which I received in 1989 from the Liverpool 8 Law Centre for help in combating the wave of racist policing which Black people in Liverpool were experiencing. Part of my response was to assist in sending Black lawyers to act as defence counsel. But when I met with Liverpool community activists, I felt that the situation which they described was so grim that more was needed. It was not enough to get people acquitted; we needed to stop them being arrested and charged. The culture of prejudice against people from Toxteth, or Liverpool 8, the area where most Black and mixed-race Liverpudlians lived, was longstanding, and police racism was only a part of the problem. So we proposed to the Liverpool City Council, a Labour Council which had recently taken over from the Liberals, that it should sponsor an Inquiry into Race Relations in Liverpool. Again I took in able colleagues: Wally Brown, former community activist in Toxteth who became a College principal, and Ruth Bundey, a solicitor with an active practice in human rights in Leeds.

The difference between Liverpool and other cities was that Black people had been settling in Liverpool for centuries. Liverpool was built on the wealth generated by the slave trade in the 18$^{t'}$ and early 19th centuries. Sailors and former slaves had married local women and raised families over the whole period since then. Charles Dickens in 1861 had reported on a visit to a public house where Black people came to relax to the music of a "fiddle and tamborine band". He was told that they kept together because "they were at a disadvantage singly, and liable to slights in the neighbouring streets". We were to discover that little had changed. In 1919, when the Black population was around 5,000, a wave of attacks took place against Black people. Up to 10,000 White rioters had been involved in these attacks, which included the murder of a Black seaman called Charles Wootton who was thrown into the sea by a mob. The *Liverpool Courier* wrote in an editorial at the time that "The average negro is nearer to the animal than is the average white man" – a bizarre comment in the circumstances.

In the years of Black and Asian immigration into Britain the 1960s it used to be said that once Black people settled down and intermarried, racial prejudice would dissipate. The history of Liverpool proved the opposite. Most Black people in Liverpool speak with the same accent, go to the same schools, and worship the same God, as White people do. Many of them are born from mixed marriages and unions. But they have been more hated, more segregated, more discriminated against in employment, more targeted by the police, than Black people in other cities. Such was the message from the vast body of evidence which hit us as soon as we opened up our inquiry. The evidence included children being forbidden to play with the children of Black neighbours; a Black four-year-old being painted white by White teenagers; a Black woman having her windows smashed and her letterbox blocked by excrement after she moved to a White area; and a Black footballer being shot in the back with an air rifle during a match. At work, when a young Black trainee complained about abuse and racial taunting, he was told that he was over-reacting and being too sensitive. A trade union official told us that this was just "working class banter". He told us that "Words such as nigger and coon are used, but they are not maliciously intended." So much for those whose job was to defend the rights of workers.

After nine days of hearing this evidence, we decided that we had to make a stand for what we believed in. We could not carry on hearing more of this and leave our comments for the end. The fact of widespread racism in Liverpool was obvious. How to deal with it was the important task of the Inquiry. So we held a press conference and published a 'Declaration of Principles'. We said that although we had long experience of racism in other cities, "we find the situation in Liverpool to be uniquely horrific". The principles which we then declared are worth repeating:

1. That every man, woman and child in the city of Liverpool is born with equal dignity and is entitled to equal respect.
2. That racism is not natural to human kind, but rather the unnatural result of prejudices instilled over the years in the family, school and society.
3. That it is particularly outrageous for Black children and youth, at the threshold of their lives, to face hostility and rejection because of their skin colour.
4. That the eradication of racism will benefit the whole of Liverpool society, both White people and Black.
5. That it is therefore a priority of this Inquiry to recommend policies and actions which will be effective in remedying the real injustices which racism has caused.

We ended by appealing to everyone in Liverpool to examine these principles and to look at their own responsibility, and use their influence, to promote the full participation of all Liverpudlians in the life of the city, irrespective of colour or race.

We published our report under the title "Loosen the Shackles". We meant that a report could not of itself free Black people from their bondage, but it could assist them to break the chains themselves. We included in the report two poems, one by local poet Levi Tafari and one by Benjamin Zephaniah, which ended:

> Ina Liverpool me see a colourful people
> forget about de Beatles
> treat everybody as equal,
> I was observing a people who can win
> they're made of bone and blood and skin
> And London are you listening?

The report was thorough, with extensive recommendations addressed to museums, members of parliament, the City Council, the police, the legal profession and the health services. We suggested doing a follow-up report after two years, as we had done at Broadwater Farm, but this did not happen, so I have no clear evidence as to the effect of our work. I have been told that the City Council did more than it had ever done before to promote equal rights. One recommendation, addressed to the museums, was definitely followed. We had been shocked that the only depiction of Black people in the National Maritime Museum was a caricature on a postcard of a thick-lipped banana boat worker. We recommended that the museums give a full and honest account of the involvement of Black people in the life of the city. Five years later I was invited to the opening of a permanent exhibition on the theme of the slave trade and its abolition. It was titled "Transatlantic Slavery: an African Story that Must be Seen, Heard and Never Forgotten", and is a moving and honest depiction of the inhuman trade which made Liverpool rich.

There was one witness to the Inquiry who I feel we let down, and I want to pay tribute to him. We had no official cooperation from the police, but one officer agreed to meet us in private. He was David Scott, who had been the community policeman in Toxteth, and was well respected by local people. He told us that he continually passed on information about dealers in hard drugs, but it was ignored. He thought that the policy was to let the community 'dope itself up'. There was no will to tackle the use of hard drugs, but lots of effort to charge people with 'public order' offences. He himself had experience of racism, as his wife's father was born in Jamaica. His helmet had been daubed with the words 'nigger lover'. His superior officer had told him to take no notice: "Your wife is not a nigger, she is a half caste." (Liverpool people love to use the term 'half caste' which I find so offensive). He said that there was an Inspector at the local police station who had a 'ferocious hatred' of 'those fucking niggers'. He signed an affidavit about all this which we published in the report.

On the very day of the publication of the report, David Scott was arrested. He was charged with an alleged fraud involving over-claiming on an insurance claim two years before. Obviously they had held it as a weapon against him to be used at the right moment. It takes courage indeed to stand up against racism when you work in the heart of a racist institution.

Every year leading members of the Black community in Britain meet at a banquet organised by the Hansib Press, publishers of *Caribbean Times* and other journals. Awards are given at the banquet to those who have served their community well. In 1989 I was presented with a Hansib

Community Award for Service and Achievement. I was one of very few White people to be honoured in this way. The award, in the shape of a beautiful silver pillar, stands proudly in my home in Jamaica today.

In the next year my association with the Hansib Press was to come in useful in a special way. The African American writer Maya Angelou was visiting London to launch one of her books. I was invited to a party given by her publishers, the Virago Press, at the home of Helena Kennedy. The party was full of literary personalities. I got talking to Maya, and asked her if she had met any of the Black leaders in Britain. "No, but I would really like to," she said. "Do you know how I could?" I told her that later in the week I was going to the Hansib Awards banquet, and would she like to be my guest. She said she was invited that evening to supper at Harold Pinter's house, but she would definitely leave early if I would come for her.

So I collected Maya Angelou from the Pinter's home in Kensington, where another White liberal gathering was in progress, and arrived with her on my arm at the banquet. Of course she was the centre of attention and had a great time. She later wrote an article in the *Times*, saying that she was amazed that a White man had been the key to her meeting the Black community. It would never happen like that in the United States.

To me, finding Maya at a party of congenial White people and then taking her to a party of congenial Black people was the most natural thing in the world, as well as being great fun. Yet the story reveals that there are still too few people in Britain who can easily cross the racial divide. Racial attitudes among White people in Britain remain deeply engrained, so that even liberals who sign plenty of anti-racist letters invite few Black people to their parties. It was sad for me to return to Britain in the late 1990s, married to a Black woman, and to find that little had changed. In the 21st century, in Britain, it is still necessary for any person who believes in the equality of all mankind, including any lawyer, to stand up and play his or her part in the eradication of British racism.

9

HUMAN RIGHTS
in NORTHERN
IRELAND

T hose who take up human rights causes in foreign lands should take care not to ignore the violations for which their own governments are responsible. I have known anti-apartheid campaigners who had little awareness of racism in Britain, and left wing activists who demonstrated loudly for freedom in Vietnam or Chile but were silent when it came to the freedom of the Irish people. Racial discrimination in Britain, and repression in Ireland have been two of the gravest areas of human rights abuse on the part of the British in contemporary history, and I have involved myself intensely with both.

I first went to Northern Ireland in January 1969, as a member of a working group of the Society of Labour Lawyers which was investigating civil rights grievances. The eruption of civil rights demonstrations had started a few months before, culminating in a New Year march from Belfast to Derry. The march was constantly harassed by Protestant opponents, and on 4th January 1969, as it approached the city of Derry over Burntollet Bridge, it was directly attacked by a gang of 'B Specials', a part-time auxiliary police force with a reputation for thuggish behaviour and Protestant bigotry. A number of marchers were injured. We reached Derry on the following day and interviewed marchers whose wounds were still bleeding.

Derry is a city unique in the world, I believe, for having two names which in themselves convey two implacably opposed views of history. To the British authorities and to most Northern Ireland Protestants it is Londonderry. To the Irish authorities, the Northern Ireland Catholics and all who sympathise with their aspirations for a united Ireland, it is Derry.

It was originally 'Derry-Calgaich' which in Irish means "the oak grove of the fierce warrior". The prefix 'London' was added in the 17th century when Derry was administered by the City of London Corporation, and it sticks in the gullet of any Catholic Derry person as a symbol of British oppression.

Derry is symbolic to Northern Ireland Protestants as being the place where their forebears in 1688 withstood the siege imposed by the army of the Catholic King James II, and thus confirmed control of the city for the Protestant King William III, his heirs and successors. The event is commemorated by Protestants every year by a march through the city. When Ireland was partitioned into North and South in 1921, it was essential for the Protestant cause that Derry should be part of Northern Ireland, even though its population was predominantly Catholic, and it was surrounded by Catholic Donegal. In 1969 the very aspect of the city which I saw for the first time reinforced the symbolism. The high city walls, enclosing the Protestant power centre of the city, dominated the 'Bogside', one of the most populated Catholic areas, poor and overcrowded and overlooked in every sense of the word.

In human rights terms Derry was a then a scandal all of its own. Two small wards where mainly Protestants lived elected twelve members to the Borough Council. One large ward where mainly Catholics lived elected eight members. The local government franchise was limited to householders, so that many adults living with their parents were disenfranchised. Businesses, mostly in Protestant hands, had extra voting rights. Thus a city whose inhabitants were two-thirds Catholic regularly returned a Protestant majority on the Council. The Council was the major provider of housing, and one the city's biggest employers, so that control of the Council by Protestants created a situation of entrenched discrimination against Catholics. Catholic families experienced multiple grievances and humiliation, which they were powerless to remedy by constitutional means. Under the Government of Ireland Act of 1920 the British Parliament had passed all control of local affairs to the Northern Ireland Parliament at Stormont. "We are a Protestant Parliament and a Protestant State," the first Prime Minister of Northern Ireland, Lord Craigavon, had boasted.

On the night of the arrival of the march from Belfast, the B Specials had continued their mayhem by going down into the Bogside and attacking the residents of some of the small back-to-back houses. We interviewed elderly residents who had been terrified. After midnight we attended an open-air meeting in the biting cold, addressed by the John Hume and Ivan Cooper, leaders in the civil rights movement in Derry. This was happening before the re-emergence of the IRA as a fighting force, and the men of the Bogside had armed themselves with staves to patrol their community and defend it against further attack

This was naked oppression, institutional and physical, carried on against a defenceless people in the United Kingdom, and virtually nobody in the British media and British politics seemed to care. For most British people the Irish problem was a tedious hangover from history. When the Irish did not fight back, they were ignored. When they did, they became terrorists to be hated. On that visit to Derry, I saw innocent and decent people being subject to bitter and unnecessary suffering. If my skills as an advocate could be of any use to them, I would never refuse them.

In July 1971 I came back to Derry as chairman of the Inquiry into the Circumstances Surrounding the Deaths of Seamus Cusack and Desmond Beattie. By then the British Army had been in Northern Ireland for nearly two years. The Provisional IRA had emerged as a fighting force, but it was still small in Derry. Civil rights demands for a reform of the franchise and the abolition of the Derry Borough Council had been accepted. But the army was seen as an occupying and alien force, and was regularly pelted with stones by the Derry youth. The army responded to the rioting by shooting 'baton rounds', cylindrical rubber bullets which were intended to bounce in front of the rioters and bruise them. The army tended to keep away from the Bogside and the other Catholic areas, and there had been a kind of stand-off which contrasted with the more violent confrontations taking place in Belfast.

The calm was shattered on the right of 7th–8th July 1971 when Seamus Cusack was fatally shot by an army rifle in the aftermath of a riot. During further disturbances on the next day, Desmond Beattie was shot and killed by another soldier's rifle. They were the first Derry men to have been shot by soldiers since the army arrived. The army claimed that Seamus Cusack had been armed with a rifle and Desmond Beattie with a nail bomb. Local eye-witnesses insisted that they had been unarmed.

When a tragic event such as this takes place, it sends waves of shock, anger and despair throughout an entire community. The trauma can only eased by an official response which recognises that a prompt, thorough, transparent and impartial investigation has to take place. The Social Democratic and Labour Party MPs of the Stormont Parliament demanded an official inquiry into the deaths of Cusack and Beattie. When the Government refused, they boycotted Stormont and set up an alternative assembly. I was then approached by Bernadette Devlin, the radical civil rights activist and Member of Parliament who was later to assault the Home Secretary across the floor of the House of Commons in the aftermath of 'Bloody Sunday'. She asked me if I would be chairman of an independent inquiry into the shootings, and I readily agreed. My fellow inquirers were Paul O'Dwyer, a veteran Irish American attorney from New York, and Albie Sachs, then a law professor in exile from South Africa where he had been jailed for his opposition to apartheid. The friendship which I then gained with Albie Sachs, now Justice Sachs of the South African Constitutional Court, has lasted to this day.

The non-official public inquiry is a weapon in the armoury of the committed human rights advocate. Its effectiveness will depend on the integrity of the people who conduct the inquiry. If you take part in an inquiry which the State does not recognise, you may be branded as a propagandist by those who fear an open search for the truth. You have to be impartial and judicial in your treatment of the evidence, but committed to the remedying of justified grievances. You cannot tell how far your report and recommendations will resonate. You will certainly have the satisfaction of knowing that the people affected by the outrage which has occurred will be strengthened by the fact that other people have cared enough to spend time with them and hear their truth. In the Cusack-Beattie report we wrote, summing up our reasons for accepting the mission:

> When a man is shot dead, whether he be a soldier or a civilian, Catholic or Protestant, his fellow-citizens have a right to search for the truth as to why be was fired upon. If the truth can be made known, then lessons can be learnt and future lives can be saved. If the truth is withheld, bitterness and discontent will flourish.

We held our Inquiry in the Derry Guildhall in the second half of July 1971. We came to the conclusion that neither Seamus Cusack nor Desmond Beattie were armed, although bombs were being thrown in the minutes preceding Desmond Beattie's death. If we could have published our report in the first week of August, I believe that it could have had an impact on the situation in Derry. It was measured and moderate in tone and it could have led to greater understanding and restraint.

But on 9th August 1971 the authorities imposed internment without trial upon Northern Ireland. The decision was made by Brian Faulkner, the Stormont Prime Minister, accepted by British Prime Minister Edward

Heath, and carried out by the British Army. Arrests were made overnight and 342 people, nearly all Catholics, were put into internment camps. Many of them had nothing to do with violence, as the police and army intelligence was out of date. It was a gross violation of human rights, and predictably it inflamed Catholic opinion. It gave rise to a series of anti-internment marches and demonstrations, but these too had been banned and were considered illegal. On 30th January 1972 when over ten thousand people marched against internment and the army blocked their route, thirteen marchers were shot dead and thirteen were wounded (one of whom later died) by soldiers of the Parachute Regiment. That was Bloody Sunday, the day which created the biggest ever motivation for people to join the IRA. From then on Northern Ireland, and Britain too, became engulfed in a cycle of violence from which it emerged only 26 years later with the Good Friday Agreement of 1998.

The years when I came to know Northern Ireland were also the years of my solidarity with the freedom movements of Southern Africa. I had actively aligned myself with FRELIMO, the ANC, SWAPO and other movements, all of whom had in varying degrees taken up arms and had attacked military and economic targets of the white supremacist regimes. I had condemned the Bantustans, attempts to partition South Africa into different tribal territories, as violating the international law principles of self-determination. I had mocked the concept that Mozambique and Angola were overseas 'provinces' of Portugal.

I had to ask myself, what was different about Ireland? Could partition be accepted as reasonable in Ulster when it was so outrageous in the Transkei? Was not the concept of an overseas province as much a colonial abomination in Europe as it was in Africa? If the freedom struggle was justified for Black people in South Africa, targets of racial bigotry, was it not also justified for the Catholic people of Northern Ireland, targets of religious bigotry? Was I holding back on support for Irish freedom only because it was uncomfortable and even dangerous to support it, since it involved opposing one's own government and armed forces?

In my analysis of the situation, both then and now, I became and remain a passionate supporter of a united Ireland and an opponent of the artificial statelet which is Northern Ireland. I believe in the right to self-determination for a people, as well as in the protection of minorities within that people. Ireland to me is a cultural, geographical and historical unit whose people have been occupied by the British and have consistently resisted that occupation. The reason why there is a substantial Protestant population in Ireland is that it was settled there over the centuries as part of a deliberate strategy to strengthen British dominance. The descendants of these settlers have the right to religious freedom and to be fully protected from discrimination, rights which today are enjoyed by Protestants who live in the Republic of Ireland. But the Protestant population has no right, according to the principles of international law, to have frontiers manipulated to give them a majority in an artificial state, any more than the South African White population or the French settlers in Algeria. The partition of Ireland was done in 1921, as an act of cowardice and fudge, and I believe that one day it will be undone.

But two factors held me back from being a supporter of the IRA in the way that I was a supporter of the freedom movements in Africa. First and foremost was my refusal to support the cruelty of the methods used by the IRA in waging its campaign. I had been schooled by Amilcar Cabral and Samora Machel, leaders who set their face against bloodshed except against carefully chosen military targets. The ANC's armed struggle, for which Nelson Mandela was serving life imprisonment, was directed at sabotaging installations and not killing civilians. The ANC refused to imitate the repression and cruelty of its adversary, and its restraint has contributed to the peaceful transition to African majority rule. The bombing of the public houses in Birmingham, Guildford and Woolwich, in which 30 civilians were killed as they were enjoying their drinks, was a detestable tactic in the eyes of my African freedom fighter friends. While these bombings were exceptional in the number of lives lost, they were not isolated aberrations. Both in Northern Ireland and Britain, there has been too much killing, too many reprisals, and too little regard for human life, which could not be justified by saying that the British soldiers or the loyalist paramilitaries did the same. And there has been too little articulation of the values and character of the united Ireland for which the struggle was waged.

I have to confess to one thrill of excitement at an IRA action, in April 1993 when a massive bomb was exploded in the City of London in the early morning. Full advance warning had been given, and there was no-one within range except one reporter who pushed past a police cordon and was killed in the explosion. The financial centre of London was devastated. The international repercussions would be incalculable. I thought then (and I was not wrong) that the government could not afford to repeat such a blow to Britain's reputation as a stable financial capital, and it would have to make peace. But this attack was not the norm. Too often the IRA's actions served only to create public enmity, as well as private grief for those who lost relatives in the 'collateral damage' of the IRA campaign.

A more pragmatic reason for my steering clear of any overt political position on the IRA campaign was that I could be far more useful to people in Northern Ireland if I made a contribution as a human rights lawyer who could be taken seriously, rather than a political activist who could be sidelined as a leftist maverick. There was plenty going on in Northern Ireland to concern anyone who valued human rights. I made another trip to Derry in 1981 on behalf of the National Council for Civil Liberties to report on the death of Paul Whitters who was killed by a plastic bullet, and of Gary English and James Brown who were run over and killed by an army Land Rover. I visited the women's prison in Armagh, and I made an unofficial visit to the Long Kesh prison, travelling in a bus with the families of prisoners from Derry, where I now had many friends.

The late 70s and early 80s were the years of the republican prisoners' protests, one of the most extraordinary stories of steadfastness in adversity in the history of political prisoners. In order to protest against being equated with ordinary criminals, and to reclaim the 'special category' status which had earlier been accorded to them, republican prisoners refused to wear prison clothes (the 'blanket protest'), then smeared their cells with their own excrement (the 'dirty protest'), and finally ten of them fasted until they died. Margaret Thatcher, in her first term as Prime Minister, saw it as a test of her 'manhood', and refused to move an inch towards acceptance of the hunger strikers' demands. The 1981 hunger strike remains for me an extraordinary display of raw selfless courage in defence of a patriotic ideal.

Internment was brought to an end with the introduction of the 'Diplock courts', courts named after Lord Diplock who recommended them, where a judge alone, with no jury, decided on guilt in cases involving violence for political or sectarian ends. Arrested people were routinely subjected to beatings and forms of torture, and the resulting 'confessions' were ruled admissible by the Diplock judges. After some years the practice of police violence against suspects was exposed by Amnesty International and others, and safeguards were introduced to prevent it. A new way of obtaining convictions was then devised, the use of the 'supergrass'. The supergrass was to be the subject of my next intervention in Northern Ireland.

What happened was that arrested paramilitary suspects would be offered the chance to go free, take on a new identity, and be set up for life in another country, if they would agree to testify against their former colleagues. (A 'grass' in British slang is an informer; thus 'supergrass' is a super informer). Some succumbed to the temptation; if they did, they would be asked to sign statements implicating dozens of people, and in due course to testify in court. The more people they could implicate, the more likely it was that a deal would be made.

The supergrass trials, of which about a dozen took place, featured indictments of enormous length. In the case in which Christopher Black was the supergrass, 38 defendants were on trial, on an indictment containing 184 charges, based on 45 separate incidents. After a trial lasting from December 1982 to August 1983, 35 defendants were convicted. The only evidence against them came from Christopher Black. The judge found that 'he was one of the most convincing witnesses that I had heard in my experience in criminal trials'. Other supergrass trials followed, both of republicans and loyalists. By the time I came to investigate, over 100 people had been convicted and were awaiting their appeals, and charges were pending against over 100 more. Fifteen supergrasses, all of them serious offenders against the law, had been given immunity from prosecution.

I was sent in 1984 by the Cobden Trust, a body linked with the National Council for Civil Liberties, to make a one-person on-the-spot investigation of the supergrass phenomenon. I was able to spend a week in Northern Ireland, and I had a booking on the first plane out of Belfast on the Saturday which I could not miss.

Once in Belfast, I was welcomed as a saviour by supporters of both loyalist and republican prisoners. I spoke with the families of the prisoners, who were organised as 'Relatives for Justice' (Catholic) and 'Families for Legal Rights' (Protestant). Their experiences and their pain were the same, but because of the sectarian divide they could not join together. I had an interview with Lord Lowry, the Lord Chief Justice, who seemed burdened by the weight of responsibility which this kind of trial imposed on the judges. I spoke to lawyers who felt that the system of justice was discredited by the use of supergrasses. I spoke to the wife of a supergrass, who gave revealing information about life in 'protective custody'.

All week long I asked whether I could speak to a supergrass. Finally on Friday afternoon Oliver Kelly, a Belfast solicitor, told me that the thought he could find Robert Lean for me. Lean had agreed to be a supergrass but had then thought better of it, retracted his statements and escaped from protective custody. After ringing a couple of priests, Kelly said that Lean was in Waterford, about six hours drive away at the very south end of Ireland. It was then 3.00 pm and my plane out of Belfast was due to leave at 8.00 am the next day. I said that I would meet Lean at 10.00 pm, got into my rented car and sped to Waterford. Three hours meeting with Lean and his wife, six hours driving back again, and I made my plane. The life of a human rights lawyer can sometimes be demanding.

The information gained was well worth the trip. Lean described vividly the power which the controlling officer had over him once he decided to cooperate. The police, he said, wrote up statements according to their intelligence as to who was involved in a particular episode. He had to sign them, whether they were true or false. He was then expected to learn the story by heart and rehearse it with the controlling officer. He was told, "It will be like a book, we will build it up chapter by chapter. It's not me, it's the man with the wig you have got to convince." Lean spoke of the 'Stockholm system' through which a relationship of trust and dependence developed between the supergrass and his controller. When not rehearsing, there was entertainment and drinking evenings, and for Mrs. Lean and her family money flowed and shopping was offered. She described it as "a working class woman's dream". But in the end it was her stubborn rejection of the new life which was crucial in persuading her husband not to go through with it.

I concluded from all that I learnt of the supergrass system that it was anyone's guess whether the evidence which emerged was true or false. I felt sure that there was a lot of suggestion coming from the police to the supergrass as to what he was expected to say. Even if the supergrass volunteered the evidence, the danger was that he would implicate not just those whom he knew to be guilty, but those whom he believed the police most desired to see convicted. I said so in my report, which caused quite a stir when I published it in Belfast. From that day on, so I was informed, every appeal against a conviction on the evidence of a supergrass succeeded; and every trial ended in not guilty verdicts, unless there was other evidence to support the charge. The supergrass system fell into disuse.

A footnote from my supergrass inquiry still troubles me. One of my friends in the Northern Ireland legal profession was the solicitor Pat Finucane, a lawyer who had a reputation for using legal remedies fearlessly to uphold justice in Northern Ireland. As is well known, Pat was murdered by loyalist gunmen in front of his wife and children in February 1989, and the truth about official collusion in his murder is still being unravelled. In 1984, Lean told me that he had been asked to sign a statement headed 'top secret' in which he was to implicate Pat and four other solicitors. He was told, "We know they feed information to the IRA, we want it just in case we need it." Lean signed, though he said it was all lies. Less than a month before Pat was killed, Douglas Hogg MP, then junior minister for Northern Ireland, 'revealed' in Parliament that a number of lawyers were known to be "unduly sympathetic" to the IRA. I was sure that he would have been given the 'evidence' of Lean, if he had asked for facts to support that statement. ("See Minister, even their own people say so.") It is only a short step from fabricating that kind of evidence to conniving at the murder of an honest, but troublesome, civil rights lawyer.

IIIIIIIIIIIIIIIIIIIIIIIIIIIIIIIIIIIII

I was called to the Northern Ireland Bar in 1984. Northern Ireland has produced some superb advocates, whose mettle was regularly tested by the legal challenges arising from the troubles. I wanted to get experience in the Northern Ireland courts if the occasion arose. I was able to take advantage of my status as a Northern Ireland barrister on a dramatic day, 19th October 1989, when the 'Guildford Four' were acquitted at the Old Bailey.

The Guildford Four were Paul Hill, Gerard Conlon, Carole Richardson and Paddy Armstrong, young people who according to the police had admitted planting bombs in pubs in Guildford, killing five people, and in Woolwich, killing two. Their case, and the linked case of the Maguire family, represent the depths to which British justice sank when it had to deal with suspected terrorists. In the Guildford Four case the only evidence which the prosecution could put before the jury was a series of conflicting 'confessions'. They were said to have been made by four vulnerable young people who lived as squatters in London. Even to the police they must have seemed unlikely members of an IRA cell.

Laymen and many lawyers often find difficulty in understanding how intelligent adults come to confess to crimes which they have not committed. But experience shows that when people are alone in a police station, beaten and threatened with death, they will sign anything to stop the intolerable pressure. The film *In the Name of the Father*, which was based on the Guildford Four and the Maguire family cases, was a brilliant evocation of the terror instilled by the Surrey detectives who, after a month of fruitless investigation, had determined that they would obtain evidence of guilt by whatever means necessary.

The bombings in London continued after the arrest of the Guildford Four and did not stop until the police cornered four IRA members in Balcombe Street in London and arrested them. By then, the Guildford Four had been convicted. The men arrested at Balcombe Street freely admitted carrying out over 20 bombing attacks around Britain, including the Guildford and Woolwich bombings. They supplied details to the police which could only have come from those who had perpetrated the attacks. They testified on behalf of the Guildford Four before the Court of Appeal in London, saying that they and no one else were guilty. To their shame, the judges of the Court of Appeal refused to accept that a miscarriage of justice had occurred. They decided that eight people were guilty – the Balcombe Street Four and the Guildford Four - even though the 'confessions' of the Guildford Four had only ever mentioned a team of four people being involved. If the 'confession' did not fit the facts, then in the eyes of the judges they must have been deliberately distorted by the wily IRA. But if they were so wily, why did they confess in the first place? The perverse obstinacy of the judges of appeal cost the Guildford Four a further 12 years in prison.

In 1987, following a campaign led by Cardinal Hume and Lord Scarman, the Home Secretary referred the case of the Guildford Four back to the Court of Appeal. A fresh investigation into the case was carried out by the Avon and Somerset police. They found in a police station cupboard a number of typed pages which appeared to be records of police interviews with the Guildford Four. The typed script contained added amendments in handwriting. The investigators compared the typed scripts, as amended in handwriting, with the 'contemporaneous' notes of interviews which had been relied on by the police officers in giving evidence at the trial. They matched. In other words, the officers had invented a script, typed up a draft, amended it to form a second draft, copied out the second draft into their notebooks, and testified falsely that these were the notes made at the time of the interviews. The only possible inference to draw was that the 'confessions' of the Four had been a work of fiction written by the police.

I was briefed as leading counsel for Paul Hill, with Helena Kennedy as my junior. We were summoned to a hearing at the Old Bailey, where we were met by crown counsel Roy Amlot, who told us of the finding of the typed interview scripts. In the light of this finding, he told us that the crown could no longer support the convictions of the four. He proposed to explain the development to the court and recommend that the convictions should be quashed immediately.

While reeling with joy at this amazing development, Helena and I saw one problem. Paul Hill had also been convicted for the murder of Brian Shaw in Belfast, and was serving a life sentence for that murder as well as for the Guildford murders. The evidence against him was another 'confession', made to officers of the Royal Ulster Constabulary (RUC) at Guildford police station, immediately before he had 'confessed' to the Guildford crime. Paul's defence at his Belfast trial in a Diplock court had been that he had been so beaten and threatened by the Surrey police over the previous day and night, that he was prepared to sign any document that was put before him. In this state of terror he had signed two 'confessions', first to the RUC for the Shaw murder, and then to the Surrey police for Guildford. So Paul was not going to be freed, but would be flown to Northern Ireland in order to go on serving his life sentences for the Shaw murder. I decided to leave Helena to enjoy the end of the Guildford appeal, while I flew to Belfast to deal with the Northern Ireland case.

I reached the Law Courts in Belfast by 3.00 pm, a few hours ahead of Paul, who was flown over handcuffed to the inside of a police helicopter. I met the crown counsel, Ronnie Appleton, who had prosecuted Paul in 1974. His attitude was that whatever the rights and wrongs of the Guildford convictions, no one had accused the RUC of brutality, so that the Belfast conviction was untainted.

I enlisted the help of my former pupil Barry Macdonald as junior counsel, and we drafted an application to appeal 'out of time'. Paul had never appealed the Belfast conviction, since he could not challenge the decision of the judge, Mr Justice Kelly, who had accepted Paul's confession as having been voluntary. We also lodged an application for bail pending appeal, and this was granted on the following day. So Paul was free, although his fight for justice was by no means over. He used his freedom to travel to the United States, to meet up with the girl who had met and married him while he was a prisoner in England.

Several years went by. The investigation of the Avon and Somerset police was still going on, and the officers who had fabricated the statements were charged with perverting the course of justice (and regrettably, acquitted). We asked the Belfast court to wait until all the material evidence was available. Eventually the Court of Appeal of Northern Ireland, presided over by Lord Chief Justice Hutton, convened to hear the appeal in April 1994.

In the intervening years Paul's circumstances had charged dramatically. The marriage to the wife he had met in prison had not worked out, but he had met and fallen in love with Courtney, the daughter of Robert Kennedy, and they were now married. Paul had become a member of the Kennedy clan, and the Kennedys are a family who stick by their own. A number of Kennedys, including Robert's mother Ethel and his son Joseph, a congressman in Massachusetts, arrived to hear the appeal, together with an international media circus.

Paul's appeal was fought over three weeks. Crucial evidence was given by a firearms officer who had witnessed a fellow officer pointing a gun through the window of a cell while Paul had been in custody in Guildford. This was important, because Paul at his trial before Mr Justice Kelly had testified that one of the most frightening experiences had been an officer threatening to let off a gun through his cell window. The difficulty was that the officer's diary showed that he was rostered for duty on the night after Paul confessed, not the night before. If he was on duty on the night after, the misconduct could not have influenced the confession.

Our other main argument was that the Surrey officers had been proved to be so corrupt that the evidence which they had given before Mr Justice Kelly could no longer be trusted. Appleton tried to rebut that argument by showing that the officers whom Paul had accused of brutality, and who had given evidence to Kelly, were not the same as the officers who had fabricated the interviews. It was a tense experience, and our hopes veered up and down as each witness gave evidence.

In the end justice was done and Paul's conviction for the murder of Brian Shaw was quashed. The officer who had seen the misconduct in the cells said that although the diary recorded the day when he was rostered for duty, he had a dim memory of being called in on an off-duty day to help guard a suspect who had just been arrested for the Guildford bombings. So the Northern Ireland Court of Appeal accepted that what Paul had alleged at his trial could well be true. In addition they decided that the degree of perjury within the Surrey force was so great that all the officers were tainted. Paul received compensation for the years of wrongful imprisonment, and he remains a member of the Kennedy clan.

Years later, Paul took part in a television programme in which he met the brother of Brian Shaw. The brother, having been briefed by the RUC, was convinced that Paul had been freed on a technicality and was really guilty. It was understandable; Paul's 'confession' had been full of detail, and the brother would have no reason over the years to doubt that it was genuine. After a tense meeting, he was ready to accept Paul's handshake, which he had refused at the start, and perhaps understand that there was at least a doubt.

I was working mainly in Jamaica during the 1990s, and I followed the peace negotiations in Northern Ireland at a distance. I read that in February 1998 Tony Blair had agreed to set up a new judicial inquiry into the events of Bloody Sunday. Two months later I watched day by day as the peace negotiations dragged on, eventually producing the Good Friday Agreement. I am not a great supporter of Tony Blair, but I believe the Good Friday Agreement to be an extraordinary achievement, which took a grim determination for which he deserves much praise. From the distance of the Caribbean I thought that my work in Northern Ireland was over. In fact my biggest commitment to Northern Ireland, which would stretch over six years, was still to be made.

10

JUSTICE *across* FRONTIERS

I wrote earlier of my mission to Portugal in 1966, which set me on the road to Africa, and introduced me to the excitement of being involved in solidarity with lawyers striving for justice in a repressive regime. I have never lost that desire to travel the world in the pursuit of justice. I commend to any lawyer who is committed to defending human rights, that he or she should look for opportunities to apply that commitment in other parts of the world. The countries which need your presence may be different from those which needed mine. But the use of legal power to repress human rights continues in many places, and a small effort on your part can make a huge impact.

After Portugal, my next journey was to Athens in 1967. Greece, the cradle of democracy whose poetry and philosophy I had studied as a classical scholar, had been hijacked by a military coup and was ruled by a junta of colonels. Thousands of leftists had been arrested and imprisoned on the island of Yaros. In Britain, the League for Democracy in Greece was actively campaigning, led by Betty Ambatielos, whose husband Tony was a political prisoner in Yaros.

In July 1967 the regime arrested Mikis Theodorakis, the Greek composer whose music had thrilled me at protest concerts which the League had organised. In June 1967 an Army Order had decreed that "Throughout the country it is forbidden to reproduce or play the music or songs of the composer Mikis Theodorakis... because this music is in the service of communism." The League sponsored a two-man delegation, myself and Cedric Thornberry, a law lecturer who later did brilliant work as a United Nations official, to go to Athens and do whatever we could to get Theodorakis released, or at least stop him being tortured.

Cedric and I met with Theodorakis' lawyer, who told us that he did not know where his client was or what was happening to him. We had a meeting with Colonel Totomis, the Minister of Security, a hard-faced man who told us nothing. We then met Colonel Patakos, the Minister of the Interior. Patakos was a caricature junta colonel, jovial and full of his own importance. He fixed me with an earnest gaze and said, "Young man, take care. You are in the House of Lords. There are communists in the House of Lords. Take care that they do not take over." I thought that Lord Milford, who was indeed a communist, the only one in the British Parliament, would be pleased to know how much he was feared. Patakos also told us nothing. They would not even admit that Theodorakis was in custody.

Cedric and I returned to our hotel, despondent. Then Cedric said, "Let's ring the *Guardian*." My first reaction was that we couldn't; the regime would be bugging all the phones. But Cedric rang the *Guardian*, and gave the paper an account of our mission. The next morning the *Guardian* ran a front page story. We ourselves did little more on that visit. Cedric was ordered to leave. I had left before him, and a few months later I was turned back at the airport when I came to observe a trial. But Theodorakis' conditions changed. His lawyer was able to see him. He was not tortured, and months later he was released. Years later, when we were both observers at a trial in Turkey, we met and he thanked me.

The lesson which I learned is as true today as it was in the sixties. Those who abuse power and oppress their people are afraid of publicity. The media can transform a local injustice into a scandal that can shame the oppressor into changing his direction. Lawyers tend to be shy of the media, but ever since that mission in 1967 I have been media-friendly. Even when my professional code as a barrister prevents me from talking about my cases, I have made sure in off-the-record briefings that the media know what I am doing. In Jamaica, where advocates are allowed to talk to the media, I always tell the media about my cases if my client is happy for that to happen. It is not to be boastful about my role as advocate. It is to spread the word, both to the abusers of power and their victims, that justice can triumph.

Not every mission would be successful. In 1980 I was invited to join a delegation from France, Belgium and Senegal to investigate human rights abuses in Morocco. Morocco was ruled by its monarch King Hassan II, who did not tolerate opposition and had jailed a number of dissidents. In addition Morocco was claiming sovereignty over the Western Sahara, a desert land which had been governed by Spain until 1975. Rich phosphate deposits had been found under the desert, which was a reason for Morocco's determination to take over the territory after Spain decolonised. A movement for independence for the people of Western Sahara, the Saharwis, had been launched in 1973 by the Polisario Front, and it was now fighting an effective guerrilla war against Morocco. I had been advising the London representative of the Polisario Front, who told me that Saharwi prisoners were being held in conditions of particular cruelty in desert dungeons. My own role in the international mission was to investigate those conditions.

The leader of our delegation was Admiral Sanguinetti, retired from the French Navy, a Corsican, proud and dignified and immaculately dressed. The Senegalese member, Mustapha Seck, was the President of the Senegalese Bar. We flew to Casablanca and took a taxi to Rabat, the Moroccan capital. Next morning we started our work, meeting lawyers who had been defending political prisoners. Returning to our hotel at midday, we found a messenger from the Mayor of Rabat, with an invitation to lunch. The Mayor's palace was like a modern version of the Alhambra, with encrusted mosaic ceilings and fountains playing in the background. We sat on vast cushions, had a feast of Moroccan delicacies, and made small talk with the Mayor. At the end of the meal, he said, "Now that you have enjoyed Moroccan hospitality, it is time for you to go home." It was a most civilised way of being deported. In vain the Admiral protested that we had not finished our business.

When we got back to the hotel we found that our bags had been packed, and taxis were waiting to take us to Casablanca airport. At the airport, all the telephones had been removed, and we could not contact our embassies. We were taken to a check-in desk and asked for our tickets. "But we have no tickets," said the Admiral, daring them to search his august person. We were taken to the head of Security, who said that if we had no tickets we must be vagabonds. The Admiral burst into laughter, saying, "Then treat us as vagabonds." One could hardly imagine a more distinguished set of vagabonds.

We spent the night on the airport chairs. A Moroccan official pleaded with Mustapha Seck to stay behind. They meant no insult to a fellow African, only to these Europeans. Seck stayed solid with us. Eventually in the morning the Moroccans grumpily produced five single tickets to Marseilles, the nearest airport on French soil, and we were ordered to board it. The angriest moment came as the police, as we left, decided to search our bags. They looked through my briefcase and saw the Polisario documents which I had brought. Their manner changed to fury. They looked as if they wanted to take me to the Sahara and dump me in a dungeon with my Polisario friends. In the end we were escorted to the plane, and so our deportation ended.

These missions, even if they end in apparent failure, have a threefold value. First, they are deeply appreciated by those who are suffering for their belief in justice and freedom. It may be the prisoner in the cell who learns that a delegation has been asking awkward questions; or the lawyer who puts his or her life and liberty in danger by standing up for human rights; or the people who support them who meet you or learn that you have been there. You are part of an invisible and immeasurable union of kindred souls who share the same ideals.

Sometimes the smallest gesture of solidarity can ripple across the world. In the early 1980s General Alexander Haig, the US Secretary of State, was visiting London. It was a time when the US was supporting the South African apartheid regime in its invasion of Angola. A group of us who had been working to help Angola and Mozambique decided to demonstrate against Haig. It was a wretched wet London day. About eight of us turned up with placards. A photographer snapped us and left. Haig was taken in on the other side of the building. We asked ourselves, why did we bother?

A few weeks later an Angolan friend came to London. "That was a fantastic demonstration which you organised against Haig," he said. "It was on the front page of the Luanda papers. It gave us tremendous strength to know what you did for us. Well done!" He showed us the front page. The photographer had managed to show the eight as if they were the vanguard of eight hundred. Thousands of readers had learned, at a time of great pressure and suffering for their country, that people in Britain stood with them. The effect is even more powerful when you have actually travelled to stand with people and do what you can to help.

The second value is that you may actually achieve something. Not every time, not your mission alone, but more often than you will ever know. Few people in authority in a repressive regime will reveal themselves as openly as the Portuguese judge. But changes will happen. You write a report and it is studied by the Foreign Office. You give a press conference and the story goes to readers everywhere. You meet a group of MPs and they raise the issues in a debate or a motion. Diplomatic representations are made by British officials to the government of the country concerned. In the end it may become necessary out of sheer self-interest for a repressive regime to change its ways. But it would not happen without you – and the thousands who take other actions inside the country and outside – having taken the trouble, given up some time and money, and stirred yourself into action.

Results were undoubtedly achieved by the British campaign on behalf of Captain Kojo Tsikata, a former officer of the Ghanaian army whom I had come to know as a friend during the years of solidarity work with Angola and Mozambique. Kojo had been a military adviser to the Angolan liberation movement, and had then come to live in London. He returned to Ghana, and was arrested in November 1975 by the military government of General Acheampong. He was charged with plotting to overthrow the government. Kojo had been well connected in London, and when a campaign for him was started, we got the support of a number of members of the Houses of Lords and Commons. We raised funds to send Jeremy Smith, one of my colleagues in the Wellington Street chambers, to be an observer at his trial before a military tribunal. Jeremy brought back a full report of the proceedings, including graphic accounts of Kojo's statement to the tribunal, in which he detailed the tortures which had been used against his body to extract a 'confession'.

Kojo Tsikata and four others were sentenced to death in August 1976. The campaign was now so well organised that a flurry of high level protests were sent to the Ghanaian Head of State. Fifty-nine Members of Parliament sent a letter urging clemency. The death sentences were not carried out, although the condemned men were still on death row when Acheampong was overthrown in July 1978 and a new military regime under General Akuffo took over. Around that time a letter from Kojo to me was smuggled out of prison. He said that he was sick, and there was a doctor responsible for the prison who was a snob who loved all things British. If I wrote a letter it might bring some results. I wrote on House of Lords notepaper, saying that the doctor's reputation was known to me and other eminent Lords. I asked for inmate Tsikata to be allowed to receive treatment from a specialist at a top London hospital.

Within two months I had a letter from Kojo, sent from Accra on 4th August 1978, saying that my letter had "worked like dynamite", and ending with words that I treasure: "I must once again express my sincere thanks to you, Jeremy and all the other friends for all that you have done for me over the past two and a half years. I am alive and free today as a result of your efforts." Kojo Tsikata later became a senior member of the government of Jerry Rawlings, and my friendship with him led to many visits to Ghana in later years.

In addition to moral support and actual results, the third value of international work is in the changes that happen in the psyche of the advocate who goes on the mission. Sometimes after weeks of slogging around the courts, an advocate can get tired and jaundiced about a career in law. Human rights missions blow away the cobwebs of cynicism. When you meet people who have been tortured because they would not confess to lies, or beaten up because they went on a demonstration, or arrested and charged because they have criticised the ruling elite, your concepts of justice and injustice, right and wrong, become clearer and purer. There are lawyers today in many countries who face harassment and imprisonment for defending unpopular clients. You come to learn that you are part of a worldwide brother- and sisterhood of dissident advocates who can be significant agents for change.

To be effective on a human rights mission, you have to be accredited by an organisation. As an individual barrister or attorney you are a busybody who can be ignored. As the representative of the International Association of Democratic Lawyers, or the International Human Rights Federation, you can stand tall, for a rebuff to you is a rebuff to the thousands of lawyers for whom you speak. So join an organisation, attend its meetings, research and write a paper about a situation which interests you – these are all ways of becoming involved. The Human Rights Committee of the English Bar has sponsored many missions in recent years, including to Iran, Colombia and Cameroon. It is active in a way which was unimaginable when I was a young barrister. The Law Society has developed training programmes in many parts of the world. There is scope for working in the international human rights field, for instance in the European Court of Human Rights, or the new International Criminal Court, or for a non-government organisation like Amnesty International or Human Rights Watch. Several members of my chambers in London have taken part in international missions and inquiries, and I continue to give them maximum encouragement.

On an international mission it is better to be a delegation, even if it is only two people, than to be on your own, for the members of a delegation can support each other when difficulties and challenges have to be faced. But it is better to go alone than not at all. In October 1990 I was asked to go to Pakistan. The Government of Prime Minister Benazir Bhutto had been dismissed by the President, who had brought charges of 'misconduct' against her in a number of courts. I was to be part of a two-man delegation on behalf of the International Human Rights Federation, based in Paris, to observe the judicial proceedings and make a report. Three days before we were due to go, the Federation withdrew its sponsorship of the mission, and my French colleague dropped out. From the briefings which I had received I knew that the situation in Pakistan was critical and the presence of an outside observer could be crucial. So I asked Lord Avebury, who was Chairman of the Parliamentary Human Rights Group, if the Group would accredit me. The Group was composed of members of the House of Commons and House of Lords who were concerned about human rights, and I had already carried out two missions for the Group, to Chile in 1987 and to Turkey in 1988. Lord Avebury agreed to support my mission to Pakistan.

Soon I was in Lahore where Benazir Bhutto's next hearing was to take place. Her lawyer was very anxious. He explained how when Benazir travelled anywhere, a huge crowd of supporters would always gather. However great the numbers, there was an unspoken discipline, which needed no police or marshals to enforce it, by which there was always a safe and respectful space in front of her as she walked. But the previous week, when she came to court, there had been a large crowd of rowdy people cheering her, and as she approached the courthouse they closed in and began to squeeze the breath from her by sheer weight of numbers. A female companion saw what was going on and pulled her into the shelter of a building, and she was safe. But she had no doubt that the intention of the 'supporters' had been to stage an accidental death, which the world would have been told was due to Ms Bhutto being crushed by her own unruly fans.

This time I accompanied Benazir and her team into the same courthouse, and there was no incident. She denounced what had happened at a press conference which I attended. I felt proud to have been there, to give at least moral support to a brave woman. I wrote a report recommending that the charges should be withdrawn, and in time they were. Benazir Bhutto survived to become Prime Minister again in 1993.

It is not only through delegations and missions that international legal solidarity is manifested. I have been involved in unofficial, but prestigious, international tribunals, where jurists are brought together from different countries to investigate a situation publicly and pronounce judgment. The philosopher Bertrand Russell founded the Bertrand Russell Peace Foundation, which organised international tribunals on war crimes in Vietnam, and on crimes against humanity committed by South American military regimes. After his death the foundation organised the Third Bertrand Russell International Tribunal, in which I took part, on human rights violations in West Germany. It met for a week in Cologne in 1978.

Its main focus was on a practice known as 'berufsverbot' by which anyone suspected of left or communist leanings could be disqualified from the public service. It also looked at the conditions in which prisoners from the 'Red Army Fraction', also known as the Baader-Meinhof group, were held.

I also took part in a War Crimes Tribunal, which was organised in New York by Ramsay Clark, the former Attorney General of the United States, into crimes committed by the US military and air forces in the Gulf War in Iraq in 1991. He invited judges and lawyers from Japan, Egypt, Europe and the American continent, an impressive gathering of legal talent. Eloquent testimony was given about the 'precision' bombing which killed civilians in shelters, the massacre of the retreating Iraq army, and the effects on the lives of children of the continuing sanctions against Iraq. The Tribunal determined that there was a case to answer of gross violation of international law by the United States.

Not a word about the Tribunal appeared in the American press or on the television. A press conference held in the United Nations building was attended only by some fringe media representatives. Up to this day, the most difficult public opinion to influence, or even reach, is the one with the greatest apparent access to information, the people of the United States. A second Tribunal was held in 2004 to consider further war crimes committed by the US and its allies in the 2003 invasion of Iraq.

Even though the Tribunal in New York had little publicity, it did not go unnoticed by the agencies which watch over us. After returning from New York, I was surprised to receive a complaint to the General Legal Council, which supervises the conduct of Jamaican attorneys, from the late Hurley Whitehorne, a respected Jamaican attorney and retired Colonel of the Jamaican army. He had learned from his friends in Britain, who had learned from their associates in US, that I had taken part in this Tribunal. He thought that it was unbecoming of a Jamaican attorney-at-law. The General Legal Council took no action, but the revelation of this network of secret service agencies, exercising their minds over my subversive actions, amused me. If you undertake human rights work, you know that you will build up a file in the computers of MI5 and other such agencies. But since the work you do is righteous, you need not worry that they are watching you. On the contrary, it is a mark of respect.

I recommend to any human rights lawyer to master some of the world's main languages. I am reasonably good in French, which has helped me on a number of missions. Spanish would have been as useful, but I have never broken through to any fluency. My French enabled me to take part in another variety of international advocacy, when I wore my wig and gown in the courts of France and Belgium, not as an observer, but as an advocate addressing the court. The rules of the European Union confer rights of audience to a lawyer from one EU country in the courts of any other, provided that the lawyer speaks the language of the country concerned, and is accompanied by a lawyer who is qualified in that country.

The continental procedure lends itself to displays of forensic histrionics. The cases in which I intervened all had a political element, and the objective of the defence team was to make a protest about the accused being charged at all, rather than to go into the details of his or her case. My first effort was in the Palais de Justice in Brussels, in a disciplinary hearing against a lawyer who had gone on radio and voiced his opinion that working class clients could not get decent representation from the Belgian Bar. For this he had been disciplined by the authorities of the Belgian legal profession. A team of lawyers from Britain, France and the Netherlands was brought together in order to defend our colleague's right to speak freely on a matter which concerned us all.

My second attempt at advocacy in French was in Paris, at a trial of French pacifists who had blocked a convoy of military vehicles transporting nuclear material. The issue was not so much whether they had broken the law, which they clearly had, but whether they should be sent to prison for protesting in a just cause. My French colleague called various eminent personalities to testify about their support for the protest. I expressed my concerns about pacifists being prosecuted for non-violent action. There were no jail sentences.

By my third appearance in a continental court I was beginning to know the ropes. It was an extradition hearing in the Palais de Justice in Paris, in which five women were wanted by West Germany for crimes associated with the Red Army Fraction. Their French lawyers were keen to make a stand against the erosion of the rights of asylum, and invited colleagues from Holland, Germany and Britain, to take part in the defence. I travelled to Paris, where my French colleague had arranged a visit to our client in prison. The lawyers had planned a joint meeting in the prison between all the lawyers and clients, but this had been prevented by the prison authorities for security reasons. The extradition hearing was fixed for a Monday afternoon. I had a case starting at the Old Bailey on the Tuesday of the same week, so I told my colleague that I would have to withdraw. "Don't worry," he said, "the hearing will start and finish on Monday."

The start time was 2.00 pm, and the legal team planned to seek an adjournment because they had not had proper facilities to consult with their clients. The three judges sat at a semicircular table, with a posse of armed police behind them. There was a space between the judges and the barristers' benches. At the side of the court was the dock, ringed with more armed police, and at the back there was an enclosure which was the public gallery, in which about a hundred supporters of the five women stood packed together.

I learned, from watching other colleagues, that the technique was to advance into the semi-circular space, eyeball the judges, and then turn and deliver a punch line to the public gallery, which would clap and stamp its feet with appreciation. Maître Vergès, who had been a defence lawyer in the Algerian war, and who later was to defend the Nazi Klaus Barbie, was one of the legal team. His method of advocacy was to start his address, or rather his harangue to the court, at the top of his voice and to get louder as he went on. Emboldened, I made a contribution by criticising the amount of overt armed security around the court, much to the delight of the gallery.

At 5.00 pm the court retired to consider the adjournment request, and the legal team adjourned for a three course supper in the Palais de Justice dining room. It was a contrast from the junk food canteens of the Old Bailey and the Law Courts in London. Well refreshed, we returned to court at 7.00 pm to learn that the adjournment was refused and the hearing would start forthwith. The Public Prosecutor spoke for about two hours. There were addresses from about eight defence lawyers. I got to my feet well after 11.00 pm. Then the clients had the right to address the court, and one of them did so on behalf of the five. We left the Palais de Justice around 12.30 am, and as my colleague had promised, I was able to catch my plane early the next morning, and reached the Old Bailey in time for the start of my trial. It had been good theatre, but it was hardly justice. It was no surprise when I later learned that the five women were duly extradited.

My last appearance in a Francophone court was more serious in its tone, and unlike the extradition hearing it may have made some difference. In 1988 an Irish priest called Father Patrick Ryan had been arrested in Belgium. He was alleged to have had associations with the IRA. A charge was pending against him in England of conspiracy to murder "for that on dates unknown, with persons unknown, he conspired to murder persons unknown". No such charge was known to Belgian law, which provided for a much more specific crime of belonging to a criminal organisation. The English common law had fashioned the much vaguer crime of conspiracy, especially in or der to prosecute subversives against whom no actual crime could be proved. I had just been defending three Irish people accused on a similar charge in England. They had been sentenced to 25 years imprisonment.

In my best French I attempted to explain the concept of 'conspiracy' to the Belgian court. The judges looked puzzled, and showed some alarm when I said that there was no limit to the prison sentence which the court might impose. I referred to the hysteria in England about the IRA in England and against Father Ryan in particular. I was very happy when the Belgian authorities decided that Father Ryan might not get a fair trial. Rather than extradite him to England, they deported him to Ireland.

My final thought on international work in the cause of justice is that one should never assume that it is only in foreign countries that human rights missions are needed. Britain has had its human rights scandals, and will have them again. After the Broadwater Farm riots of 1985, when dozens of Black youth were being charged on dubious evidence, a delegation headed by Margaret Burnham, one of Boston's first Black judges, observed some of the trials and wrote an excellent report. The procedures of the common law system do not lend themselves so easily to direct advocacy by foreign lawyers in our courts. But international intervention in British cases can be decisive.

I have written of being part of the defence team for the Birmingham Six. I never thought that my advocacy in the courtroom in that case made much difference. But I do take pride in a day in Washington in the summer of 1990, after the Six had lost their second appeal, and any hope of release seemed to have been dashed. Following sustained pressure from the supporters of the Six, their case was publicised in the United States. The Human Rights Caucus of the United States Congress decided to hold a public hearing on the case. I flew up from Jamaica to present the legal arguments. Gerard Conlon, one of the Guildford Four recently freed after 15 years of wrongful imprisonment, was to speak on the experience of being an innocent man in jail.

The Chairman of the Caucus, Congressman Tom Lantos, explained to us that this was the first time that the Caucus had investigated human rights violations in an allied country. He said that the British Embassy had made representations to them to abort the hearing; but "whenever a government asks us not to investigate, that's when we know that we have to investigate". About 25 Congress members came to the hearing. Gerry Conlon was eloquent and moving. I described the flaws in the prosecution case which had been exposed in the appeal before Lord Lane.

A month later the Home Secretary announced that the Devon and Cornwall police would conduct a further investigation into the

Birmingham Six case. That investigation led to the scientific tests on the police officers' notebooks, proving that the 'confessions' had been fabricated after the event rather than recorded contemporaneously, and that in turn led to the third appeal. I cannot prove that the intervention of the US Congress forced the UK Government to re-open the case, but I think it likely. No government can be comfortable if the US Congress is breathing down its neck.

After the hearing Gerry Conlon expressed surprise that none of the Congress members who attended the hearing had been Black. He recalled the solidarity which had existed in prison between Black and Irish prisoners, and the help given by Black families in giving accommodation to visiting Irish relatives. He knew that injustice in the British system struck at Irish and Black prisoners alike. He asked me to go with him to lobby African American leaders. We saw Reverend Jesse Jackson and went to the offices of several Black members of Congress. We learned that the Irish community in the US had given little support to African Americans; on the contrary, the Irish were often regarded as the oppressor. But Gerry had made an important statement. In the context of Britain, the two most scandalous areas of human rights violation in recent history have concerned Irish freedom and racial injustice. Gerry showed true vision in refusing to allow the quest for justice to be compartmentalised into separate causes.

By the time I appeared for the Birmingham Six in Washington, the focus of my life and legal practice was changing. Until 1990 my various interventions had been based on my status as a British barrister, operating out of the United Kingdom. However much I was a dissident, I had been part of the British professional establishment, using that status to try and obtain justice for the underdog. In my work in the 'third world', whether in Mozambique or Morocco or Pakistan, I was a representative of the privileged world who chose to act in solidarity with the underprivileged. If I could through my representations influence the British authorities to speak or act differently in response to foreign injustices, I would be influencing a government which had still had real power in the world.

From 1991, although still a British barrister, I was also a Jamaican attorney-at-law working mainly in Jamaica. I was no longer working from the outside in solidarity. I was inside one of the countries of the 'third world', living every day with its poverty, its debts and its comparative impotence in the world system. In the next part of this book I will try to show how my role as a human rights advocate has changed and adapted to this radically new environment.

Part Two

Attorney-at-law, Jamaica

11

MISSION *to* GRENADA

In February 1984 I made my first visit to the Caribbean as a human rights lawyer sent on a mission to Grenada. Apart from a holiday, I had experienced the Caribbean only at second hand through friendships with activists living in Britain. The nearest I got to the revolutionary government of Grenada was to attend a sensational meeting addressed by its Prime Minister Maurice Bishop at Kensington Town Hall in the early part of 1983.

Maurice Bishop spoke for two spell-binding hours. I have never heard a finer political speech. He described the achievements of his New Jewel Movement (NJM) government since it deposed the autocratic Eric Gairy in 1979. He spoke of the simple improvements in rural roads, health services and education which his government had made. He described the new airport, then under construction with the help of European money and Cuban experts. The airport would open up Grenada to tourism, but the Reagan administration in the United States had described it as a Cuban base. He spoke as a man devoted to the upliftment of the people of his country, using the power of government to deal with the people's basic needs. He mocked Ronald Reagan's description of little Grenada, with its population of 100,000, as being a danger to US security. Behind the mockery he was warning us that Grenada was under threat.

Those who have heard of Fidel Castro attest to a similar combination of intellectual mastery and manifest love of the people. In my own experience Samora Machel was also a leader who captivated audiences with the power of his loving and ebullient personality. But this leader was an English-speaking revolutionary. The worry for the United States was that Grenada's example of people's power would spread to other parts of the English-speaking Caribbean and beyond. Early in 1983 the US staged a military exercise near Puerto Rico, which took the form of a simulated attack on 'Amber and the Amberines'. Since Grenada lies close to the island group called the Grenadines, the purpose of the exercise was obvious.

On 19th October 1983 the Grenada Revolution imploded upon itself in the most awful way. Maurice Bishop was murdered with a number of other leaders, including Jacqueline Creft, Minister of Education, who was pregnant with his child. They were executed by a firing squad of their own soldiers. Their bodies were dumped in an unknown grave. The NJM leaders continued in government for a week before being overthrown by the United States military, which invaded the island and quickly subdued a people who were in mourning and shock. They arrested anyone who could be linked to the NJM government.

Why had this catastrophe happened? Part of the answer can be found in the minutes of the meetings of the Central Committee of the NJM in the months before October 1983. The NJM was in reality a party organised along Leninist lines, with a small membership of faithful socialists. Not all the government ministers were in the NJM, but the NJM controlled the levers of power and made the crucial decisions about the direction of the revolution. In September 1983 the Central Committee had agreed that the leadership of the NJM should be shared between Maurice Bishop and Bernard Coard, Grenada's Minister of Finance. They were to be joint leaders. Coard was said to be strong in his ideology and organisational skills, while Bishop was a great communicator and was loved by the people.

At a meeting on 30th September 1983 Bishop went along with the idea, although he must have seen it as an attack on himself as leader. He had then gone on a foreign tour to Eastern Europe, returning via Cuba. It was rumoured that while he was abroad he had decided to withdraw his agreement to the joint leadership plan, and that on his return 'blood would flow'. Unusually, none of his close colleagues came to meet him when he arrived home. Within a week of his return, the majority of the Central Committee ordered that he should be placed under house arrest. A meeting of NJM members on 16th October condemned him for violating the principles of democratic centralism, the Leninist tenet by which a decision once made had to be loyally observed.

Maurice Bishop's arrest put the country into turmoil. On 19th October a popular demonstration arrived at Bishop's house and released him, without opposition from those who were guarding him. The jubilant crowd marched with Bishop at their head to Fort Rupert, the principal army barracks. They disarmed the soldiers and took over the Fort. The members of the Central Committee were gathered at another Fort, Fort Frederick. The military commanders viewed Bishop's action as a rebellion and ordered a detachment of soldiers to take back the Fort. There was a short battle with shooting on both sides, and a number of civilians died trying to escape over the walls of the Fort. Maurice Bishop and the leaders who were with him were seized. Soon after they were lined up in a courtyard inside the Fort and shot. Martial law was imposed and Grenadians were ordered to remain in their homes. A week later United States forces invaded Grenada and arrested the members of the Government and many others.

Those bare facts beg a lot of questions. Did the Central Committee order the death of Bishop and the other leaders? If not, why were they summarily executed? Why, and on whose orders were their bodies dumped and hidden? How could responsible leaders order the arrest of a leader who was loved by the people? How, indeed, could a movement of comrades who were seemingly united in their goals destroy their achievements through internecine strife and killing? I remember demonstrating outside the US Embassy in London, angry about the invasion but unable to understand what had happened. The invasion was illegal, sure enough. It was not justified by self-defence or by any other principle of international law. But I could feel little solidarity with the leaders who had wrecked the revolution and handed such a golden opportunity to the United States.

Three months later I was on my way to Grenada with a British solicitor, Sarah Burton, to join up with a Jamaican attorney, Jacqueline Samuels-Brown. We had been asked to go there as a legal team representing about forty prisoners who were still detained under the authority of the US forces. I was briefed about the mission by Fennis Augustine, who had been the Grenadian High Commissioner in London. He cautioned us against taking sides between the supporters of Maurice Bishop, who were denouncing Bernard Coard as one of the architects of the killings, and the supporters of Coard, many of whom (including Coard himself and his wife Phyllis) were in detention without trial. Our mission was to act strictly as legal representatives.

I began by presenting my credentials as a barrister and seeking admission to the Grenada Bar. Many British barristers had appeared in the Grenadian Courts, and I was admitted without difficulty. The next day I was told that my admission to the Bar had been challenged and was to be revoked. At a hearing before the Supreme Court of Grenada the Attorney General argued that I did not have the Caribbean Legal

Education Certificate, so I was not eligible. The Judge agreed with him, so I was disbarred after one day at the Grenada Bar. I later appealed the decision and lost again. It turned out that on a strict interpretation of the treaty which set up the Caribbean Law Schools in Jamaica and Trinidad, lawyers from Commonwealth countries needed to study for six months before being qualified to join a Caribbean Bar. Grenada had not enforced the rules strictly in the past, but the opportunity was taken to put the barrier up against me.

Since Jacqueline Samuels-Brown was already admitted to the Bar and had all the necessary credentials, our work could go ahead, and this initial hiccup did not hold us back. We faced a situation where forty people had been locked up for over three months. They were being questioned without a lawyer being present. Some of them were said to have been beaten. None had been taken before a Court. In such circumstances the ancient remedy of *habeas corpus*, which for centuries has been used to release people from illegal detention, was most appropriate. We worked day and night to prepare forty *habeas corpus* applications, and we served them on the authorities. Jacqueline could not get access to her clients, so we brought a separate case against the prison governor. We were lawyers doing the business of justice.

One day as we were driving through St. Georges, Jacqueline cried out "That's Phyllis!" Phyllis Coard was in the car ahead of us with three men, driving towards the Police Headquarters. We followed the car, as we knew that the prisoners were being taken one by one from the prison to be 'interrogated'. Our attempts to secure Phyllis' rights to consult an attorney were soon thwarted. As the police car went through the gate the barrier was slammed down and we could not get through.

But the pressure had worked. The next day there was a flurry around the Supreme Court building and we gathered that some of our clients were being brought to Court. Twenty of the detainees, including Bernard and Phyllis Coard, were in the dock, having been charged with the murder of Maurice Bishop and the other leaders. The prosecutor announced the charges and asked for a remand in custody. Jacqueline Samuels-Brown made a most eloquent and courageous speech, complaining of the beatings which the detainees had suffered, and urging the Magistrate to exercise his authority to prevent any recurrence. Phyllis told me later that the police had started to beat her in order to extract a confession, but they had stopped because she had to go to Court and she could not be allowed to appear in public with the marks of violence visible. In the courtroom I was able to exchange some words with Bernard Coard in the dock, and even in a short conversation I became aware of his powerful personality and intellect.

The bringing of charges meant that legality and due process had been restored to a situation which had been lawless. I do not know how much longer the detainees would have stayed in detention without charge or trial if we had not gone there. The remaining twenty detainees who were not charged were soon released. So the ancient remedy of *habeas corpus* had got results. Our mission as a legal team was over, but Jacqueline was to return for trip after trip in the years which followed to take part in the trial and appeal of the people who were charged.

Grenada is one of the most beautiful islands which you can imagine. The capital St. Georges is built around a little harbour, with streets winding up hills and churches of different denominations on the skyline. Grand Anse, where many of the tourist hotels are built, is a classic picture postcard beach. So it was bizarre to see military helicopters flying over the churches, barbed wire along the beach around the hotel used by the Americans, and US marines in their jeeps checking Grenadian women. The people we spoke to did not resent the occupying force. Rather they mourned the passing of Maurice Bishop and cursed those who had killed him.

After the work in Grenada was done, I was asked to go to Jamaica to give a report on the situation to Jamaican lawyers and political activists. In a short visit I met several people who were to become good friends. I met Dudley Thompson and Carl Rattray, lawyers and former ministers in the government of Michael Manley administration, then in opposition; and Trevor Munroe, leader of the Workers Party of Jamaica (WPJ) which had had close relations with the NJM. My trip to Jamaica was organised by Elean Thomas, a journalist and leader of the WPJ, who had worked in solidarity with the NJM in Grenada, assisting the Grenadian radio station with training and advice. After the US invasion she had travelled to the island and had rescued the three children of Bernard and Phyllis Coard. She had escaped with them from the island, minutes before the American forces could stop her.

Back in London I continued to be involved with Grenada. I was one of the founders of the Committee for Human Rights in Grenada, formed by people in Britain who opposed the US invasion and were concerned to see that those accused of murder should get a fair trial. Some of the Committee's members formed a separate group to support Phyllis Coard, who as the only woman in the Grenadian jail was effectively in solitary confinement.

The Committee for Human Rights steered a course which stopped short of adopting the Grenada accused as political prisoners, but supported their right for a fair trial. This was an ideological compromise, since there were many in the Committee who saw the Grenada accused as victims of US imperialism who should be defended as comrades. The three most active members of the Committee were Richard Hart, a Jamaican socialist who had been Attorney General in Bishop's government; Carol Davis, a teacher from Guyana who had worked for the Grenada Ministry of Education and had been stranded in London at a conference when disaster struck in October 1983; and myself. Driving in a car together after many years of working together, I asked an awkward question: "Would you still support the Grenada accused if you knew they were guilty as charged?" "Yes;" said Richard Hart without hesitation, "they were comrades who may have made mistakes but they are fighting the common enemy." "No," said Carol; "if they killed Maurice Bishop and Jacqueline Creft they did a wicked act for which they should be punished." I agreed with Carol.

Seventeen of those who had been charged were convicted after a long trial in a court specially built near the Richmond Hill prison. Fourteen of them, all members of the Central Committee of the NJM, were convicted of murder and sentenced to death. Three soldiers who had actually carried out the executions were convicted of manslaughter and sentenced to thirty years imprisonment. This was a strange verdict, for those who carry out a murder are legally as guilty as those who give the orders. It must have reflected the jury's view that the leaders and not the foot-soldiers bore the real responsibility for the executions.

After the seventeen had been convicted, I wrote a pamphlet for the Committee called 'No Case for Hanging'. I explained why I did not regard the seventeen as political prisoners. I contrasted the case of Nelson Mandela and the other prisoners condemned at the Rivonia trial in South Africa. Whether or not they were guilty of treason against the apartheid state, the prisoners of the African National Congress had been fighting for a just cause. In the struggle of their people for equality and justice, they had been denied any other means but armed resistance. Their guilt or innocence in relation to the charges did not matter. The real criminals were those who ran the apartheid system. By contrast the murder of Maurice Bishop was a crime by any standards, and there was no excuse for it. It was right that those who were suspected of being involved in the executions should stand trial. The issue was whether the trial had been fair.

In the pamphlet I showed how the trial was fraught with unfairness. The jury was not selected in accordance with Grenada law. The Registrar who dealt with the empanelling of the jury had been a member of the prosecution legal team a short time before. The jurors themselves had hissed their teeth and shouted abuse at the defendants and their lawyers at the outset of the case, showing manifest bias which should have resulted in their disqualification. The defendants, in protest at these and other events, dismissed their legal team and refused to take part in the proceedings. When they disrupted the trial, the judge sentenced them for contempt of court and proceeded with the trial in their absence.

In addition, the evidence itself was weak on the critical issue of who had given the orders to kill Maurice Bishop. The prosecution relied heavily on a witness named Cletus St Paul, who had been Bishop's chief security guard. He had been taken into custody by the NJM, and he was at Fort Frederick under guard on the morning of 19th October. He claimed that all the members of the Central Committee had huddled in a meeting in front of him. At the end of the meeting they all shouted "Long live the Central Committee! Long live the Revolution!" Soon after that a detachment of troops was sent to Fort Rupert. The evidence of this meeting, which the accused leaders denied, was crucial to the prosecution's case that the executions resulted from a deliberate Central Committee decision.

The prosecution also relied on confessions by some of the soldiers that they had been told that it was 'Central Committee orders' that they should carry out the executions; and on a statement by Kamau McBarnette, one of the Central Committee members, that he had been party to a Committee decision. They all alleged that they had been tortured before signing the confessions, and that the confessions were not true.

There was another potential witness named Errol George. He was not called at the trial, but he had given evidence at a preliminary inquiry, so that the judge knew about him and could, in the interests of justice, have summoned him to testify. He had said that he too was at Fort Frederick, close to Cletus St. Paul, and that St. Paul could not have seen and heard what he claimed. Because the defendants were unrepresented, and took little part in the trial in protest against the unfair rulings, this important evidence was never heard by the jury.

All these arguments were put forward to the Grenada Court of Appeal by a legal team headed by Ian Ramsay, which worked tirelessly over many years, advancing about twenty separate grounds of appeal. I observed some of the sessions of the appeal. In 1991 the Court announced that the appeals were dismissed. Its written judgment has never been made known to the accused men and women, or to the public, which is in itself a disgrace to the judicial system. How can people know if justice has been done, if a court refuses to publish its reasons? The Committee joined with people across the world to petition the government of Grenada for a reprieve from the death sentences. This was granted in 1991, and the sentences were commuted to life imprisonment. Thirteen of the Grenada 17 remain in prison. Phyllis Coard was granted compassionate release in 2001 on a temporary basis to obtain medical treatment, and she now lives in Jamaica. The three convicted of manslaughter were released in December 2006.

To this day I am deeply troubled by the Grenada case. Having read all the evidence that was before the Court, I would not accept that all of the fourteen Central Committee members were guilty of murder, in the sense that they took a deliberate collective decision to execute Maurice Bishop. Some of them must have been guilty, including the military commanders who gave the orders to the detachment of soldiers. Others in the leadership claim to have been so distraught at the unfolding events that they were overwhelmed, and took no part. If so, they would not be legally guilty of murder.

But the events of October 1983 are not just about criminal guilt. The fall of the New Jewel Movement exposed the flaws in the communist ideology and practice which the Movement espoused. The party which fought itself to death was a small fragment of the Grenada people. The records of its meetings are full of elitist references to X being a good socialist while Y has petit bourgeois tendencies. At the end of one meeting a member of the Central Committee was ordered to reform himself by reading the works of Stalin. Maurice Bishop himself was criticised for his lack of discipline and ideological depth. They behaved sometimes like a caricature of a left-wing cabal.

Although the NJM championed the interests of the people, it never put itself forward for the approval of the people in elections. There is no substitute for a free and democratic election. It gives the people the chance to approve or reject what the leaders claim to be doing in their interests. The failure to hold an election was one of the New Jewel Movement's greatest mistakes. Although the revolution in Grenada, while it lasted, gave Grenadians an immense sense of pride and achievement, its leaders were collectively guilty of destroying the people's dreams. I may not be convinced of their legal guilt, but I hold them morally and politically responsible for killing one of the finest leaders which the independent English-speaking Caribbean has produced, and for the failure of a radical experiment which might have transformed the English-speaking Caribbean, had it been carried out in a more democratic spirit.

Through the Grenada case I was introduced to a group of Jamaican lawyers who made their impression on me long before I joined the

Jamaican Bar. I observed Ian Ramsay's team in Court and attended some of his pre-court brainstorming meetings during the late 1980s while the appeal was being heard. Ian Ramsay had a pure lawyer's approach. He expressed no views on his clients' political wisdom. He looked at the conduct of the trial and fastened on everything which was not done according to the law. He drove his team to research every precedent which might support his arguments. He did not argue all the points himself, but entrusted members of the team with the responsibility of being the advocates on particular issues. The members of his team have continued to shine in the legal profession: Howard Hamilton became Jamaica's first Public Defender. A.J. Nicholson became Attorney General and Minister of Justice of Jamaica. Norma Linton succeeded Ian Ramsay as President of the Advocates Association of Jamaica. Jacqueline Samuels-Brown, whom I had admired so much in Court in February 1984, remains one of Jamaica's best advocates. The careers of all of them were shaped by Ian Ramsay. They lost the appeal, which was hardly surprising given the prevailing hostility with which their clients were regarded. But their dedicated advocacy must surely have contributed to the saving of their clients' lives from the gallows.

The other consequence of Grenada on my life was that I met Elean Thomas, who had been the organiser of my first trip to Jamaica. Elean then went to work in Prague as the representative of the Workers Party of Jamaica on the *World Marxist Review*, the journal which was edited by members of all the Communist parties of the world. She made frequent visits to London, where she launched her second book of poetry and short stories, published by Karia Press. The press was run by Buzz Johnson, who strove against massive difficulties to provide an outlet for Black and Caribbean writers. I saw her often, and I was excited to have such a creative and radical woman as my friend.

The 1980s were years of personal upheaval. By 1983 my marriage to Kate had broken down, and we had separated. On my lecture tour of Australia I had met a childhood sweetheart, Helen Mary Sawyer, and we were engaged for several years, mostly at long distance. I accepted a visiting lectureship in Human Rights Law at Latrobe University in Melbourne in order to be with her. This continued over three summers, in which I travelled through different parts of Australia, including the central part where I met with aboriginal leaders. I was appalled at the conditions in which the indigenous Australians lived, into which they had been forced by two centuries of brutal and arrogant occupation by Europeans. I was shocked at the lack of conscience and concern shown by the vast majority of Australians, my mother's people. I spoke out about aboriginal rights in the Australian media. Had my life worked out as I then planned it, part two of this book might have chronicled my life as a human rights lawyer in Australia.

But it did not happen that way. Helen Mary insisted that we wait for some years so that I would be sure what I wanted to do. She also became increasingly devoted to her New Age religious beliefs, which I could not share then. By 1987 I wanted to explore my growing friendship with Elean, and I broke off the engagement. I went to Prague to visit Elean, and over several visits my Jamaican friend became my lover, and then my fiancée. She moved to London and worked on her first novel. We were married in September 1988 in the Church of Our Lord Jesus Christ in Kingston, where her father was the Bishop. This marriage was the key to my being able to live and work in Jamaica. Within a few years I had used the key and opened the door to the second part of my life.

12

MOVING *to* JAMAICA

September 1988 was an eventful month, which included two human rights missions, a hurricane and a marriage. It started with a return visit to Grenada, where the appeal of the Grenada 17 had started. I observed the proceedings for a few days and met the President of the Court, Mr Justice Haynes of Guyana, a gentle and wise man. Regrettably he died while the appeal was still being heard, and the appeal had to be re-started before a new panel consisting of Haynes' two colleagues and a new judge. His death was a blow to the cause of justice. He had made a ruling shortly before his death that the key witness Cletus St. Paul should be called before the Court of Appeal to explain various inconsistencies in his evidence. The new Court declined to follow his ruling. I am sure that he would not have given a judgment and then refused to publish it in writing. He was a jurist of the old school, for whom the study of written judgments was central to the just development of the law.

I then went to Puerto Rico, to investigate the detention by the United States of a leader of the Puerto Rican independence movement, Filiberto Ojeda Rios. He was a colourful rebel, who had been arrested in the United States in 1984 and charged with a bank robbery in Hartford, Connecticut. It was said that he had taken seven million dollars from the Wells Fargo bank, some of which had been distributed publicly to the poor of San Juan. He had been granted bail after nearly three years, only to be re-arrested and flown to Puerto Rico on a charge of wounding an officer of the FBI. His attorney in the US was my friend Richard Harvey, a British barrister who had moved to a progressive law practice in Harlem. I linked up with Richard and with Ojeda's Puerto Rican attorney, who had been denied access to his client. We spoke at a press conference, protesting that he was being detained at a military base and prevented from seeing the attorneys of his choice. I returned on a later occasion to observe his trial in San Juan, in which he was acquitted of the wounding charge. (He refused to return to Hartford and was convicted of the bank robbery in his absence, and remained on the FBI's most wanted list until he was wounded and left to die by United States marshals who attacked his Puerto Rico home in 2005.) I experienced a taste of the contradictory society which is Puerto Rico, bound economically and politically to the United States, but fiercely independent in culture and spirit.

I then reached Kingston, where Elean was preparing for the annual congress of the Workers Party of Jamaica, and at the same time issuing invitations to our wedding which was to be two weeks later. On the second day of the congress, the news began to spread that Hurricane Gilbert was heading for Jamaica and likely to hit the island within 24 hours. I was sent off to search for kerosene and candles and stock up with food.

The experience of a full-blown hurricane is truly terrifying. We were staying with friends, Cyril and Linnette Vassell. The wind and rain built up over hours, lashing one side of the house, seeking out every weak spot, hammering against the windows, screaming in the intensity of its gusts, breaking down branches and trees. Then there was a period of calm as the eye of the storm passed over us. The rain stopped and the wind died, and we nailed down loose sheets of zinc roofing as best as we could. After twenty minutes the eye passed, and the storm crashed with renewed ferocity against the other side of the house. Finally night fell and the rain continued to pour, entering through every hole in the roof which the hurricane had opened up.

In the days following the hurricane we drove through streets littered with fallen debris to visit friends, many of whom had suffered worse damage than we, but all were safe. It was a time when Jamaicans were rallying round to help each other. We had planned a wedding reception at a Kingston hotel, but we cancelled it, as an expensive function did not seem appropriate. Elean's father's church and home were packed with guests, and the wedding was a warm spontaneous party rather than a formal affair.

All these experiences helped to knit me closer to Jamaica and the Caribbean, but at that point I had no intention of making our main home there. My expectation was that I would continue in my legal and political work in London and Elean would develop her career as a writer. She had left Czechoslovakia and enrolled in a diploma course for writers at

Goldsmiths College. But my growing fascination with Jamaica could not be ignored. In 1989 I decided that at least I should get qualified as a Jamaican attorney, and obtain the Caribbean Legal Education Certificate, the lack of which had kept me excluded from the Grenada Bar. With that certificate I would be entitled to appear in court in any part of the Caribbean.

This required me to do a six month course at the Norman Manley Law School, including being an intern for two months with a law firm. I did the course and my internship was with the firm of Gaynair & Fraser, headed by W.B.Frankson QC. By the end of the course we had taken the decision that while I would continue to have law chambers in London, our main home and working base would be Jamaica. In 1990 I was called to the Jamaica Bar, and in 1991 I started the firm of Gifford, Haughton & Thompson, setting up offices in Duke Street, not far from the Supreme Court in downtown Kingston. In 1994 I became a citizen of Jamaica, in addition to retaining British citizenship.

I am sure that there are still many people in England who wonder why a successful barrister at the peak of his career, a member of the House of Lords as well, should uproot and move to the Caribbean. Even in Jamaica the question is asked. At the start, a colleague who was thinking of joining my firm wondered what would happen if my marriage did not last. He must have thought that my move was simply born of romantic excitement. In fact the marriage did not last, but my commitment to Jamaica did. As the economy of Jamaica gets worse, it debt burden larger, and its crime rate steeper, the question is renewed. Why do you want to stay here? When I started spending more time in England during the Bloody Sunday Inquiry, I had to reassure people constantly that this was not the beginning of a move out.

The truth is that once I put down roots in Jamaica, there was little doubt in my mind that this was to be my permanent home and my professional base. Given the choice of two countries in which my wife and I could legally settle, I find the quality of my life in Jamaica to be much more satisfying. I am healthier and happier. I live in a land of incredible beauty and a near perfect climate. I have a professional skill which is seriously in demand. I do a range of work which is amazingly varied and constantly challenging. There are possibilities, still largely untapped, of extending my practice into other parts of the Caribbean. I am here to stay, and if I can keep myself strong I would like to practice law in this region for many years to come.

Breaking down some of the elements in this picture, I would start with the quality of the people among whom I now live and work. Jamaican men and women are among the most passionate, life-loving, exuberant, proud, respectful people I know. One of the founders of Jamaican independence, Norman Manley, described his people in words which I cannot improve, cited in Philip Sherlock and Hazel Bennett's book *The Story of the Jamaican People* (1998):

> I affirm of Jamaica that we are a great people. Out of the past of fire and suffering and neglect, the human spirit has survived – patient and strong, quick to anger, quick to forgive, lusty and vigorous, but with deep reserves of loyalty and love and a deep capacity for steadiness under stress and for joy in all things that make life good and blessed.

On settling in Jamaica I did not feel pre-judged. When I arrived and set up my practice, I was neither put down nor exalted. People just waited to see how I would get on, whether I could cut it socially and professionally. Having shown that I could, after a year or so I became part of the society and part of the Bar, liked by many and respected by most. Above all, I am not made to feel White. A leading talk show host, Barbara Gloudon, said once that I had become a Jamaican 'by osmosis'. I took it as a great compliment. It reciprocated what I had come to feel, that Jamaica was where I was at home. I was not an 'ethnic minority'. I was simply a person who had migrated from Britain to become part of Jamaica. 'Out of many, one people', as the Jamaican motto puts it.

Contrast what happened to my wife Tina (yes, I married a third time, but more of that later) when she came to live for a time in London. Life for her, as for huge numbers of Black people in Britain, became a constant daily battle to validate her identity. She could hardly ever escape from the awareness that people were labelling her as Black. The issue of race dominated. Store detectives followed her. Passers-by in the street looked surreptitiously towards her. Teachers at her college urged her not to be so colourful. Liberals talked to her about race. Black friends swapped stories about racism. And if she ever raised her voice to complain – as she did – then people looked embarrassed, as if this was not the done thing and she must have a chip on her shoulder. Her experiences were not unusual. Similar things happened to Elean.

When I have listened to Jamaicans talking about their times in Britain, I have found it uncomfortable to the British. Everyone has a story to tell, stories of racial stereotyping which are funny and absurd in retrospect, but were bitter insults when they happened. Fortunately, most Jamaicans have such immense confidence in their own dignity and equality that they can laugh at the crassness of the British. For Black children in British schools and Black youth in British streets, their experiences of racism are more shaming and more destructive.

I love the directness of Jamaicans. They look you in the eye and appraise you, and expect you to do the same, rather than look to the side or over their shoulder. I love their courtesy, even though sections of the youth have become much ruder than their parents and grandparents. I love their outspokenness, the passionate arguments about cricket or politics which are always loud but rarely malicious. I love the patriotism, the love of one's country without the desire to beat up anyone else's. Jamaicans sing their National Anthem as if they mean every word of it, down to the ringing climax:

> Justice, truth, be ours forever,
> Jamaica land we love.
> Jamaica, Jamaica, Jamaica land we love.

Jamaica's history is a proud story of resistance to inhuman and barbaric treatment, first under slavery and later under a repressive colonial government. Jamaica's heroes, who are celebrated every year on National Heroes Day, are people to teach one's children about with pride. Nanny of the Maroons, who fought so successfully against the British that she secured the freedom of her people by treaty in 1739. Sam Sharpe, who led the rebellion of the slaves in 1831 which, though it failed and he was hanged, was the precursor to emancipation. Paul Bogle and William Gordon, two pastors who confronted one of the worst tyrants of the colonial era in 1865 and were also executed. Marcus Garvey, whose message of the beauty and dignity of the Black race echoed around the world, a prophet far ahead of his time. Finally, Norman Manley and Alexander Bustamante, the founders of modern independent Jamaica.

I mention these great names because their example has inspired Jamaicans of all classes with a sense of justice and freedom, the antithesis of the imperialist values which still permeate the education and culture of Britain. The ethos of 'Rule Britannia, Britannia rules the waves' inspires the hooligans in the football grounds, the racists in the British National Party, and the jingoistic editors of the *Sun* and the *Daily Mail*. "God Save the Queen" is a national anthem which reads as a monarchist hymn of triumph, and conveys nothing of the positive values of Britain and her people.

Of course there are things I hate about Jamaica. I hate the readiness of many Jamaicans to use violence to settle quarrels. I hate the way many

Jamaica men abuse their women, oppressing them in the home or breeding a baby and disappearing. I hate the repeated murders by police officers shooting suspects who they could have arrested. I hate the prejudice against gay men and lesbians. I hate the death penalty, although thank God there have been no executions since I came to live in Jamaica. But all these hates are issues on which I can and do raise my voice and - unlike in Britain when I have been often labelled an extremist – I am respected and not reviled for standing up for what I believe to be right.

Along with the quality of the people is the quality of the environment. Jamaica is constantly beautiful. Every day of the year is warm, and when the days are not sunny you get showers and storms which refresh the earth and renew the greenery. Kingston is a green city, on a plain between mountains and sea, where even humble homes have mango and other fruit trees in their back yards. I live high on a hill overlooking Kingston and its harbour. I get up as the sun rises over the Blue Mountains, take my child to school, put in a full day's work and get home for a walk in the hills before sunset. If a test match is playing, I can end the day with a couple of hours watching cricket at Sabina Park, where I am a member of the Kingston Cricket Club. For diversion I can go on a trip to the beach or into the country, or in the evenings a jazz concert or a performance of Jamaica's superb Dance Theatre. For a weekend break I can go to a cottage on a peaceful beach or a retreat in the Blue Mountains. Jamaica can be a glorious place to be.

And Jamaica is only one of dozens of places in the Caribbean which are full of beauty and history within easy reach. When I lived in London I delighted in the freedom to travel through Europe and feel the warmth of other cultures and see the beauty of their lands and buildings and their art. France, Italy, Greece, Ireland are all places which I have loved. The Caribbean region is no less wonderful in the attractions which the passionate traveller can enjoy. Since living in the Caribbean I have had vacations in Cuba, Dominican Republic, Mexico and Guyana, and each one has been an experience to treasure. I have made business trips on legal work to Trinidad, Barbados, Antigua, Curaçao and the Turks and Caicos Islands. I have yet to visit other jewel islands like Tobago, St Lucia and Dominica, or the French islands of Martinique and Guadeloupe. Do you wonder now why I am happy to be where I am?

At a deeper level I feel that my coming to Jamaica has been a direct continuation of my work in and for Africa. Working in solidarity with the freedom fighters of Mozambique and South Africa was one of my life's formative experiences. I later had close relationships with Ghanaians who opposed military rule and Kenyans who stood up against the dictatorship of President Moi. So coming to a country inhabited mainly by the descendants of Africans was not strange. I responded to the Africanness of Jamaica. I made friends with Rastafarians like Jah Lloyd, for whom the return to Africa was an article of faith. I saw what many Jamaicans try to deny, that they are formed from Africa and have retained African characteristics which go far beyond colour and physical features. I was reinforced in this view by reading Philip Sherlock and Hazel Bennett's great work, *The Story of the Jamaican People* (1998), in which they trace the Jamaican virtues of resistance and endurance back to the values of West Africa:

> The West African people belonged to different language groups, communities and tribes, but they shared certain basic cultural similarities, such as a strong sense of community, a powerful attachment to the land, a concern for children as the 'buds of expectation and hope', as well as for their ancestors, for personal dignity and a respect for the tribal leaders and for the freedom enjoyed within the boundaries of tribal obligations. These are all a part of the rich religious heritage of the West African people and they explain the immediate, widespread and long-sustained struggle of the dispersed African-American people for freedom.

As well as being African, Jamaica is also accessible and in many ways familiar to a migrant from Britain. The colonial occupation has left behind the English language which many Jamaicans deploy in literature and oratory with great skill. To love Shakespeare, as I do with a passion, is not out of place in Jamaica. The native language of Jamaica is the Jamaican language, sometimes called patois. It has its own grammar and vocabulary, much of it derived from the languages of West Africa. I do not try to speak it, but it is not difficult for a speaker of English to understand. The game of cricket is supported and discussed with a passion. I love both the African and the English elements of Jamaica; and through the migration of peoples, China, India and Syria are also part of the rich Jamaican mosaic.

I am trying to reach down further to explain why I am at home in the cultures of Africa and Jamaica. To find the whole truth I have to acknowledge the spiritual dimension. Sherlock and Bennett are instructive in showing how the spirituality of the African people was continued and adapted by the African-Jamaicans. Writing of the African spiritual traditions they say:

> The physical and the spiritual were seen as two dimensions of one and the same universe, and the African experienced this religious universe through

acts of worship, sacrifices and offerings, prayers, innovations, blessings and salutations. Also, and this prevails throughout Black America, music, singing and dancing run deep into the innermost parts of African peoples and many things come to the surface under musical inspiration which otherwise may not be readily revealed.

I find this difficult to write about, since I have throughout my life rejected religious dogma, bigotry, exclusiveness and hierarchy. I turned away from the Church of England indoctrination which I received at school as its rituals were formalistic and dull. For my parents Church was a social responsibility rather than a genuine faith. They had a deep love of their neighbours, but it came from an ethical commitment rather than Bible study. Through my marriage to Kate and my conversion to the principles of democratic socialism, I became a humanist, passionately committed to social justice but rejecting any notion of a divine or religious foundation for my beliefs. While I could admire individuals whose faith led them to be fighters for injustice – like Archbishop Tutu and Archbishop Huddleston and Canon Collins, all leaders in the resistance against apartheid – I could not join their churches. I still can not abide any church which proclaims that women may not be spiritual leaders; or any church which insists that salvation can only be found by submitting to its interpretation of the truth; or any church which teaches that human beings are sinners, condemned to hell unless they acknowledge the gospel as preached by its pastor. The intolerance of religious authorities against those they consider to be heathen or infidels has caused war and death and persecution throughout history. Jamaica, which is said to have more churches per head of population than anywhere else, has no shortage of dogmatic church leaders who hate gays and demean women and preach that salvation can come only through them.

And yet, and yet… I feel glad to be in a place in which a recognition of the spiritual dimension is almost universal. I like it when a meal is blessed or a prayer is said at the start of a meeting. I respond to the reggae singer who invokes 'Jah Rastafari' as his inspiration. I feel the power of the anthem which begins "Eternal father bless our land" and continues as a prayer to God to bring wisdom and justice. I look at the Britain which I left behind and find that it has become very materialistic. I wish constantly that Jamaica could have some of Britain's wealth, and that Britain could have some of Jamaica's spirit in exchange. I have developed a deep friendship with Bishop Peter Morgan, a radical priest whose commitment to the upliftment of Jamaican people is infectious and unquenchable. He considers me to be a man of God who will not acknowledge that I am. I love him for who he is and what he does, without having any wish to join his church.

I have come to recognise that I am a spiritual being, although I still find it difficult to describe what that means. It means at the least that there is in me, and in everyone, a miraculous power to do good, to radiate positive energy, to change the environment in which we live. I believe in a God within me rather than a God 'out there'. I have enormous respect for the teaching of a spiritual leader like Deepak Chopra, who himself draws on the wisdom of Indian spiritual masters; but I have never had the patience to meditate or do yoga or discipline myself in a spiritual way. I believe also that we have a soul which survives the death of the physical body. How that happens, whether we reincarnate into other bodies, what happens after death, is a total mystery to me. But from the evidence of people who have had near death experiences and psychic conversations with the dead, I believe that something happens, and I look forward to finding out what it is when it is my turn to die.

The purpose of these musings is not to articulate a philosophy, but to explain the deeper attraction of the non-European, God-centred traditions of Africa and Jamaica on my psyche. I can only talk about it at all because of the influence in my life of my wife Tina. She has herself been on a journey through Catholicism and the fundamentalism of the evangelical churches, and has turned away from both. Unlike me she devotes time to meditation and yoga. We came together as a couple in 1997, after my marriage to Elean collapsed. She has been the beautiful, loving, radiant beacon of my life ever since.

On the occasion of my 50th birthday in May 1990, Elean together with my colleagues in the Wellington Street chambers organised a birthday party in the Middle Temple Hall. The Hall is a magnificent 16th century building where students eat their dinners and barristers chat about their cases over lunch. The coat of arms of the first Lord Gifford is emblazoned in stained glass in one of its windows. It was a good place to celebrate what was not just a birthday but a turning point in my life.

The guests represented every aspect of my life to date. Members of my Australian family. Nicholas Phillips, the judge who had nearly died in the crevasse. A message from President Chissano of Mozambique. A tribute from the representative of the African National Congress. A song from three Kenyan women – the husband of one of them was still in a Kenyan jail. Gerry Conlan and Paul Hill from the Guildford Four – the Birmingham Six were still in prison. The pacifist Albert Beale whom I had defended at the Old Bailey. Barry Macdonald, my former pupil from Northern Ireland. Turks, Jamaicans, Trinidadians, Grenadians, Ghanaians, trade unionists, Black activists and radical lawyers. The great Black poet Benjamin Zephaniah and the great Black diplomat Emeka Anyoku, then Secretary General of the Commonwealth. The Jamaican socialist and historian Richard Hart, speaking in moving terms of the contribution which he believed I could make to Jamaica. My son Tom and my daughter Polly and my wife Elean, all giving their toasts and tributes. So many nice things were said and sung that there was too little time for the dancing at the end.

In the decision to leave Britain, the real wrench was leaving behind such a kaleidoscope of wonderful people. Nearly all of them had come to know me as a result of some political or legal struggle. I have spoken before of how advocacy in a just cause can educate the advocate. It also creates friendships and bonds of love between the advocate and the people whose cause you champion. However much I resolved to keep in touch with all these friends, I knew that the links with many of them would weaken when I stopped being a London-based barrister whom they could easily reach. I felt that they were a send-off party, sorry to see me go but wishing me safe travel and a happy landing in this new world where I had chosen to go.

13

JAMAICAN ATTORNEY

The first client who came into my Kingston office was Dorothy Lewis, Acting Principal of Hampton School in the parish of St Elizabeth. Hampton is a prestigious girls' boarding school favoured by the Jamaican middle class. Ms Lewis had risen through the ranks as a working class teacher, and her style was probably a bit abrasive for the school governing board. She had been promoted to the office of Principal for a probationary year, but when she consulted me in April 1991, she had been told that her appointment would not be confirmed. The Board had given her no reasons, and she believed that it was a matter of simple prejudice.

I checked the Education Regulations and found that there were strict procedures which governed the situation. If a probationary principal was not to be confirmed, clear reasons had to be given, as well as a proper opportunity for her to respond to any criticism before the decision was taken. I wrote to the Permanent Secretary at the Ministry of Education and to the Chairman of the Board pointing out that my client had rights to natural justice and fair procedures. The Board went ahead in June and demoted her back to the post of Vice-Principal, without giving reasons. By July I had filed an application for judicial review. I asked the Supreme Court to make orders that the Board's decision should be quashed and Ms Lewis reinstated. In October the case was heard, and we won. Dorothy Lewis was able to resume her post shortly after the start of the school year as Principal on a further year's probation.

For Dorothy Lewis it was, unfortunately, only a temporary victory. She caused genuine offence in her second year, and a new Board went through the correct procedures. They held a formal hearing at which I represented her, but I could not save her a second time. The chairperson of the Board was Donna Parchment, a thoroughly fair person who since has been the driving force behind the mediation movement in Jamaica. Ms Lewis left Hampton for the United States, and has since died.

But for justice in Jamaica it was an important success. At that time judicial review procedures were not much used. It was reported in the press that the Ministry had been ordered to climb down. It is good for the rule of law when citizens see that unlawful decisions of the authorities can be struck down by the courts. For me it was a great start to my practice in Jamaica, and it was an example of the value of the 'fused' legal profession. In Jamaica lawyers are not divided into barristers and solicitors. All qualified lawyers are attorneys. In this case I was able to see the client, understand the problem, write the appropriate letter which was then ignored, and put the letter in evidence before the court. In the end I had the satisfaction of reading the judgment of Chief Justice Rowe, which quoted from the letter. I had been able to give good service from beginning to end.

Ira Rowe, President of the Court of Appeal, was acting Chief Justice during my first year at the Jamaican Bar. He was a man of immense kindness and humanity. He presided over my first trial in the Jamaican Supreme Court, and resolved for me a problem which had been bothering me. The problem was, where should I sit? Should I sit in the front row, reserved for Queen's Counsel, or in the second row where other attorneys sit? The problem may seem petty, but in a new country I did not want to do the wrong thing. I had not been appointed a Queen's Counsel in Jamaica, so that in theory I did not have the right to be in the front row. However, many were saying that recognition in the name of the Queen should be accepted universally, and that my dignity would be demeaned if I did not go to the front row. So I went to see Chief Justice Rowe in his chambers, and asked for his guidance. After reflecting for a moment he advised me to ask a Queen's Counsel to move a motion before him, that as a distinguished English QC who had settled in Jamaica, I should be permitted to sit in the front row. I took his advice, the motion was moved and granted, and I have sat in the front row without question ever since.

There is of course a degree of absurdity in Jamaica retaining a title which derives from the British monarchy. Trinidad and Tobago and Guyana, which have both become republics, have changed the title to 'Senior Counsel'. Jamaica remains chained to its past, in spite of many promises of constitutional reform from our leaders, so that the Queen remains Jamaica's nominal Head of State. Jamaica's leading constitutional lawyer Dr Lloyd Barnett has found this to be so unprincipled that he has refused to accept the title of Queen's Counsel, even though he is one of Jamaica's finest attorneys. Ian Ramsay, who was appointed QC at a young age, renounced the status in 1969 after the Court of Appeal had rejected the appeal of his client in the case of his client Warwar. He considered this to be such an injustice that he could no longer bear a title bestowed on behalf of the Jamaican state. These acts of conscience do their actors great credit. My own position as I started my new career was that as I had been a QC for eight years in England, I should remain a QC in Jamaica.

Lloyd Barnett and Ian Ramsay were two of my many role models and highly respected colleagues at the Jamaican Bar. One of the richest benefits from my experience of Jamaican legal practice has been the fellowship of such colleagues. Moving to Jamaica has not involved any lowering of standards in the quality of the advocacy around me. On the contrary, in Jamaica I have learnt how to be a better advocate. Lloyd Barnett always seems to have done meticulous research before he stands up in court, and his grasp of constitutional and civil law is phenomenal. He has combined a busy practice with chairmanship of the Independent Jamaican Council for Human Rights, among other public positions. In civil law both Dennis Morrison and Hilary Phillips stand out as advocates who are thorough in their work, always ready to give advice, and models of that honesty and integrity which all attorneys ought to demonstrate. Both have been distinguished Presidents of the Jamaican Bar. R.N.A. Henriques and Pamela Benka-Coker are senior counsel who I have not known well, the former urbane and well connected and the latter passionate and radical. Both sprang to the defence of my firm in 2002 when our office was invaded by police to execute a warrant which we claim to be utterly unconstitutional.

Among seniors practising in criminal law, Frank Phipps is an advocate with a superb touch who has given me great encouragement. He asked me to join with him in arguing the case of John Franklin, in which the Privy Council laid down the principle that in cases in the Resident Magistrates' Courts, the prosecution must normally disclose the statements which it is going to rely on, so as to enable the defence to know the case which it must answer. The ruling has been followed in Jamaica ever since. Frank is President of the Farquharson Institute, a law reform group which contributes to the ongoing debate on the quality of justice in Jamaica.

Ian Ramsay was the colleague to whom I was closest. Ian was the finest advocate that I have met in any jurisdiction. He was the most generous of men, who shared his cases, and his fees, with a number of younger colleagues at his chambers at 53 Church Street. He prepared his arguments with the greatest ingenuity, challenging his team to look at every possible angle to vindicate his clients' innocence. His style in court was masterly, at times bitingly sarcastic, always passionate in defence of his client. In the appeal of the Grenada 17, where he lead a team of ten, he showed an unwavering commitment, year after year, visit after visit, in front of an often hostile and cynical court. His death while still in active practice was a bitter loss.

His closest colleague, in Grenada and countless other cases, was Howard Hamilton, the first Public Defender, an office which he held with great distinction and commitment, taking up the causes of those with little voice. AIDS victims, Rastafarians, prisoners, neglected children, street people with mental problems, are among many whose unjust treatment he has brought to light. Howard is another icon to me, an accomplished criminal advocate who was always speaking up for the have-nots. He like so many Jamaican professionals is also fun to be with. His irrepressible energy infuses me, and helps me not to feel old.

It should not be surprising that Jamaica has so many outstanding advocates. One of Jamaica's national heroes is Norman Manley, a world class advocate who became one of the architects of Jamaica's independence. The stories of his courtroom victories are legends at the Jamaican Bar. Then there was Dudley Thompson, who in 1952 drove 900 miles from his law office in Tanganyika to a remote town in Northern Kenya, where Jomo Kenyatta was about to be tried by a British judge. He reached just in time, and was able to gather a team of lawyers who later fought the case. Dudley later became one of Jamaica's most combative advocates.

It will be seen that many of the people I have mentioned as being fine lawyers were also fine citizens, making their contribution to the public good, taking their beliefs about justice into the national sphere, advocating social justice as well as legal justice. These were people I could admire, and whose company I have much enjoyed. During the years which I spent in Britain, the dominance of white ruling class attitudes, which I hated, meant that I never felt that I belonged to the mainstream of the legal profession. To be an advocate with a conscience meant opposing much of what the mainstream stood for. In Jamaica the Bar has welcomed me. While there is still much to be angry about, I feel integrated as I never did at the English bar.

My first major criminal brief was to defend a much loved attorney, Michael Lorne. I had met 'Miguel', as he was known, at an anti-apartheid meeting some years before. He was a soft-spoken, dreadlocked attorney who was known for his fearless representation of poor people who had been harassed by the police. He was charged with receiving stolen goods, a motor car which he had bought which turned out to have been stolen from a University professor. At his first court appearance, dozens of attorneys turned up to represent him. I was asked to lead the team, and took it as a high honour. Miguel was convicted after a long trial, and lost his appeal. He served a year at the Tamarind Farm prison, where he soon got a reputation for being a respected adviser to his fellow inmates. He remains a good friend, the proprietor of the Headstart bookshop, and a prominent campaigner for the movement for reparations. The experience of defending him brought me close to some of the radical young attorneys at the Jamaican bar, and although we lost the case, I gained in experience.

I was terrified at the start of my Jamaican practice that I would not be able to understand the language spoken by working class Jamaicans, especially the witnesses who I had to cross-examine. The Jamaican national language, or 'patois', has its own grammatical forms and vocabulary, some of them African in origin. I have never attempted to speak it, for I would sound foolish. But I have heard attorneys, and even judges, break into patois in order to make themselves understood by a witness. In one of my early cases, defending a farmer from the parish of St James in the Montego Bay court, I could hardly understand a word of what my client was saying, and I relied on Hugh Thompson, my partner and junior counsel, to translate. Our client was accused of killing a man and throwing his body down a deep well, where it had stayed for two years before the crime came to light. He had made a signed confession, in which he said that he had been stealing coconuts from a tree when the deceased came by and asked him for a coconut. He had thrown one down which had landed on the man's head and knocked him senseless. In a panic, believing that he had killed him, he threw him down the well.

Studying the evidence I realised that there was no case for our client to answer. If the deceased was killed by the coconut, his death was an accident. If he was killed by drowning, then our client had thrown a live body into the well, and he would be guilty of manslaughter at least. But the skull had not been recovered, so the cause of death was not known. The case was prosecuted by Paula Llewellyn, one of the most forceful and dedicated prosecutors whom I have met in any jurisdiction. We clashed in the first of many encounters, and I won. Mr Justice Walker agreed that the prosecution had not proved how the deceased had died, so it might have been an accident, and the accused had to be set free. He ran out of the court without even thanking me. I was relieved to have got a decision from the judge, since I was not confident of winning over the Montego Bay jury, who looked as if they could not wait to convict the accused.

In Britain I used to enjoy jury trials enormously. I felt that the jury shed the light of humanity into the courtroom. The judges and barristers, dressed in their antique wigs and gowns, perform the rituals of justice, day after day, and it is hard for them not to become cynical and case-hardened. For the jury, the case they are trying may be the only case they will ever try. I once spoke to a juror who had sat on a case where I had been defence counsel, which concerned the attempted murder of the Israeli ambassador by a Palestinian group. The evidence was overwhelming against my client, and the jury convicted him, but only after three days of deliberation. My client was sentenced to 30 years imprisonment. The juror who I met later explained why they had taken so long. She said that they all had agreed that this could be the most important decision which they would take in their lives, and they had to go through the evidence methodically, however long that might take. That is the spirit of commitment which I have observed in many British juries over the years. As an advocate, it is vital to treat the jury with respect and connect with them as fellow human beings. Especially when the judge and the prosecutor are behaving as if they were superior human beings, I have been able to address the jury on the footing that they, and I, and my client, are the reasonable, down-to-earth people who can empathise and agree with each other.

In Jamaica I value the jury system just as much, but I feel less confident in my ability to relate to the jurors. In Jamaica the judge and the prosecutor have more experiences in common with the jury than I have. I have known prosecutors to talk in patois or quote Jamaican proverbs, deliberately to show that they are more in tune with the good sense of the people than I am. In addition to that, Jamaican juries are infected with the anxiety that all of us feel about the rising murder rate in the country, so that it is hard to get across concepts such as reasonable doubt or the presumption of innocence. So I have been reluctant to take on many jury trials. I feel more confident in criminal appeals, or even cases before Resident Magistrates, where advocacy is a battle of wits, an intellectual dialogue before judges who are closer to me in training and mental outlook.

When I have won cases before Jamaican juries it has often been through good tactics rather than silver-tongued advocacy. In my first jury trial, I defended a teacher accused of indecently assaulting a girl pupil. The evidence of the girl was very muddled, but I thought that I needed to strengthen the teacher's hand by calling a number of character witnesses, including the principal of the school. After retiring for an hour, the jury of seven told the judge that they were deadlocked four to three in favour of guilt. They were told to go back and deliberate further. My client and I were gloomy, as a five to two majority would be enough for a conviction according to law. An hour later, they returned a unanimous not guilty verdict. One of my colleagues spoke later to a juror, who said: "The three of us who thought he was innocent held firm. The four who thought he was guilty prayed to God. God's message was that he was a good teacher who would not do it again. So we were all happy to acquit." The evidence about his good character had been decisive.

As well as seeing some of the best attorneys at work in Jamaica, I have seen some of the worst. Lawyers who take large fees from their clients and deliver a shoddy service or no service at all. Lawyers who come to court unprepared. Lawyers who weary the court with hopeless arguments. Lawyers who keep their clients in ignorance of what is going on with their cases. And worst of all, lawyers who have been dishonest with their clients' money. They may be only a few, but they fuel the cynicism in the public which tarnishes the whole legal profession.

For barristers in the divided profession which exists in England, one of the incentives for you to do your case well is that you will please your instructing solicitor, who will then brief you again. You have a professional client, the solicitor, as well as a lay client, the litigant. In the fused profession of Jamaica that can happen also; in many of the cases which I argue I have been briefed by an attorney in another firm, and I enjoy the teamwork which is required. But most of the time as the attorney you are interfacing directly with your client, and you have a solemn ethical duty to secure the best resolution of that client's problem which the law will allow. To me letting down a client is painful. Clients are the not just the source of your livelihood, but human beings with problems who deserve to be treated with respect and with compassion.

The Bar has Canons of Ethics which run to many pages, and which have to be learned by every student. Even so, I would like to push down the throats of many attorneys my personal code of basic principles:

Listen to your client. When a client first comes to see you, you will probably have no idea of what his or her problem is. You have to listen hard, sift the details to find out what is important, and take a good note. I have a collection of hard-backed note books which contain every important detail of the cases that I am doing. The notebooks have page numbers and a running index. Weeks or months after seeing a client, I may have to appear in court for him, or write a letter or draft a claim. My memory will have forgotten the details, but my notebook has them all.

If the client is in custody, the requirement of listening is even more necessary. It is difficult to obtain coherent instructions from the dock of a crowded courtroom. Spending time with the client who is in custody is crucial. But far too few defence attorneys actually visit their clients in the remand centres or prisons. Prison visits not only enable the attorney to get proper instructions, but they can be a lifeline to the client. Most clients in custody need desperately to see their attorneys, even if only to get a basic understanding of what is happening to their case.

Study the documents in the case. In most civil cases and many criminal cases, the essence of the case may be in documents. Employment cases may depend on a written contract or on a company's grievance procedures. The terms of a business contract may depend on a written agreement or a series of letters. Every criminal appeal depends on whether grounds for an appeal can be found in the transcript of the trial. My method is to read the documentary material and make notes about every important document in my hard-backed notebook. In that way I can pick up the file weeks or months later, look at the notes, and it all comes back to me.

Look up the law. When you have listened to your client and read the documents, you will know what his or her problem is. The next step will be to decide whether the law provides a solution to that problem. The longer I practise law, the more I realise how much law I do not know. I keep a basic library, which includes the All England Reports, the Jamaica Law Reports, the West Indian Reports, Halsbury's Laws, the Laws of Jamaica and some basic text books. I use that library several times a day. Often before I advise a client or write a letter, I will have checked to see exactly what the relevant Act of Parliament, or text book, has to say on the subject. If a matter is before the Supreme Court, I refer constantly to the Civil Procedure Rules. Again, I note any useful cases or quotations in my hard-backed notebook.

Explain what you can and cannot do. Having listened to your client and read the documents and looked at the law, you should be in a position to give advice. You must be frank about what can and cannot be done. If a course of action is hopeless, do not pretend that it might succeed. If the chances of success are slight, make sure the client knows that the action may fail. Clients will not thank you for building up false hopes which will be dashed in the end. I try to be clear and honest in my advice, and once again I note down in my hard-backed notebook the advice which I have given.

Tell clients what they must pay and what they are paying for. Having advised your client what you can do, you have to tell him or her what it will cost. Sometimes you can do no more than estimate what the total costs might be. But do not ask for lump sums without any explanation of what you will do for the money and how you will account for it. Try not to justify the public perception that lawyers are sharks. Be open about how much per hour your time is worth. One of my partners gives each client a written document setting out her terms of business. I prefer to explain the details across the table, noting what I have said in my notebook. Either way the client goes away knowing that for a certain outlay of funds he or she can expect a certain quantity of work to be done.

Treat the client's funds as sacred. When the task which you have undertaken involves the receipt of funds on trust for a client, that money must go into your clients' trust account and never be used for any purpose other than the purpose for which the client paid it. This principle is so fundamental that it should not have to be spelled out. To use these funds for your own purposes is to commit a criminal act of fraud. Several attorneys have gone to jail for this, or been disbarred for it, during the time when I have been practising in Jamaica.

Report to the client on what is going on. It is natural for a client to worry. What is happening to my case? is a question at the forefront of their minds. But too many attorneys treat enquiries from clients as an intrusion. They get their secretaries to answer, and refuse to see the client who comes for an appointment. There may be some tiresome clients, but in truth most clients will not pester you if you have explained what is going on, and if you have done what you promised to do. If you write a letter or receive a letter, or file a claim or receive a defence, give the client a copy. If there is an unexpected delay, tell the client what has happened. Often when clients complain to the General Legal Council, it turns out that the problem is not bad service but bad communication.

Prepare for every court appearance. I have seen too many lawyers stand up in court who have evidently not thought out what they are going to say. Improvisation has its place in advocacy, and sometimes you have to scrap what you were going to say in order to deal with an intervention from a judge or an unexpected answer from a witness. But improvisation can too often be a cover for laziness. An unprepared advocate risks looking foolish before the judge, and may lose a case which should have been won. I always jot down the essence of the argument which I intend to advance or the questions which I intend to ask, even in the simplest court appearance. If you are applying for bail, make a note of all the reasons why bail is justified. If you are pleading in mitigation, list all the arguments why your client should not go to prison. If you are going before a judge on a procedural matter, check the relevant sections of the Civil Procedure Rules. If you are arguing a point of law, look up the authorities that you will cite, identify the relevant passages, and have copies available for the judge and for your opponent. Judges will soon recognise a badly prepared advocate, and if your preparation is weak the judge may well decide that your case is weak as well. Like most advocates, I love to win and hate to lose; so I take care to maximise the chances of winning.

During fifteen years of practice in Jamaica I have shaped and applied these principles to a variety of cases in courts ranging from the Resident Magistrates' Court to the Privy Council. I have become familiar with areas of law which I knew little or nothing about before, such as libel law, industrial relations, constitutional rights, land disputes, and business arbitration. In England as a young lawyer I revered the leaders of the Bar who could turn their hand to any kind of case. Then we were all told that we had to specialise. Now in Jamaica I rejoice that if you are respected as a leading counsel, you will be expected to turn your hand to any branch of the law. In truth being an advocate is a speciality in itself. As well as all the other reasons why I am glad to be in Jamaica, my professional life has become vastly more varied and fascinating.

When I started off I went into partnership with Antonnette Haughton and Hugh Thompson. Antonnette was a fiery radical champion of the underprivileged, practising mainly in the parish of St. Mary. She scared many of her male colleagues with her feminist zeal. I believed that her potential was enormous, and we made a good team in the early years. As most Jamaicans know, she made her impact on Jamaican life as one of our most popular talk show hosts. She was spending less time as an attorney, which I thought was a pity, and this led to our separating as partners in 1998.

Hugh Thompson has remained my partner and good friend, and I value him greatly. If I am a legal brain, he is a social being with a conscience, which he can translate into impassioned advocacy in the criminal courts. He has a vast network of friends and acquaintances, nurtured greatly through his devotion to the Kingston Cricket Club. He keeps me in touch with Jamaican 'runnings', which I might not appreciate as a comparative newcomer to the scene. Our third partner is Sandra Graham-Bright, who was a successful barrister in England until she decided to relocate to the country of her parents' birth. She runs our office in Montego Bay. She is someone I can rely on to be efficient and totally trustworthy.

I work out of an office in Tower Street in downtown Kingston, directly opposite the Supreme Court and a stone's throw from the Court of Appeal.

I have employed a succession of associate attorneys without whom I could not manage the volume of work which comes through the office. My office is also a law chambers, with independent attorneys who have acted as my juniors in a number of significant cases. Over time I hope that the practice will expand further. My aim has been to gather round me a team which can give a service of the highest standard, and be an agency for the remedying of injustice. My aims have not fundamentally changed since the days when I founded a radical cooperative of barristers, over thirty years ago.

14

THE EXALTED *and* *the* MEEK

When I arrive at my office and my secretary has two or three appointments for me to see new clients, I still feel a shiver of excitement, for I know not what dramas may unfold. The highest and the lowest have come through my chambers door. Political leaders, public servants, police chiefs, businessmen, trade unionists, attorneys, doctors, Rastafarian healers, Italian chefs, associations of nurses and herbalists and bank managers, wronged wives, bereaved parents, families disputing over land; mothers and girlfriends and brothers of men who have been locked up; people who have been suffered at the hands of brutal policemen, or negligent doctors, or reckless drivers. All have a story to tell, an injustice to be remedied, and usually an experience of humiliation or loss which cries out for redress. The practice of a people's lawyer in Jamaica is a constant challenge.

Most law students today, I am told, are ambitious to be business lawyers, to work for a big firm or to be the in-house lawyer for a financial institution. That is the top of the ladder for them. If they are interested in criminal law, they would rather prosecute than defend. If their career is to be in litigation, then the Attorney General's chambers attracts them. The age of the radical law student seems for the moment to be over. Many of my most able Jamaican colleagues studied in the 1970s when the radical socialism of Michael Manley's government infused many students with a sense of mission to fight for justice. Salary scales to them were a secondary consideration. These colleagues are now the cutting edge of the Jamaican Bar, and incidentally most of them seem to be earning reasonable fees. I look out for their young successors, and some of them have become interns and associates in my office. My firm has donated an annual prize for the student at the Norman Manley Law School who shows the greatest commitment to projects in furtherance of human rights. I want to fire students and young attorneys with the zeal to be people's lawyers rather than business lawyers or the state's lawyers. When your client is a living individual rather than a corporation or a ministry, the satisfaction of winning is indescribable.

Of course an attorney has to be conscious of the need to earn money. I often have to tell people that my office is not a legal aid clinic. Given the range of incomes of my clients, the rich in effect subsidise the poor. I am sure that I earn much less than the senior partners in the big firms. I am constantly impressed at the way in which Jamaican families will support a member who is in trouble. The real legal aid system in Jamaica is family support. Many of my fees are paid by the clients' extended family in Britain or America.

Some of my most grateful clients have been the people at the bottom of the pile, the inmates in our penal institutions. If an inmate writes to me, I always reply, usually to ask him or her to tell a family member to come and see me. If members of a prisoner's family ask to see me, I do not charge a consultation fee. The families of prisoners suffer, often more grievously and unjustly than the prisoner. They make daily journeys to leave food at the prisons. They suffer the agonising experience of seeing their loved ones on visits where they can only communicate by shouting for a couple of minutes through a cage. They have to bear the responsibility for the children left behind. When they believe the prisoner to be innocent, the pain is all the greater.

So I always see these families and give them preliminary advice. If the prisoner has been duly sentenced and has lost his appeal, there is little to be done. Some families want the case taken to the Privy Council, but are daunted when you tell them of the massive costs involved in travelling to London and instructing a London solicitor. When the prisoner has been convicted and wants to appeal to the Court of Appeal, then the costs are more affordable; but even then I am reluctant to charge a large fee before I know whether there is any basis for an appeal to succeed. That will not become apparent before I read the transcript of the trial. So I charge a retainer for reading the transcript and seeing the client, on the basis that if there are good grounds for the appeal, a second fee will be needed. It is not sensible for an attorney to demand a large fee and then have to come to court with arguments that are obviously doomed to fail. An attorney's reputation with the judiciary depends to a great extent on his or her arguments being worthy of respect.

Some of the most poignant cases concern long-term life sentence prisoners. There are hundreds of such prisoners, who spent years on death row before their sentences were commuted to life imprisonment. Many of these prisoners appear to have been radically transformed by the experience of the death cells. Some have become excellent artists and craftsmen, and my office is adorned with their works. Others have taken a lead in the 'Reverence for Life' organisation in the prisons, organising themselves to defuse conflicts and encourage spiritual growth behind bars. I have no doubt that there are many men and women in the prisons who are thoroughly rehabilitated after twenty or more years, and ready to start a useful life. The prison system in Jamaica should take credit for this, for in spite of the brutality of some warders and the overcrowding of the cells, the correctional authorities have done much good work in promoting employment, art and music, training and education.

The one thing that a lifer needs to know is when he will be able to apply for parole. Jamaica operates an enlightened law on parole. The Parole Board has a duty to investigate all applications. It deploys probation officers to visit the prisoner and his family, obtain reports from the prison, get a psychiatric report, and make an evaluation as to whether the prisoner will be a danger to society. If the sentence is for a fixed number of years, parole may be granted after one-third of the sentence has been served. If the sentence is life imprisonment, the position is more complicated.

In the days when every murder attracted a mandatory sentence of death, those whose sentence was later commuted to life imprisonment could apply for parole after seven years from the date of commutation. In 1992, the law was passed which divided murders into capital and non-capital; there were defined categories of capital murder, and the rest were non-capital. In the case of the non-capital murders, the sentencing judge was given the power to specify the minimum number of years which the convicted person should serve before being eligible for parole. There has been no guidance given as to the principles to be applied; the number of years seems often to depend on the personality of the judge.

This power to impose a minimum sentence has worked injustice in some cases. For instance I was retained by the family of Mary Lynch, after she had been convicted of murdering her husband and her appeal had been turned down. She had been sentenced to life imprisonment and ordered to serve a minimum of 20 years. There was no remission on this period; she had been sentenced in 1994, so however well behaved she was, she could not apply for parole before 2014. My first move was to petition the Privy Council, since I believed that the courts had paid little regard to a defence of provocation which was relevant to her case. On the evidence she may well have lost her self-control and lashed out at a husband who had abused her. But the Privy Council refused to grant leave to appeal.

I then considered her sentence. In the days when every convicted murderer was sentenced to death, a woman was never hanged in Jamaica. So under the old law Mary would have been sentenced in 1994, and after two or three years appealing her conviction, she would have been commuted at the latest in 1997. She could then have applied for parole after seven years, in 2004. So she had suffered – ten more years in prison – by not being sentenced to death. Since her case had been through the courts, the only thing to do was to petition the Governor General for him to exercise his powers to reduce sentences. The Governor General, after being advised by the Jamaican Privy Council, accepted the arguments and ordered that she would be eligible for parole in 2006 instead of 2014. She had hoped for a better result, but a reduction of eight years was still very welcome, and in my view very just.

When the new law was passed, it included a transitional provision to deal with all the murder cases which had been completed before 1992. The cases would be reviewed by a judge who would decide whether they fell into the capital or non-capital category. If non-capital, the judge would decide on the minimum sentence. If capital, there would be a further review before three judges of the Court of Appeal at which the prisoner would be represented. The three judges would review the case and if they thought that the case was non-capital, they would impose the minimum sentence.

The first problem that arose was that the judges who conducted the first review imposed long minimum sentences on those who were adjudged to be non-capital, and the sentences were not backdated. So a man who had been sentenced in 1985 might get a 20-year sentence running from 1992, leaving him in prison without hope of parole until 2012. And this had happened without the prisoner having had any right to make representations through an attorney. Some years later when a case called *Huntley v Attorney General* came before the Privy Council, the government conceded that it was wrong for these penalties to have been imposed without the prisoner having been heard. So all the cases had to be reviewed again, which did not happen until 2000. At that point Justice Rattray, President of the Court of Appeal, gave guidance that all the minimum orders should be backdated to the date of the original sentence. I took part in many of these reviews, and the Independent Jamaican Council for Human Rights organised a panel of attorneys to provide pro bono representation.

Meanwhile the cases which had been classified as capital had been reviewed in 1995 by the three judges of the Court of Appeal, who reclassified many of them as non-capital, but again imposed long minimum sentences which were not backdated. Representing some of the inmates, I found myself thinking that some of the judges were so opposed to the removal of the mandatory death penalty that they were determined to visit the commuted murderers with heavy prison terms.

After 2000 I was visited by the families of these prisoners, who not unnaturally complained that their relatives had not had their sentences backdated, but all those who had been reviewed in 2000 had benefited from the Rattray decision. The law had been unequally applied. Since there was no further appeal or review which these prisoners could demand, my strategy was to draft petitions to the Governor General, pointing out the inconsistency. The Governor General in all those cases has appreciated the injustice and allowed the sentence to be backdated.

There was a further category of prisoners, those who had been confirmed as capital cases on the second review in 1995. By then the case of Pratt and Morgan had been decided, and all these prisoners were entitled to be commuted as they had been on death row for more than five years. About 50 of them were commuted in June 1995. According to the amending Act, a judge of the Court of Appeal was required to examine each of these cases and make an order as to the minimum period which they should serve before parole. If no order was made by the judge, they were entitled to apply for parole after seven years.

The families of some of these prisoners came to me for advice. I told them to tell the prisoners to sit tight and do nothing. While arrangements were made for the review of all the non-capital cases, nothing was done to review the cases commuted under Pratt and Morgan. In 2003, after the seven years had passed, I was approached by the family of McCordie Morrison, one of the 1995 commutees who had applied for parole but had been told that his case would have to be reviewed by a judge. Together with Nancy Anderson, Secretary of the Independent Jamaican Council for Human Rights, I decided to make this a test case. We argued that after the seven years had passed, Morrison obtained an entitlement to apply for parole. If the system had not got around to reviewing his case in seven years, that was not his fault. Justice Wesley James in the Supreme Court could not accept this reasoning, but in the Court of Appeal we sailed home. The Court ruled that it was up to the system to arrange the hearing, and if the system had failed, the prisoner obtained a right to apply for parole which could not be taken away.

It can be seen that the cases of life sentence prisoners can pose legal conundrums which need a lot of creative thought. Some prisoners had a right to a review, some could petition the Governor General, some had cases to be taken to the Supreme Court. In other cases I have had to advise that there was nothing to be done. Each of these cases involves human liberty and the welfare of family members. They are worth the effort. Prisoners whom I visit in the prisons are encouraged by the opportunity of getting good advice, and often when I go to visit three prisoners I end up seeing six. The end result is that prisoners know how long they have to serve, and what is their parole date to aim for. Many have had that date brought forward. This means that prisoners who in the end have to return to society are treated with a measure of justice, and this must help in their rehabilitation and welfare, ultimately creating safer conditions for their release.

Most cases in the criminal courts are fraught with tension. The stakes are high for the client, and the advocate needs to be committed and passionate and sometimes angry on the client's behalf. One reason why I do such a mixture of civil and criminal cases is that criminal work can be so stressful; and when you lose a case and a client starts a long prison sentence, the advocate can feel very depressed. But there was one criminal case which I fought over days in the Half Way Tree Resident Magistrates' Court in which, unusually, there was much to laugh about. I was retained by Ben Munroe, a blind community activist, and his brother Frank. They were charged with conspiracy to export ganja. The evidence against them was to be given by two agents of the US Drug Enforcement Agency (DEA), who had tape recordings of their meetings with Ben and Frank and their phone conversations with Ben. The DEA men were posing as American drug dealers who wanted Ben to use his contacts on the Kingston wharf to ship large quantities of ganja. They were talking in code about catching fish. Ben's voice could be heard agreeing to the deal, and telling the Americans that the fishing captains would need a lot of money up front. Eventually they paid Ben US$30,000 in cash, which was handed to Frank and counted.

Ben's defence was that he knew from the start that they were DEA agents and decided to play along with them, in order to extract from them as much money as possible which would be distributed to poor people in the community. The ganja which he promised to ship was non-existent. When the Americans asked to be taken to the place where the ganja was stored, they all drove into the countryside, only to be told that the ganja had just been moved into the hills for safety. Of course it never existed in the first place. The ganja was meant to be shipped in cans of pineapple juice, but when Ben finally produced shipping documents, they turned out to be bogus. On the last tape the voice of one of the agents could be heard saying plaintively, "I want my money Ben, you got my money." Ben was heard asking him to be patient, suggesting that with a bit more money the deal could still be successful.

I remembered the case of the Sikhs who had been accused of plotting to murder Rajiv Gandhi, especially my client Marwaha who pretended to agree with the plot. In the same way, if the Munroes had no intention of shipping any ganja, they could not be guilty of conspiracy, which required proof of a genuine agreement to commit a crime. When the tapes were played one could sense the interplay of devious minds, each playing a part and trying to dupe the other. The main DEA agent gave his evidence, but while he was still in the witness box the case was adjourned. Frank Phipps, who was in the case defending another alleged conspirator, suggested that I apply for an arrest warrant against the agent, on the charge of soliciting the commission of a crime.

I thought about this and the idea seemed very logical. If you try to persuade another to commit a crime you are guilty of soliciting the crime. The DEA agent had tried to persuade Ben and Frank to export ganja. The evidence was there on the tapes. So I drafted a warrant and it was signed by a resident magistrate. The agent faced arrest when he returned to Jamaica. When the court convened again the agent did not appear, even though he had been bound over to attend. It was reported to the court that he was in fear. Frank and I applied to have the case thrown out, but the resident magistrate decided that she should continue to hear it. Some weeks later the Director of Public Prosecutions entered a *nolle prosequi*, meaning that the prosecution of the agent had to be terminated.

The resident magistrate was Shirley Lewis, who later became the Clerk to the Jamaican Parliament. She said that it was one of the most interesting cases which she had tried. In her judgment she said that she could not rule out the possibility that Ben had been tipped off about the DEA agents and had set out to deceive them. If so he and Frank could not be guilty of conspiracy, and the so charge was dismissed. Ben Munroe was free to continue his leadership of the Low Income Family Foundation, a controversial project which ultimately brought him back to the Half Way Tree Court on charges which are still to be resolved.

My practice in civil law has also produced fascinating challenges, of which the still unfinished saga of the National Transport Co-operative Society must be one of the most demanding. In 1998 I was retained by Ezroy Millwood, President of the co-operative, a client who has become a friend and someone I greatly respect. He has shown passionate energy in defending the rights of the 350 bus owners who made up the co-operative. He is also a most public-spirited person. He was responsible through the Kingston Kiwanis for raising funds to pay for the medical treatment of a small boy who was dreadfully scarred by burns. Although he did not know it, the boy's mother was a member of my staff.

In 1995 the Transport Minister Robert Pickersgill had invited bus companies to bid for the franchises which were being offered for five zones in the Kingston area. The franchises would be for ten years, and would replace the previous free-for-all system which had failed to provide the public with a decent service. The problem for the prospective franchisees was that under the law, it is the minister who determines the bus fares, so that the viability of the franchises depended on the level fixed by the minister. He made a solemn written promise that the fares would be fixed and then maintained at a level which would provide the franchisees with a 15 per cent return on their capital investment. On the faith of this promise, which was expressed to be legally binding, the co-operative agreed to operate two of the five franchises.

However the minister never honoured the promise. The level of the increase which would have been necessary was so high that the government feared the political consequences of agreeing to it. The co-operative operated the best service it could, but with the fares set at an uneconomic level, the service suffered. By May 1998 there was a lot of public discontent at the state of the bus services in Kingston. A new minister, Peter Phillips, decided to terminate the franchises and to operate the bus system through a state-owned monopoly, the Jamaica Urban Transit Corporation (JUTC). He offered to negotiate with the franchise holders, and I was called in to lead Patrick Bailey as legal advisor to the co-operative.

The government was offering to compensate the co-operative for the profits it would have earned in the remaining seven years of the franchise. We argued that in addition the government had to recognise the losses which had been suffered as a result of the breach of the promise to set the fares at a profitable level. When the accounts of the co-operative were audited, it emerged that these losses were running at about a billion dollars a year. The negotiations then stalled. The government settled with the other franchise holders, but the co-operative continued to run the service in their areas.

By August 2000, as nothing was happening, Ezroy Millwood instructed me to sue the Ministry for damages for breach of contract, covering the losses from 1995 to date. The claim was filed in the Supreme Court for over $3 billion, the accumulated losses of the 350 members over the five years. The government hastened to resume negotiations, and by March 2001 an agreement was reached for the co-operative to cease operations. The compensation for the loss of the franchise was agreed, but the Supreme Court claim was referred to an arbitration panel of three arbitrators.

When the arbitration panel convened in 2002, it consisted of three judges of impeccable reputation: Justice Boyd Carey, former judge of appeal and a sharp legal mind; Justice Ira Rowe, former President of the Jamaica Court of Appeal; and Mrs. Angela Hudson-Phillips QC, an attorney of great integrity. The ministry team was led by Stephen Shelton, who on the day before the hearing came up with a preliminary objection. All the franchises were illegal, he said, because the law under which they were granted provided for the Minister to grant 'an exclusive licence'. Since the Minister had granted five licences, he had acted unlawfully and the whole operation had been illegal from the start. What is more, argued Shelton, any preliminary point of this kind had to be determined by the Supreme Court, as stated in a leading textbook, *Mustill's Commerical Arbitration* (1991). These arguments were attempts to derail the whole arbitration before it started, and they had to be taken seriously, even though they seemed far-fetched.

Since we had only a day in which to respond, I sought help from my chambers in London. I asked one of our pupil barristers to check whether the law had changed since 1991. Given the time difference, he could work on it all day until 3.00 pm, and fax the results to me in my Kingston chambers when it would be 9.00 am. He faxed me the 2001 edition of Mustill's book, in which the passage relied on by Shelton had been completely rewritten. A new case had established that all preliminary points should be determined by the arbitrators themselves. It was so sweet to quote the latest edition of the very tome which my opponent had thought was his trump card. The arbitrators rejected the preliminary point and proceeded with the hearing. In 2003 they ruled that the co-operative's claim was soundly based in law, and that its accounts were to be relied on. They awarded the phenomenal sum of $4,544,764,113.00, which with interest added came to over $8 billion – or about US$150 million.

The story of the case of NTCS v Government of Jamaica is not over, and I cannot comment on it further. The government claimed that the arbitrators had made errors of law, including the ruling on the 'illegality' point, and Justice Brooks in the Supreme Court found for the government. The co-operative has appealed against his decision, and the case may well end up in the Privy Council. But even as an unfinished story, it is valuable as a demonstration of the power of the law. Here was a situation which the members of the co-operative thought to be terribly unfair. They had been deprived of the promised fare, but they were being blamed for the poor service. We invoked the law as a remedy for the unfairness, and we achieved a ruling from three eminent jurists. And I had applied a rule that all attorneys should observe, that you should always quote the most up to date edition of a law book.

Even so there are limitations to the reach of the law, as I was to learn when representatives of the Portmore community came to consult me early in 2005. Portmore is a large suburb of Kingston, situated across Kingston Harbour and accessed by a causeway bridge. The government, as part of its highway development programme, intended to replace the existing road across the bridge with a six lane toll road. The Portmore citizens, most of whom worked in Kingston, would have to pay a toll which was to be $60 dollars (just under US$1.00) for each journey. The alternative was a slow and circuitous route via the Mandela Highway, seventeen kilometres instead of seven by the toll road. The residents felt that the plan would place an unfair burden on them. Collecting boxes were rattled around Portmore to fund a legal challenge.

I looked at the law and found that the Toll Roads Act stipulated that there must be an alternative route "in the area in which the toll road is to be established". The proposed alternative was nowhere near that area, so there was a strong case for saying that a toll could not be imposed unless a legal alternative was provided. Then, just to be thorough, I checked the volume of 'statutory instruments', where one can find the various ministerial orders which are made from time to time. To my surprise I found that the minister had made an Order back in May 2002, designating the new road as a toll road and naming the Mandela Highway as the alternative. This was serious news, since if you are challenging the legality of a ministerial order you must come to court within three months, unless there is a good reason for the delay. The contractors, who had been building the new road for the past two or three years, had proceeded on the basis that the Order had been duly made. It would be very hard to challenge it three years later.

The representatives of the community had never heard of this Order. It had been published in the *Jamaica Gazette*, the official journal which few people ever read. It was not mentioned in the government's website or in any official handout, so the people could hardly be blamed if they did not know about it. I attended a meeting of hundreds of Portmore citizens, who were in effect my clients, and gave them my opinion: you have a good argument but you may be too late. The citizens were so angry that they were prepared to raise the money, and an application for judicial review was filed promptly in the Supreme Court.

The Government argued that the alternative route was legal and that in any case we were too late. Over US$60 million had been spent by the contractors, and the Government would be liable if the road plan had to be aborted. Justice Gloria Smith ruled against us, and the question then was, can we take this case any further? Even if the Court of Appeal found against us, would the Privy Council give us justice? By then I had done further research, and found a recent case in the House of Lords where the claimants had failed, even though their claim was correct, because two years had passed and much had been done under the assumption that the ruling which they challenged was lawful. It did not matter that the claimants had no means of knowing that the ruling had been made. The judges of the House of Lords are the same as those who make up the Privy Council.

In keeping with my principle that you must not mislead a client, I had to say that I saw no prospects of success in a further appeal. I advised the Portmore organisations to make the political and moral case that there should be a reduction in the toll paid by Portmore residents. I still believe that it would be unfair to visit the costs of the highway on the Portmore people without giving them a viable alternative, and I hope that a compromise will emerge. But this time the weapon of the law could not help them.

I have ventured into business law in Jamaica, but even in this part of my practice there is an element of acting for the underdog. I have often been consulted by business people who have been wronged by financial institutions. The 1990s in Jamaica were years of runaway inflation and soaring interest rates. Borrowers had to pay up to 40 per cent on their loans, which increased to a penalty rate of up to 90 per cent if they were in default. I heard many sad stories of people losing the houses which they had put up as security, when they could not get out of a spiralling situation of debt. Often there was little help to be given, since the small print of many mortgages gives extensive freedom to the banks to vary their interest rates. But when Stephen Hew came to see me, I believed that there was a good case to take to the Supreme Court.

Stephen Hew was an elderly man who banked with the National Commercial Bank (NCB). He had an ambition from childhood, to be able to borrow a million pounds. By the time he was 75 years old, he had succeeded in purchasing over a hundred acres of prime land in Ironshore in Montego Bay, and so he had security on which to borrow. He spoke of his dream to the local NCB manager, who suggested that he develop another, less desirable piece of land with a loan from the bank. The Ironshore land would be mortgaged as security for the loan. Even though Mr Hew had no worked out plan for the development, he went ahead and borrowed two million dollars from NCB. The development soon ran into difficulties because of Mr Hew's inexperience. The interest on the loan escalated, and there were no more funds with which Mr Hew could repay it. By the time the case came to court, NCB was claiming $132 million from him. All his beautiful land in Ironshore would be swallowed up in paying the compound penalty interest which the bank had charged.

I believed that a case could be made that NCB had exercised undue influence over Mr Hew. He was a naïve man with little experience in developing land. He took the bank's advice which turned out to be disastrous. I resisted the bank's claim and counter-claimed for the money which Mr Hew had paid in interest on a loan which should never have been made. In cross-examination the NCB manager admitted that Mr Hew had spoken of his childhood ambition to borrow a million pounds, but he denied that the Bank had taken advantage of his simple and trusting nature. Justice Reid rejected the Bank's claim and awarded Mr.Hew $18 million on the counter-claim. The Court of Appeal upheld the judge's award.

I wish the story had a happy ending, but it did not. Mr Hew died after the Appeal Court's judgment. NCB appealed to the Privy Council. I was able to secure payment of the $18 million, but I took no further part in the case. For some reason Mr Hew's sons did not retain me to represent his case in the Privy Council, and the Privy Council reversed the Jamaican courts' decisions. It ruled that a bank has no duty to dissuade a customer from making an unwise investment. I have always thought that Mr Hew's case was an exception to that rule, and that I could have successfully defended the judgments before the Privy Council, but perhaps that is my conceit.

In 2004–05 I had three victories in the Privy Council which encapsulated for me the glory of the rule of law in protecting the weak against the strong. The first was for Anthony Abrahams, who is now the host of the popular *Breakfast Club* morning radio programme. In the early 1980s Tony had been Minister of Tourism. In 1987 the *Gleaner*, which was then the only Jamaican daily morning newspaper, published an article suggesting that while serving as Minister he had received 'kickbacks' in return for tourism promotion contracts. The article was repeated in the *Star*, the popular evening newspaper owned by the Gleaner Company. The Gleaner Company claimed that the articles were true, but it was unable to provide any evidence to support this claim. Eventually its defence was struck out by the Court of Appeal, and a jury was empanelled to consider the proper level of damages. The jury awarded $80.7 million, which was reduced by the Court of Appeal to $35 million. Even this sum – the equivalent at the time of about half a million pounds – was far higher than any previous award in Jamaica, and it was over twice as high as the ceiling of £200,000 which the English courts had recently fixed for damages for loss of reputation. The Gleaner Company was claiming that an award of this magnitude struck a blow to the freedom of the press, and it briefed Lord Lester of Herne Hill, my old room-made Anthony Lester, who was now Britain's leading libel lawyer.

Abrahams had been ably represented by Winston Spaulding QC, who asked me to lead him in the Privy Council. On reading the transcript and talking to Tony Abrahams, I learned why the courts had awarded so much. The Tony Abrahams who was now a much respected and popular broadcaster, had been for five years following the publication of the libel an isolated, ostracised and unemployed man, hissed at in shops and shunned in social functions. The libel had made him an outcast, and his health had suffered severely. The power of the press to ruin a reputation in a small country was never more clearly displayed. Because for years the *Gleaner* was trying to justify the truth of the libel, it made no apology until 1995, and even then it was an apology which one of the judges in the Court of Appeal described as "unorthodox and less than sincere but moreso 'tongue-in-cheek' causing greater hurt".

I quickly saw that against all the high-flown expressions of principle which Lord Lester was likely to expound to the Privy Council, what was needed was a true and detailed account of one man's suffering at the hands of an irresponsible piece of journalistic behaviour. In drafting the written submission which all Privy Council judges read carefully before the hearing, Winston and I extracted from the transcript all the telling details of Tony's anguish, including the loss of a promising career which he had been building as a tourism consultant. We suggested that the Jamaican courts were in a better position than the Privy Council to understand and evaluate the devastating effect of a libel such as this in a Jamaican context. We said that when one took into account the loss of professional income over five years, the award as reduced by the Court of Appeal was fully justified. What we were reflecting, in appropriate legal language, was the pain of a human life, a rising star for whom a broken reputation had been more shattering than a broken limb.

The Privy Council accepted these arguments so comprehensively that after Lester had finished his submissions, they did not even call on us to respond. In his judgment Lord Hoffmann said that, "For nearly sixteen years the defendants, with all the prestige and resources at their command, have doggedly resisted the attempts of Mr Abrahams to clear his name." The judges unanimously upheld the award of the Court of Appeal, and dismissed the *Gleaner*'s appeal with costs. It is to the *Gleaner*'s credit that it paid the damages, with interest and costs, within a few months of the decision.

My next client before the Privy Council was Clinton Bernard. In 1990 he had been waiting in a line to make an overseas telephone call from a public phone booth. Just as he started to make the call, a man came up saying 'police' and tried to grab the phone. Mr Bernard resisted, at which the other man pushed him away, took out a revolver and shot him in the head. Mr Bernard lost consciousness, and woke up in hospital handcuffed to a bed and under arrest. He was charged with assaulting a police officer, a charge which was later dropped. The shot caused an injury to the brain and weakness in his limbs. The shooter turned out to be Constable Morgan, an off duty police officer using his service revolver. He was charged with causing grievous bodily harm, but fled the country and never returned.

Bernard sued the Attorney General on behalf of the Jamaican Government which employed the officer, on the principle of 'vicarious liability', according to which an employer is liable for wrongs done by his employee acting in the execution of his duty. The Attorney General argued that Morgan was not executing his duty, so that the Government was not liable for his actions. Bernard was awarded over $2 million by Justice McCalla of the Supreme Court, with interest and costs, but the Court of Appeal overturned the judgment "with reluctance". Justice Bingham referred to Mr Bernard as being one of the "many innocent victims of the barbarous conduct of some agents of the state", and Justice Walker called for "a meaningful ex gratia payment to be made by Government". But they thought that the law required them to reject Mr Bernard's claim.

There was such a public outcry about the case that the government did pay the damages of $2 million to Mr Bernard, but not the interest and legal costs which amounted to nearly $3 million. At this point Mr Bernard asked me to take his case to the Privy Council. After consulting with a solicitor in London, Earl Chambers, who was as shocked as I was about the judgment, we agreed to take the case on a 'no-win, no-fee' basis. We wanted justice to be done and if possible, a new precedent to be set, since unjustified killings by police officers are only too common in Jamaica.

The Privy Council includes judges from Scotland, Northern Ireland and South Africa, and sometimes judges are assigned from other parts of the Commonwealth. So it was important to look at cases from all parts of the common law world. I found that the law on vicarious liability had been developed in recent years in both Canada and England in cases involving people who had responsibility for children and had sexually abused them. According to the old interpretation of the law, the abusers were acting outside the scope of their duty. But the courts had taken the line that since they had been employed to care for the children and had failed to care for them, they had failed in the very duty which they were employed to carry out. So the child abuse victims had recovered damages from the owners of the institutions.

In the same way, I argued, Morgan had been employed to keep the peace and had been given a gun for that purpose, and he had failed in that duty. He had abused the authority, and the weapon, with which he had been entrusted. With the help again of a pupil from my London chambers, I found a useful case from South Africa in which a police officer had committed criminal acts against a member of the public, and the state had been made liable to pay. I was helped also by a recent report which had been made on Jamaica by a Special Rapporteur of the United Nations Committee on Human Rights, in which the prevalence of illegal police shootings was highlighted. I quoted the report in the written submission. In due course I was happy to see both the South African case and the UN report referred to in the judgment of the Privy Council, delivered by a judge who had practiced in South Africa, Lord Steyn. As human rights lawyers, we need more and more to draw on international norms and precedents, for human rights issues transcend national frontiers.

The Privy Council upheld the judge's award and overturned the Court of Appeal's decision. The judges said: "It is of prime importance that the shooting incident followed immediately upon the constable's announcement that he was a policeman, which in context was probably calculated to create the impression that he was on police business." They followed the reasoning in the child abuse cases and held that the State was liable for the act done by Morgan with a service revolver under the cloak of his authority as a policeman. Mr Bernard got the whole of the interest due to him, and Earl Chambers and I were paid our fees.

The third case in this series was the Jamaica Flour Mills case which I describe in the next chapter. In these three cases, individual citizens had taken on big institutions and won. Mr Abrahams had taken on the *Gleaner*, which wields great influence in Jamaica. Mr Bernard had taken on the Jamaican Government. The Flour Mills workers through their union had taken on a powerful American company. Justice had been slow in coming – sixteen years for Abrahams, fifteen for Bernard. Their own tenacity and determination had been remarkable. I was proud to be there for them to ensure that the highest court did the right thing.

I have mentioned cases which have had a high profile or which teach useful lessons. Behind them is the often unglamorous day to day work of a human rights attorney. In fifteen years of practice in Jamaica I have met the highest and the lowest in the hierarchies of power and wealth. Some of my more well-known clients may never be known, because their cases did not come to court and they are entitled to my professional secrecy. I have learned that injustice can strike the rich and the poor, the well connected and the incarcerated, and all can usually find remedies through the law. My practice has reached out to them all, and my doors continue to be open to the exalted and to the meek.

15

JUSTICE *at* WORK

---

hen I was a barrister in England I longed to be an advocate for the trade union movement. I was a keen member of the Labour Party, the origins of which were rooted in trade unionism. The party had been formed to represent the organised working class at a time when the ruling class were doing their utmost to crush workers' protests at their miserable pay and working conditions. The law had been used as a weapon of the ruling class. The English courts in the 19ᵗʰ century had ruled that to strike was to break your contract of employment, and to organise a strike was to take part in an unlawful conspiracy. The harshness of these common law rules was relieved by legislation, notably the Trade Disputes Act 1906 which protected peaceful picketing by workers at their place of work. But when I started at the Bar the prejudice of the judiciary against organised labour was evident.

I admired the small number of lawyers who were committed to the defence of the trade unions and their members. One was solicitor Jack Gaster, a veteran of the Communist Party with experience of trade union cases going back to the 1930s. When he briefed a young barrister, his habit was to come to court and sit behind the barrister, like a general testing a new recruit. I was more terrified of him than of any magistrate or judge. In 1973 he briefed me to defend Peter Kavanagh, who was a member of the Electrical Trades Union, whose members were on strike at St Thomas' Hospital in London. The striking electricians had organised a picket at the hospital in order to persuade non-union electricians not to break the strike. They thought that they were protected by an Act of Parliament which said that picketing for the purpose of peaceful persuasion 'shall not of itself constitute an offence'. The police, however, had formed a cordon which prevented the pickets from approaching the strike breakers. Mr Kavanagh tried to push through the cordon and was promptly arrested and charged with assaulting and obstructing the police in the execution of their duty.

To Mr Kavanagh, and to me, it seemed to be a clear case in which his right to picket peacefully had been violated, so that the police were not acting in the execution of any duty when they stopped him. But the magistrate convicted him, and we appealed to the High Court. The Lord Chief Justice, Lord Widgery, delivered a judgment in which he made a distinction between a 'right' and an 'immunity': "I am of the opinion that the true view of this subsection is that it is one creating immunities where required, and not one creating positive rights capable of being infringed by the police officers in this case."

I felt outraged by the decision. The Lord Chief Justice was saying that although workers were allowed to picket peacefully, they were not allowed to prevent the police from preventing them from picketing peacefully. If that were the law, the police could stop picketing altogether. We applied to the House of Lords for leave to appeal. The presiding judge was Lord Dilhorne, former Conservative Lord Chancellor and a thorough reactionary. His name before he became a Lord was Sir Reginald Manningham-Buller, commonly adapted by lawyers to 'Sir Reginald Bullying-Manner'. His hostility to everything I said was palpable, and leave to appeal was refused.

When the National Union of Mineworkers called the strike in 1984 which was to last for a year, the Wellington Street chambers were part of a core of radical lawyers who defended miners who were charged with rioting. I have described some of the cases in which we were involved. The experience of working to represent trade unionists over a protracted period intensified my belief in the necessity that trade unions should exist, and should be free to protect their members against exploitation and arbitrary dismissal.

Without trade unions there is an intolerable imbalance of power in the employment relationship. Management holds nearly all the cards. It can dictate levels of pay and conditions of work. It can hire and fire at will, and if it chooses it can shut down a factory or an industry. In Jamaica there have been cases of management firing the whole work force overnight and recruiting non-unionised workers instead. The workers can respond to oppressive management by threatening and implementing strike action, but this can be a risky strategy. The British miners' strike, for all its heroism and sacrifice, failed to stop the closure of the majority of Britain's coal mines.

Whereas in Britain I represented individual trade unionists from time to time, I was not a specialist in trade union law and did not get briefed in the big cases. In Jamaica I am proud to say that employment law, including the representation of trade unions and their members, has become one of my areas of expertise. It has given me the highest professional and personal satisfaction to win cases which have not only done justice to the individuals involved, but which have set benchmarks and standards to be observed by employers throughout the country. These are cases which show that the law can do justice in favour of the small low paid worker, in spite of the opposition of the economically mighty employer. They are cases which have resonance in other fields of law, for they give confidence to the citizen that the justice system can work.

An explanation is needed of the basic law governing labour relations in Jamaica. Jamaicans have had unusually cruel and brutal experiences of working for a boss – the 'backra massa', as the overseer was called. Most Jamaicans were slaves until emancipation in 1838. Thereafter, although theoretically free to leave their jobs, they were in reality prisoners of the contract which the bosses imposed upon them. The notion of a contract in English common law is that a bargain entered into between free men and women is sacred. If you agree to work for me for ten dollars a week, then you must work the work and I must pay you the pay. But since I have only agreed to pay you for a week at a time, I can terminate the contract on giving a week's notice. It does not matter if you go on working week after week for me for twenty years. Under the common law I can still give you notice, for any reason or none. You also can give me notice; but if I employ a thousand people in this industry, and jobs in the industry are scarce, your right to quit is hardly equal to my right to fire you.

In Jamaica as in Britain, this gross imbalance of power was confronted by the growing effectiveness of the trade union movement. The Bustamante Industrial Trade Union (BITU), allied to the Jamaica Labour Party (JLP), and the National Workers Union (NWU), allied to the People's National Party (PNP), through mass recruitment in Jamaica's major industries such as sugar, were able to empower the working class through the threat that if the employers did not accept their demands for better pay and conditions, the industry would be paralysed by strike action. But while the emergent trade union movement obtained huge gains for the Jamaican worker, as well as a sense of dignity and pride in place of colonial subservience, relations between management and labour were full of conflict, and the conflicts which were not resolved erupted into strikes.

In the 1970s the PNP government led by Michael Manley enacted a series of laws which collectively amounted to a new charter of employment rights. The Employment (Termination and Redundancy Payments) Act provided for minimum periods of notice, the amount of notice depending on length of service. In the case of redundancy further payments had to be made, two weeks pay per year for an employee of up to 10 years standing, and three weeks pay per year thereafter. So an employee who had worked for 20 years and was made redundant would have to get 12 weeks' notice or pay in lieu, and also 50 weeks' redundancy pay. For the first time recognition was given to the value of long service. Other Acts passed in this era for the benefit of workers were the Maternity Leave Act and the Holidays with Pay Act.

The cornerstone of the reform programme was the Labour Relations and Industrial Disputes Act. The Act required employers to recognise trade unions, and provided for a ballot procedure by which the workers could vote to be represented by a union which would have the right to bargain on their behalf. It also set up a machinery aimed at replacing industrial conflict with a system of discussion, conciliation, mediation and – if all else failed – arbitration. Any dispute which could not be resolved by negotiation would be referred to the Minister of Labour, whose negotiators would invite the parties to take part in round-table talks and hammer out a settlement. If the dispute was still unresolved the minister had the power to refer it to the Industrial Disputes Tribunal (IDT) for settlement. The IDT could issue back to work orders which ensured that production continued while the hearing before the IDT was pending. The IDT, composed of a chairman with experience of industrial relations and two members appointed by organisations of employers and employees, would make an award which was to be final and binding and could not be impeached except in case of an error of law.

This system has been in operation since 1975, and in my view has contributed enormously to industrial harmony and the prevention of strikes. The IDTs deal with two main classes of dispute, both of which can generate an acute sense of grievance if they are not fairly resolved. First, disputes about pay and conditions. If the employer is prepared to increase pay by 5 per cent and the union is asking for 10 per cent, and the gap cannot be bridged by conciliation, it is the IDT which must make the award which it considers to be right having regard to all the evidence, including pay in comparable companies and the financial viability of the employer. Even if one side or the other may disagree with the award, they have to accept it as the binding decision of an independent body which has given both sides a fair hearing. This area of the IDT's jurisdiction is not to be found in Britain, where pay disputes are often only settled after bitter and damaging strikes. I have no doubt that Jamaica's system is better.

If the IDT makes a mistake in the interpretation of the law, the Supreme Court can intervene. In 1995 I was approached by the Jamaican Association of Local Government Officers (JALGO), which represented Jamaica's firefighters. Their wages were pitifully low, and the Government had stated that it could not afford to pay more. The IDT upheld the Government's view, saying that "Cabinet's final approval constitutes a policy decision which is not subject to modification by the Tribunal." This was based on the Tribunal's interpretation of a section of the Act which says that it may not make any award which is "inconsistent with the national interest".

I took the case to the Supreme Court, arguing that what the Government thought it could afford was not the same as the national interest. The Court agreed and ordered a new hearing, at which a reasonable award was eventually made. Justice Cooke in a memorable passage of his judgment encapsulated the value of the IDT as an independent arbiter of industrial conflict:

> As I write our schools are closed – teachers have taken strike action. The water in our pipes may soon be no more as certain categories of persons employed to the National Water Commission have withdrawn their labour. The workers in the Bauxite Industry have only just gone back to work, having taken industrial action. Seething murmurs of employee discontent pervade the land. In all this, resolution there must be, and perhaps there may be references to the IDT. On all accounts the Tribunal created to settle disputes which have defied hitherto conciliatory efforts and procedures has played an invaluable role in the conflicts which arise from time to time between employers and employees. No doubt it will continue to do so. It is therefore important that the Tribunal recognises its independence – an independence that can only add to the confidence of those persons or parties who appear before it.

The IDT's other main area of jurisdiction is over dismissals. Where a dispute arises over the dismissal of one or more employees, the IDT must make a judgment as to whether the dismissal was 'unjustifiable'. If, having looked at all the background, the IDT considers that the dismissal was unjustifiable, it may order the reinstatement of the employee as well as compensation for lost wages. (Until recently the

IDT was obliged to reinstate the employee if he or she wished to be reinstated, but an amendment to the law now gives the IDT a discretion whether to order reinstatement or compensation or both.) In this area of its jurisdiction the IDT plays a similar role to that of the industrial tribunals in Britain. As in Britain, the Act required Parliament to approve a Labour Relations Code which should be observed by employers and workers, in the interests of a partnership in which communication and consultation were essential.

Dismissal from a job can give rise to the most heart-rending personal consequences. The very dignity and worth of a person is assailed if he or she is sacked for no good reason. Years of faithful service may be ended by a thoughtless exercise of power. In Jamaica, where news travels fast and jobs are scarce, to be dismissed from your job may result in your being rejected by every other employer in the same business. Where one parent is the sole wage earner, dismissals may mean that children starve, miss school, and can no longer be treated if they are sick.

My baptism of fire in the IDT came through the 'Grand Lido' case. Grand Lido Negril is a luxury hotel, one of the finest in Jamaica's premier resort, part of the Superclubs Group founded by the Issa family. The workers were represented by a staff association, and they were concerned that the association was not securing their interests. There was talk of joining a trade union, and there were allegations that employees who were in favour of joining a union had been dismissed. The staff association asked for a meeting between workers and management, and a time was agreed for one morning. When the time came the employees assembled, but the management did not appear. The managers were upset by the fact that Pearnel Charles, representing the BITU, had come to Negril and was talking to employees at the hotel gate. The employees who had assembled refused to go to their posts, and there was a stand-off for a few hours. Just when they had agreed to return to work provided there was no victimisation, the management announced that they were all dismissed – both the employees on the morning shift and those who came in the afternoon to join them. In all 225 employees were fired. Most of them had been working for the hotel for many years. Before long the dispute had been referred to the IDT.

Normally the arguments for the employees at IDT hearings are presented by union officers who are extremely capable advocates. But the staff association had no experience of the IDT, and I was asked to represent it together with attorney-at-law Wentworth Charles, brother to Pearnel. It was clear that the dismissed employees had no funds to pay for attorneys, and we took on the case for a token payment. We felt the justice of the employees' case to be overwhelming.

The hotel management was represented by Emil George QC. Emil and I have become good professional colleagues, but when appearing against him I can never escape the feeling that he represents a planter class which should have become extinct. If the case is going well for him, he is charming, but if crossed he can be truculent and bullying. In the Grand Lido case he clearly believed that the management had done the right thing. The employees, he argued, by refusing to return to work had repudiated their contracts of employment. They had, in effect, sacked themselves, and the management had done no wrong in accepting their repudiation. It was an argument which was well founded in the old common law, and indeed in another hotel case, relating to the Four Seasons Hotel in Kingston, the Court of Appeal had upheld the case of the management when workers had been dismissed after a strike.

Wentworth and I argued that the IDT was not limited to applying the old common law. The Act required it to look at all the circumstances, and at the Labour Relations Code, and to make a judgment as to whether the employer had acted fairly. The Code encouraged management to meet with workers who had grievances, and this had not happened. The IDT in the Four Seasons case had been dealing with a strike of several days, and had not surprisingly found that the dismissals were justifiable. In this case the strike, such as it was, had only lasted a few hours, and it was about to end when the dismissals were ordered. The management had acted high-handedly and dictatorially towards workers who had given excellent service over years.

In those days the IDT sat in stiflingly hot rooms in Slipe Road in Kingston. For 20 days we battled in the heat for the dismissed employees. Some of them were in tears as they recalled the care which they had given to the guests of the hotel. It had been the centre of their lives for years. The witnesses from the management insisted that the workers had been unreasonable, and that a hotel could not function if workers downed tools for even a day. The chairman of the IDT, Clinton Davis, was a kindly man who presided even-handedly and patiently over the proceedings.

The IDT decided that all 225 workers had been unjustifiably dismissed and should be reinstated, with 60 per cent of their pay from the time of dismissal to the time of the decision, and with full pay until the time of reinstatement. The deduction of 40 per cent was a recognition that the workers had been at fault in not returning to work, but the IDT placed the greater part of the blame on the insensitive conduct of the management. They found that: "The management did not demonstrate the understanding and compromise which the circumstances demanded *ab initio* and throughout."

The hotel challenged the IDT's decision in the Supreme Court, where they lost, and again in the Court of Appeal. They relied on the old common law doctrine that the employees had repudiated their contract, and therefore their action was 'justified' at common law. They said that the word 'unjustifiable' in the Act was not the same as the word 'unfair' in the British statute, but meant that the dismissals could not be justified under principles of the common law. I could see that this interpretation would drive a coach and horses through the legislation, since many dismissals are 'justified' under the strict common law, but blatantly unfair. I did a search through legislation in other countries, and found that in New Zealand the word 'unjustifiable' was used in relation to dismissals in employment statutes. A request to a legal colleague in New Zealand revealed that judges had interpreted the word to mean 'unfair'. So we cited several New Zealand cases to the Court of Appeal.

Presiding over the Court of Appeal was the President, Justice Rattray. As Carl Rattray, he had been Minister of Justice and Attorney General in various PNP governments. His appointment as President by Prime Minister Patterson, whose partner he had once been in the firm of Rattray Patterson Rattray, was criticised by some as an act of political nepotism. But the legal profession had come to greatly admire his courtesy, his fairness and his wisdom as a judge. His judgment in the Grand Lido case eloquently set the Labour Relations Act in the context of Jamaica's history:

> For the majority of us in the Caribbean, the inheritors of a slave society, the movements have been cyclic – first from the status of slave to the strictness of contract, and now to an accommodating coalescence of both status and contract, in which the contract is still very relevant though the rigidities of its enforcement have been ameliorated. To achieve this Parliament has legislated a distinct environment including the creation of a specialist forum, not for the trial of actions but for the settlement of disputes.

Sitting with him was Justice Gordon, a judge of the old school who could not accept that the common law principles of contract, which he had imbibed as a student and expounded through his long career, had been so radically disturbed. The Act, he said in disagreement with the President of the Court, "did not take away the common law rights of an employer under a contract of employment".

The decisive vote was that of the most junior judge, Justice Bingham. He was a judge whom I had always liked. He would always listen carefully to the arguments, and once convinced of the justice of your case he would be with you unshakeably. He said that having read both of the judgments of his brethren, he thought that the approach of the President was correct. Parliament had introduced "some degree of equity and fairness" into the law of employment. The worker now had "an interest in his job akin to an interest in property". The Act had given remedies to the aggrieved workers which were "hitherto unknown to the common law".

The saga of the Grand Lido case was not quite over. The Hotel obtained leave to appeal to the Privy Council. We were confident that we would be able to defend the judgement of the Court of Appeal, which was in line with judicial decisions in many countries. But then a strange event happened in the House of Lords in London which intrigued lawyers all over the world. The former dictator of Chile, Augusto Pinochet, had been arrested in Britain on an extradition warrant issued by a judge in Spain. His challenge to the extradition order had gone to the House of Lords, where various organisations including Amnesty International had been allowed to intervene and make submissions. The House of Lords upheld Pinochet's extradition.

Pinochet's lawyers then challenged the House of Lords ruling on the grounds that one of the five Law Lords, Lord Hoffman, was biased. Lord Hoffman was chairman of a charitable company set up by Amnesty International to do charitable work. A different panel of Lords had to determine whether the decision of their brethren was tainted with bias. They held that it was. Amnesty was a party to the proceedings, so any judge who was closely connected with an Amnesty affiliate was automatically disqualified, however open-minded he may have been. The Pinochet appeal had therefore to be reheard.

Emil George told me that he intended to raise before the Privy Council the argument that Justice Rattray, when Minister of Justice, had been one of the architects of the Labour Relations and Industrial Disputes Act, and should have disqualified himself under the Hoffman principle. This had me worried, since I was sure that Carl Rattray had believed passionately in the legislation which he had interpreted in the Grand Lido case, and could well have made speeches on the issue. On the other hand, there was no institutional connection between him and any party to the case, which was the decisive factor in the Pinochet case. I reflected that the workers had already waited for over four years for justice. A hearing before the Privy Council, with the possibility of a further hearing before a new Court of Appeal, with possibly another Privy Council appeal after that, would be intolerable.

I spoke to Pearnel Charles, who was still the unofficial representative of the workers. He said that the hotel was prepared to settle on the basis of paying the greater part of the four years' back wages, and costs. There would be no reinstatement, but most of the workers were already established in new jobs. I recommended the settlement. Apart from the problems which might arise in the Privy Council, I wanted Justice Rattray's judgment to be the leading decision on industrial relations law, and so it has proved. The Grand Lido case came to an end, and one of the benefits of its ending was that not only the employees but also their attorneys at last got paid.

Some years later, the Grand Lido judgment was scrutinised by the Privy Council, in the Flour Mills case. In 1999 Jamaica Flour Mills Limited, the dominant producers of flour in the country, had been taken over by a US company, ADM Milling. The new management decided that some of the work at the wharf would be outsourced to an independent contractor, which would entail making three men redundant. One had worked for the company for 28 years, the other two for 13 years. They were told at 2.30 pm that they were to be dismissed with immediate effect on the grounds of redundancy. They were represented by the National Workers Union (NWU), which had not been consulted about the redundancy situation. The Union called a strike, which ended when the dispute was referred to the IDT, which made a back to work order.

The Labour Relations Code contains clear provisions that in a case of redundancy there must be consultation with the workers or their representatives, and efforts should be made to avoid undue hardship and to secure alternative employment if possible. The manager who signed the dismissal letters admitted that he had no knowledge of the Code, and said that the Union had not been told in advance because of the fear of acts of sabotage. The IDT took a dim view of the disregard of the Code, and rejected the argument about sabotage. They said that it was "unfair, unreasonable and unconscionable for the Company to effect the dismissals in the way that it did". It showed "very little if any concern for the dignity and human feelings of the workers". Assuming that there was a redundancy situation, the manner of the dismissals made them unjustifiable. The IDT ordered that the three men be reinstated, with full pay. But they directed that two of the men, who had cashed their redundancy cheques because of the needs of their families, must offset the amount which they had received against the back pay. It was a clear cut decision in a blatant case of unfair dismissal, and it should have ended there.

However the management of Jamaica Flour Mills appeared to resent the IDT's decision. They challenged it in the Supreme Court, where the Chief Justice and two other judges decided that the IDT was right. They appealed to the Court of Appeal, where the President of the Court of Appeal and two other judges decided that the IDT was right. Justice Walker described the dismissals as "an outstanding example of man's inhumanity to man".

Still refusing to accept defeat, the company took the case to the Privy Council. By the time the case was heard, five and a half years had elapsed since the dismissals. One of the workers was desperately trying to fend off moves by his bank to foreclose on his mortgage and sell his house. Of course the Union could not afford to pay lawyers to appear before the Privy Council, which is usually a costly exercise. I enlisted the help of Mark Stephens, senior partner in a leading London firm of solicitors, as well as two English barristers who were expert in employment law, and we all agreed to act for the Union on a 'conditional fee agreement', by which we would be paid only if we won.

The points of law which the company had presented to the Jamaican courts appeared to have little substance. They claimed that the two men who had taken their redundancy cheques had waived their right to compensation. We answered that they only did so after the dispute had been referred to the IDT, and then only because of their need. They claimed that the IDT had put too much emphasis on the Labour Relations Code, and that consultation with the Union would have made no difference. We answered that respect for the dignity of the workers demanded that some notice should have been given, and that the company should have listened to what the Union had to say. As Justice Paul Harrison put it in the Court of Appeal, "The company does not have a monopoly on wisdom."

When the company asked for leave to appeal to the Privy Council, it disclosed that part of the basis for its appeal would be that the Grand Lido decision was wrong. We had cited that decision, and the courts had relied on it. Because of the doctrine of precedent, by which previous decisions are binding in later cases, the company could not dispute the decision in the Jamaican courts. But the Privy Council, as the highest court in the Jamaican legal system, had the power to overrule the Grand Lido decision. It was interesting that Jamaica Flour Mills' attorneys were the firm of Livingston Alexander Levy, a firm whose attorneys have been worthy opponents in many of my cases. One of their partners, Angela Robertson, a doughty defender of the rights of employers, had often complained to me that she considered the Grand Lido decision to be wrong. Now they had the chance to put that argument forward at the highest level. Had this, I wondered, been the real purpose of all these appeals in what seemed to be a hopeless case?

Together with my legal team, which included a Professor from Oxford University, we made a study of industrial relations laws all over the Commonwealth. Without exception they recognised that a dismissal carried out in defiance of proper procedures could be ruled to be unfair, even if there was a reason for it such as redundancy. We presented a detailed written argument for the Privy Council to read before the hearing began. We were supported by the Government's attorneys, who were in the case representing the IDT, who also put in a strong written argument.

When it came to the hearing, I almost felt sorry for Donald Scharschmidt QC, the Jamaican attorney who presented the company's case. Five eminent Law Lords dissected each of his arguments, courteously but ruthlessly, and found them wanting. Each of them fired polite but barbed questions which he was unable to answer. In his confusion, his notes slipped off the sloping podium and fell to the floor. Having been vanquished on all the points which had been raised in the lower courts, he backed away from attacking the Grand Lido judgment. At the end of the morning, when it was clear that his appeal had failed, he asked me whether I had been surprised at the way he was treated. Knowing from experience how the Privy Council treats a poor case, I had to say that I was not.

The Privy Council's judgment upheld the decision of the IDT and the Jamaican courts, and to my delight, approved the judgment of Justice Rattray in the Grand Lido case. The decision was headline news in the Jamaican press, and I did several media interviews. I believed it to be important that the Jamaican public, who are so often sceptical about the legal system, should know that the Jamaican courts had got it right, and had been able to do justice for the small man against the mighty corporation.

Working as a trade union lawyer has brought me to meet many wonderful clients, from senior bank managers to humble waiters. When groups of workers do not have an experienced trade union to represent them, I have acted for them at negotiations at the Ministry of Labour. I have come to respect the process of mediation, which can be long and tedious, but often achieves a settlement at less cost and delay, and with less pain than would be suffered in a long tribunal hearing. It calls for different skills from the advocate; you have to know when to be tough and when to make concessions. Mediation is now becoming more used in Supreme Court litigation, and it is now mandatory for parties to seek a settlement by mediation before a case is set down for trial. It is eminently sensible;

you try to reach an amicable settlement with the help of an experienced mediator, and if that fails you still have your right to a decision from the court.

The most difficult problems in the Jamaican employment scene are those faced by non-unionised employees who are unfairly dismissed. The IDT only has jurisdiction over disputes which are referred to it by the minister, which in practice means disputes which are brought by a trade union or a staff association. The value of group representation is increasingly being recognised by senior managers and executives, some of whom have formed staff associations and applied for affiliation to trade unions. When a group of senior managers of the National Commercial Bank were in dispute over pay and conditions, they applied to join the BITU, which sought bargaining rights through the holding of a ballot. The bank was appalled, claiming that as they were managers they could not join a trade union. The managers drew attention to the Constitution of Jamaica, which enshrines the right of every person to belong to a trade union. The case went to the IDT which supported the bank managers. The decision would have been challenged by the bank in the Supreme Court, if there had not been a settlement which avoided the need for union membership to be claimed.

The problem for the employee who has no trade union or staff association is that he or she is limited to the rights available under the common law. Normally this means that however unfairly an employment is terminated, the dismissed employee may only recover pay in lieu of notice. The common law does not permit a court to order reinstatement, or to pay damages for distress, or even to pay compensation for lost wages in the period before the employee can find a new job. Ideally Jamaicans need a right of individual access to an IDT, as is the case in Britain. But this can be ill afforded by a country whose public services are all under stress because of the poverty of the national budget.

I believe that the best way forward is for the courts to develop the common law creatively, and this is beginning to happen. There was a case in England in which the House of Lords ruled that in every contract of employment there was an implied duty of trust and confidence, and neither side should act in a way which betrays that trust. If an employer victimises an employee by dismissing him or her without cause, or on a trumped-up charge, that is a betrayal of trust and a breach of the contractual duty. In that case, said the House of Lords, the damages should cover all the consequences of the breach; so that if, as is often the case, an arbitrary dismissal results in the employee being blacklisted and unable to get a new job, the employer who betrayed the trust should pay full damages for the lost salary. The Jamaican courts have not yet considered a case of this kind, but given the philosophy which was expounded by Justice Rattray, I am hopeful that they would look on such a case positively. One way or another, I aim to continue to get justice for the Jamaican worker.

16

HUMAN RIGHTS
in JAMAICA

T he "Fundamental Rights and Freedoms" of the Jamaican people are set out in Chapter III of the Constitution of Jamaica, which was adopted at the time of that country's independence in 1962. Unfortunately, any Jamaican citizen who bought a copy of the Constitution and tried to grasp the meaning of Chapter III would soon give up in despair. It starts with a sentence containing twenty lines and a number of clauses starting 'whereas' and 'subject to'. It continues by setting out various rights but subjecting them to multiple exceptions, so that you end up needing to consult a lawyer to appreciate the extent of your rights. This is not healthy for a free society. If people do not know what rights they possess, they will not stand up for them when they are abused. A Charter of Rights needs to live in the minds of the people. Its core provisions should be grounded in the consciousness of young people before they leave school. It should be written in clear and resonant language, not turgid legalese.

The need for reform of the Constitution was recognised in 1992 when a Constitutional Commission was set up. It held public meetings and reported in 1994. Its report included a draft Bill of Rights for which the Commission's Chairman Dr Lloyd Barnett was responsible, with input from Edward Seaga and David Coore. In clear language the draft set out seventeen rights which neither Parliament or any organ of the State could abrogate or infringe. The rights included many which are not to be found in the 1962 Constitution; such as the right to vote; the right to a healthy environment; the rights of children to protection and to free primary education; the right to a passport; and the right to fair, humane and equal treatment from any public authority. Instead of a list of exceptions, the draft Bill simply provided that rights could be qualified by laws which were required "in periods of public emergency or as may be demonstrably justified in a free and democratic society". It was an excellent draft, but it has not been enacted into law. Both the Opposition and the Government have tabled bills which drew on the Commission's draft, but each time there have been disagreements over details. Recently a Joint Select Committee of Parliament has been debating the draft again, so I hope that Jamaica will eventually have the Bill of Rights which the people need.

The Commission's draft dealt with a serious flaw in the 1962 Constitution. Section 26(8) declared that nothing contained in any law in force before 1962 could be held to be inconsistent with the provisions of Chapter III. In other words the pre-1962 colonial laws were assumed to conform with the rights contained in the Constitution, so that only laws passed after 1962 could be challenged as unconstitutional. This provision freezes constitutional rights in the mould which was shaped up to 1962. It makes no allowance for the possibility that Jamaican judges might find that pre-independence laws were less than perfect in their protection of human rights. Among the laws which cannot be challenged because of this provision are the Flogging Regulation Act (not used in practice) which permits flogging as a punishment; the sections of the Offences Against the Person Act which criminalise homosexual acts; and the Vagrancy Act which allows for the imprisonment of 'vagrants' who are 'found wandering abroad'. It is high time for this constitutional shackle to be unloosed.

With all its shortcomings, Chapter III of the Constitution does guarantee most of the essential freedoms which underpin a democratic society. It protects the right to life and liberty; the right not to be subjected to torture or inhuman or degrading punishment or treatment; the right not to have property seized or premises entered; the right to a fair trial; and the rights of freedom of religion, expression and association. But does the reality conform to the promise of the law? Taking stock of the state of human rights in Jamaica today, looking at how far Jamaicans actually enjoy their fundamental rights and freedoms, the picture is uneven and at times appalling.

On the positive side, freedom of speech in Jamaica is alive and well. People in high places are criticised and often vilified on a daily basis on talk shows and news programmes. Freedom of association is well developed, so that trade unions, human rights groups and numerous professional and social organisations are part of the life blood of Jamaican society. Freedom of religion is enjoyed by the adherents of thousands of churches and other places of worship. The right to property is generally respected.

A Jamaican's home, like the proverbial home of the Englishman, is still his castle. Those who criticise Jamaica's human rights record should recognise the value of these rights which Jamaicans sometimes take for granted.

But there are other rights which are violated on a daily basis. The right to life rings hollow in a country which has the second highest murder rate in the world – 1674 murders in 2005 in a population of two and a half million people. Innocent lives are taken not just by criminals, but by the police. The police killed 168 people in 2005, some no doubt in self-defence, but many in cold blood or through gross misuse of firearms by officers who tend to shoot first and think of the explanation later. The right to liberty is constantly denied to poor suspects who are locked up for weeks and not brought to court 'without delay' as the Constitution requires. Those who can afford an attorney can make a habeas corpus application which will normally bring their illegal detention to an end. Those without an attorney languish in police lock-ups until the police determine whether to charge them or release them.

The right not to be subjected to inhuman or degrading punishment or treatment means little to Jamaica's prisoners who are held in overcrowded and often hellish conditions. The prisons where convicted prisoners are kept are bad enough, with inmates crammed into insanitary cells where many have no room to lie down; but at least there are long periods of association in the open air, where various kinds of work and creativity and recreation take place. The remand centres and police station lock-ups, where prisoners awaiting trial or extradition are kept, are the worst. There is no place for exercise or fresh air, and prisoners sit in their cells for the greater part of the day and night.

As for the right to a fair trial within a reasonable time, the position is dire. The courts try to be fair, but they have given up on keeping to a 'reasonable time' because the system both for criminal and civil justice has become clogged with overload. Three years is not unusual for an accused person to be in custody awaiting trial. The civil justice system was recently reformed by the introduction of case management conferences, which take place after a claim has been filed and a defence has been served. But there are delays of up to a year to get a case management date, and when you get to the case management conference, the date which will then be fixed for the trial of the case is likely to be another two or three years ahead.

The overarching consideration about justice in Jamaica today is the state of the Jamaican economy. Over the years since independence Jamaica has borrowed and borrowed. Much of the borrowing was for essential projects, particularly in the field of education, which had been neglected under colonialism. Experts differ as to whether all the borrowing was necessary or wise, and I am no expert in economics. The stark reality is that over the last few years between 65 and 70 per cent of all of Jamaica's tax revenues have had to be allocated to debt servicing. The Jamaican government has to run all public services – including education, health, policing, road maintenance, and justice – with a mere 30-35 per cent of its revenues. To use a Jamaican phrase, any minister coming into government today is given 'basket to carry water'. Every public service is underfinanced and under intense strain. There is a shortage of teachers in the schools, beds in the hospitals, police on the streets, and a surplus of potholes in the roads. The justice system has its share of shortages: too few judges, court buildings in disrepair, no Jamaican law reports for any year since 1998, delays in the payment of legal aid fees. Although Jamaica has first world ambitions, its economy has many of the features of the third world.

In the face of all the difficulties I constantly urge my colleagues in the legal profession not to despair. The system may be slow but it has not broken down. The judges must be given credit for presiding over a court system which retains the essential hallmarks of justice. The judges are not corrupt. Most of them do their best to be fair. There are younger judges coming through the system who give me confidence in the future because of their independence of mind and their legal ability. Chief Justice Wolfe has shown commendable zeal in getting the system to work efficiently, including getting the courts to start on time. The judges of appeal have a gruelling workload, which has led to delays in the writing of judgments; but the quality of their reasoning remains high, and several of their judgments in recent years have been praised by the Privy Council. But the judges can only uphold human rights in cases which are brought before them. If those whose rights are abused cannot get representation, then justice is an unattainable fantasy for them.

I see hope in recent developments in Jamaica which have widened the possibilities of justice. The position of Public Defender was created by Act of Parliament in 2000, as a result of recommendations made by the Constitutional Commission and in particular Edward Seaga. The Public Defender has powers to investigate cases of injustice as a result of administrative action, and cases of infringement of constitutional rights. He or she is to be a champion of those whose grievances would not otherwise be redressed. Howard Hamilton QC, the first holder of the office, used his mandate to speak out for many of the least favoured Jamaicans. When a case needs court action he refers it to an attorney, and he and I have worked together on many issues.

The Public Defender introduced me to the case of Kevin Hall, an inmate of the St Catherine prison who wanted to join the Church of Haile Selassie I, a Rastafarian church. The ministers of the Church were only able to see him as ordinary visitors, which meant a few minutes shouting through a grille in conditions of minimal privacy. The ministers of all the Christian churches had the facility of using the prison chapel to conduct services, but this was denied to the Rastafarians. I brought a constitutional motion complaining that Mr Hall's right to freedom of religion had been violated. The right in the Constitution expressly includes "the freedom, either alone or in community with others, and both in public and in private, to manifest and propagate his religion or belief in worship, teaching, practice and observance". Shortly before the case was due to be heard the Government's attorneys suggested a settlement. A solemn agreement was reached which recognised the Church's right to hold services in the prison on the same terms as other churches. Assurances were given that ganja would not be used in the services. As a result, there is now a service taking place every month in the St Catherine Adult Correctional Centre, attended by several dozen inmates, complete with chalices and incense-burning and the colourful rituals of Rastafari.

Non-governmental organisations have begun to play a remarkable role in bringing injustices to light and holding the State to account. The Independent Jamaican Council for Human Rights (IJCHR) researched the plight of inmates in the prisons whose cases had been forgotten. Many of them had been declared 'unfit to plead' and remanded indefinitely on minor charges. Some had been in prison without trial for decades. Several cases were taken to court. Inmates were freed and a system agreed with the authorities for monitoring such cases. IJCHR has also taken up the cases of Haitian and Cuban refugees and filed claims for asylum where appropriate.

Lawyers used to the Legal Aid scheme in England have the luxury of knowing that if they take the cases of the despised and downtrodden, the mentally ill and the refugees and others whose human rights are in jeopardy, they will usually be paid from public funds. As a result the English law reports are full of cases involving critical human rights issues for poor litigants. Jamaica simply does not have the resources to pay legal aid in civil cases. The rates of pay for criminal legal aid were improved some years ago, but even then they are low and paid late. So the involvement of civil society organisations, which in turn mobilise attorneys of good will, is crucial if a just society is to be created.

The organisation Jamaicans for Justice (JFJ) has been conspicuous in bringing abuses of power by the police and other authorities to light, and pursuing remedies for the victims. The organisation has worked effectively with pathologists from Britain, who have brought an independent element into the investigation of police killings. It was tireless in the case of Michael Gayle, a young mentally ill man who was cycling along a Kingston street in 1999 during a period of curfew, when police and soldiers stopped him, set upon him and beat him with gun butts, punches and kicks, so that he died two days later from peritonitis following traumatic rupture to the stomach. When no one was prosecuted for his death, JFJ took the case to the Inter-American Commission on Human Rights. The Commission made a ruling that Jamaica was responsible for violations of five articles of the American Convention on Human Rights: the right to life, to humane treatment, to liberty and security, and to an effective hearing and remedy. Many other well-known cases of police shooting would have received little attention if JFJ had not existed.

The organisations reflect and articulate a widespread conscience in the Jamaican people. One also hears it from journalists, church leaders, academics and others who speak day after day in the media, wringing their hands at the injustices of the system and offering their advice as to what we can do to rescue our sinking society. If words alone could change a country, Jamaica would be a paradise. When a major human rights scandal occurs, the outcry can move the authorities into action. This happened one night in 1999 when 32 mentally ill and down-and-out 'street people' in Montego Bay were rounded up, herded into a truck and dumped a hundred miles away in the remote countryside. The action was outrageous, and it was met with public outrage. After a lot of prevarication the Government set up a full judicial inquiry.

So when I am asked about the state of human rights in Jamaica, I say that it is a work in progress, repeatedly set back by gross abuses, but fostered by the efforts of good people in strong organisations. My experience in Jamaica even more than in Britain is that everyone can make a difference. Human rights are upheld by the judges, but often after inordinate delays and only in cases which attorneys are willing to bring to court. Speaking directly to Jamaican lawyers, I say that every lawyer can made a difference to the advancement of human rights in Jamaica. However much people lobby and campaign and expose injustices, it is the law which provides the concrete remedies which the victims of injustice need. Many of the lawyers who take cases with the support of the human rights organisations are veterans whose record goes back through the decades. I would like to see more young attorneys fired with the zeal to take up human rights cases. If you are not sure about how to fight a case, ask for guidance from one of the veterans. Do the research and ask a senior to be your leader when the case comes before the court. Take some cases for no fee, or for a reduced fee, or on a contingency fee. Whether or not you are properly paid, make sure that those whose rights are abused can get access justice.

Human rights violations do not happen only at the hands of the agents of the State. If one were to do a survey among Jamaican citizens as to the ways in which their rights have been violated, I would bet that spousal abuse would head the list. The love of justice which most Jamaicans profess has to be contrasted with the brutal injustices perpetrated by so many Jamaican men upon their partners in the privacy of the home. The reality of thousands of Jamaican women is the domestic hell of living with men whose idea of a personal relationship is that they should be in absolute control; they can lust after other women while their women must stay at home; they should be obeyed at all times; and they can enforce their dictates by violence if their desires are flouted. The concept of equal rights and justice does not enter the heads of these would-be all-powerful males.

As with every example of historical injustice, the victims in the end refuse to bow down. Jamaican women are fighting back. Their liberation struggle may not be organised under any banner, but women today are making better use of education and employment than ever before. Three-quarters of the graduates from the Norman Manley Law School in recent years have been women, and this proportion is mirrored in other fields. This development is treated by some men as presenting a crisis for the Jamaican male. In a way this is right, for demands for freedom always cause a crisis for the oppressors. But the crisis is simple to resolve. Once men are able to accept the concept of equality and justice in their personal lives – equal respect for each others' views, equal rights to a career, equal responsibilities towards children, an equal say in sexual activity or non-activity, and a total end to violence – they will find that a new and joyous world will open to them.

I recall the words of Jamaican academic Cecil Gutzmore, who said at his wedding to the equally learned academic Carolyn Cooper that he had been asked by many men how he was going to manage with such a strong woman: "I could never imagine marrying a weak woman. Carolyn is part of a movement gaining power throughout the world. The world is becoming more feminised, and I welcome it." I agree with him. The prospect of real equality is a challenge to be grasped eagerly by men as well as by women. So many men are blind to the real beauty of their women. The beauty of a woman lies in the interweaving of her mental brilliance, her bodily form and her spiritual fire. Men who simply pant after the body are doomed to fail. They disrespect the mind and may never reach the spirit.

Living in an equal relationship is not easy. We all carry baggage from our upbringing, much of it reinforcing male chauvinism. We all have moods, desires, temptations, tendencies to wield power in different ways. But when it works it is pure joy. Two equal partners supporting the family. Two creative minds giving each other space, challenging each other to do better, rejoicing in each other's success. Embracing freedom and justice in the home will benefit mankind and womankind alike.

Children too have rights. The International Convention on the Rights of the Child provides a comprehensive statement of the rights which children should enjoy, but there are far too many abandoned and abused children who grow to be teenage criminals or prostitutes. It pains me when I hear, as I do too often in Jamaica, of children being sexually abused, children roaming the streets, children being sacrificed in parental wars. I was happy to have been able to use my contacts with English lawyers to secure justice when a father took his children away to London without their mother's consent. Within a week the father was traced through Interpol and served with a writ from the High Court of Justice, which soon ordered their return to Jamaica. Cases involving spouses and children are more demanding than almost any others. The emotions of your client are intense, and the whole future of the children may depend on the decision of the judge. I greatly admire Jamaican attorneys such as Margarette Macaulay who fight for the rights of women and children on a daily basis, as well as the women's organisations which provide refuge and support to women in crisis.

No review of human rights in Jamaica can ignore the fact that homosexual acts between men are criminalised. The law penalises "the abominable crime of buggery" by a prison sentence of up to ten years, and being party to "any act of gross indecency with another male person" with up to two years. At a time when civil partnerships between gay couples are becoming recognised around the world as being legal relationships having the same status as marriage, Jamaica remains bound by the laws of the Old Testament. While there are few prosecutions for homosexual acts between consenting adults, the prejudice in the society is widespread. International protests against homophobic lyrics have been effective in restraining musicians who have stoked up the hatred of gays, but few gay activists dare identify themselves in public. The main political parties have refused to consider changing the law.

I implore Jamaicans to look at the situation of gay men in the context of human rights and justice. The Constitution of Jamaica proclaims that every person in Jamaica has the right to "respect for his private and family life". Each of us would demand as much for our own private relationships. The law should intervene only when the right to private life is abused, for instance by spousal violence or child molestation. Subject to that, what adult people do in their private consenting relationships is up to them, and in principle the Constitution protects them. Indeed, fundamental rights need the most vigilant protection when they are claimed by vulnerable and unpopular sections of society.

Gay men in Jamaica face a similar barrier of prejudice to that faced by gay men in Northern Ireland in the 1970s. The law in England, Wales and Scotland had been amended so as to repeal the criminalisation of sexual acts in private between consenting adults aged 21 and over. But in Northern Ireland the power of the churches had prevailed. This was one issue on which Catholics and Protestants in Northern Ireland were united. 'Save Ulster from Sodomy' was the slogan of Protestant leader Ian Paisley. To avoid antagonising both sides of the religious divide, the British Government had agreed to keep the old laws on the statute book.

I was retained in 1981 by Jeff Dudgeon, secretary of the Northern Ireland Gay Rights Association. He claimed that his right to respect for his private and family life, to which he was entitled under the European Convention on Human Rights, was violated by the very existence of a law which made his sexual activities criminal. He approached Terry Munyard, a gay barrister in my chambers in Wellington Street, as he wanted a gay lawyer to argue his case. Terry said that what he needed was a team of human rights lawyers, whether they were gay or straight. I was asked to lead the team on a journey to the Court of Human Rights in Strasbourg.

We appeared before the full court of 19 judges, and scored a notable victory. The Court ruled by fifteen votes to four that Jeff "had suffered and continues to suffer an unjustified interference with his right to respect for his private life". The lawyers for the United Kingdom had argued that the law reflected the conservative moral attitudes of the Northern Ireland people, and that it was not enforced against consenting adults. But, said the Court, "the restriction imposed on Mr Dudgeon under Northern Ireland law, by reason of its breadth and absolute character is, quite apart from the severity of the possible penalties provided for, disproportionate to the aims sought to be achieved". Shortly afterwards the British Government changed the law in Northern Ireland. It was a classic case of the human rights of the individual being upheld by the judiciary in a hostile and prejudiced political environment.

To bring a similar successful action in Jamaica would at present be difficult if not impossible as a result of section 26(8) of the Constitution. Until that section is repealed, Jamaican gays will continue to live and love in secret. For them the words of Oscar Wilde's lover Lord Alfred Douglas, written in 1896, still ring true: "I am the Love that dare not speak its name."

||||||||||||||||||||||||||||||||||||||||

When English colleagues ask me about my Jamaican practice they assume that much of my work is on death row cases. In fact I have done very few cases which involve the death penalty, and this is because there are comparatively few such cases in Jamaica at all. No one has been executed in Jamaica since 1988, so that in my 15 years of practice I have not had to experience the emotions of having a client who has been killed by the State. I once had a client who had a warrant of execution read to him, to be carried out in the following week. I visited him in the death cell which is situated within the same small compound as the gallows. He had the appearance of a man who was already half dead. The colour and lifeblood appeared to have drained from his face as he sat alone in the tiny cell. In his case there was in fact no cause for alarm, since an appeal to the Privy Council had been lodged for him, and the warrant had been read by mistake.

Through a series of decisions by the Government and the courts, the possibility of the death penalty being applied in Jamaica has been narrowed to a tiny number of cases. When I started practice in Jamaica in 1991, there were over 300 prisoners on death row. In October 2005 there were only three. But the issue is still hotly debated. A majority of the public believes in the death penalty, and politicians from time to time promise to change the laws which prevent the imposition of this penalty, or which impose conditions on its implementation. I will first explain the decisions which have been made, before arguing why I believe that Jamaica should abolish the death penalty altogether.

The first move came from the Government in 1992, when it introduced the Offences Against the Person (Amendment) Act which divided murders into 'capital' and 'non-capital'. A murder would only be capital if it involved the killing of a person of a particular status in the law enforcement system such as police officer, prison officer, judge or prosecutor; or if the murder was committed in the course or furtherance of rape, burglary or arson; or if it was done in the furtherance of terrorism. Even in these cases only the person who actually caused the death or personally used violence would be guilty of capital murder. Contract murders were also made capital, both for the hitman and the person who contracted him. Finally anyone guilty of two murders, of whatever category, would be sentenced to death.

After the amending Act was passed, all the pending death row cases had to be re-examined to see what category they fell into. The amending Act was a compromise between those in the Cabinet who were pro and anti the death penalty. It had the effect of sharply reducing the number of prisoners on death row. The charge of capital murder was laid in about one tenth of all murder trials; all the others were trials for non-capital murder where the sentence would be life imprisonment with a minimum term to be served before parole. Interestingly, there has been little public protest about the amending Act and its effects.

In 1993 came the historic decision of the Privy Council in the case of *Pratt and Morgan*. The seven judges ruled that it amounted to inhuman and degrading punishment, in violation of the Constitution, for a person to be kept on death row after 'unconscionable delay'. A delay for more than five years would normally be considered unconscionable. Even though the delays were caused by the prisoner taking advantage of the various appeal processes, the judges said that a humane system had to make sure that the appeals were disposed of within a reasonable time frame. Their rationale was that:

> a State that wishes to retain capital punishment must accept the responsibility of ensuring that execution follows as swiftly as practicable after sentence… Appellate procedures that echo down the years are not compatible with capital punishment. The death row phenomenon must not become established as a part of our jurisprudence.

This decision has been controversial, and in Barbados a specific constitutional amendment has been passed to annul its effect. A similar proposal has been made by the Jamaican Attorney General. I support the *Pratt and Morgan* decision because of my experience in talking to clients who have been through years on death row, waiting week after week for court decisions which may hasten their death, clinging for life but preparing for death as each year goes by and each appeal fails. Earl Pratt and Ivan Morgan had been convicted in 1979 and had been removed to the condemned cells on three occasions. The Privy Council drew attention to the agony of mind that these men must have suffered as they have alternated between hope and despair in the fourteen years that they had been in prison facing the gallows. When the case was decided there were about fifty prisoners whose cases had been categorised as capital in the review process. Most had been on death row for over five years, and their sentences were all commuted to life imprisonment in obedience to the decision.

The next landmark Privy Council decision was the case of *Lewis and others v Attorney General*, decided in 2000. Neville Lewis was one of two men who murdered Vic Higgs, an Englishman who had settled in Jamaica and had been admired for his work in promoting golf in the Island. He gave a lift to two young men who killed him, robbed him of his gun and dumped his body in a lake of mud. I had acted for Lewis at his trial, which was a trial I did not enjoy, since I felt keenly that I could have given that lift and met that fate. His case was that he had been forced to take part by his co-accused, a defence which the jury rejected.

Other lawyers took his and some other cases to the Privy Council on a constitutional motion, arguing that they should not be executed because (a) they had made petitions to the United Nations Human Rights Committee and the Inter-American Commission on Human Rights, which were still pending; and (b) they should have had the right to make representations to the Jamaican body (also confusingly called the Privy Council) which advises the Governor General on the exercise of his powers of clemency. Both these arguments were upheld by the judges of the Privy Council.

These decisions have led the Attorney General of Jamaica to complain that it is now impossible to execute anyone. Even though the Government has removed the right to petition the UN Human Rights Committee, every convicted person has rights of appeal to the Court of Appeal and the Privy Council, as well as the right to petition the Inter-American Commission on Human Rights. When you add to that the right to make representations to the Jamaican Privy Council, argues the Attorney General, the five-year time limit will have passed. That is why he wants to follow Barbados and repeal the effects of *Pratt and Morgan*. I do not agree with him. It is not right that people's rights should be abused because the legal system is slow. If you are proposing to take a man's life, you should not impose on him the additional agony of long delay. If the appeal processes were fast-tracked in the small number of capital cases, then the two judicial appeals could be over within fifteen to eighteen months, leaving ample time for the other petitions and representations to be made.

The final reform in the death penalty process was perhaps the most fundamental. It is no longer mandatory, even in a case of capital murder or double murder, for the death penalty to be imposed. The Privy Council ruled in the case of *Lambert Watson* in 2004 that imposition of a mandatory sentence of death would be an inhuman punishment. The nine judges said that "basic humanity required that a person convicted of murder should be allowed the opportunity to show why sentence of death should not be passed on him". The Government passed a further amending Act in 2005 to give effect to the decision. The present position is that in a case which used to be capital, the judge who presided over the trial may either pass the death sentence or a sentence of life imprisonment with a minimum of twenty years to be served before parole. In the cases which used to be non-capital, the judge may pass either a life sentence or a sentence of fifteen or more years imprisonment. Judges are now faced with the awesome responsibility of deciding between life and death. I do not think that I could do it. It is significant that in the majority of cases dealt with so far, judges have chosen life rather than death. That is the final reason why the number of death row inmates had fallen to three by the end of 2005.

But can it be right in any case for the State to deliberately, in cold blood, end the life of a human being? The world is moving away from the death penalty as being either useful or moral as a sentence for crime. European countries have abolished the death penalty without exception, and it is now a protocol of the European Convention on Human Rights that the death penalty should not be resumed. Jamaica's neighbours in Central and South America have nearly all abolished the death penalty. The only countries in the Americas to retain it are the United States and Guatemala. Does Jamaica want to follow the sinister example of the US where at the end of 2005 there were 3,383 prisoners on death row, all poor, many Black, many of them there for decades? Does Jamaica want to emulate the system in which Stanley 'Tookie' Williams, a former gangster who repented of his ways and became an author of children's books, was executed in 2005 by lethal injection, 24 years after the murders of which he was convicted, on the say-so of Governor Schwarzenegger of California?

Look instead at the example of the countries of Africa from which the forebears of most Jamaicans came. Half of them have abolished the death penalty, including South Africa, Namibia, Mozambique and Angola. In the case of *Mankwanyane* in which the South African Constitutional Court declared the death penalty to be unconstitutional, Justice Sachs drew on the evidence of precolonial African traditions. He examined the history of the indigenous South Africans and found that the death penalty was hardly ever imposed. Their reasoning was, why sacrifice a second life for one already lost? It was the Dutch and the British who imported cruel forms of execution into Africa. Death by hanging was the fate of three of Jamaica's national heroes: Sam Sharpe, Paul Bogle and George William Gordon. Must Jamaica continue to copy the colonial barbarians?

My life as a human rights advocate has taught me so many lessons relevant to this issue. First, I know that the judicial system is not infallible. The Birmingham Six and the Guildford Four would undoubtedly have been hanged if the death penalty had been available when they were convicted. The whole of Britain was revolted by the crime the Six were found guilty of committing. Public clamour would have demanded their death. But years later they were all found to have been innocent. The Jamaican system, starved of resources as it is, is still more fallible. Witnesses can lie, and confessions can be fabricated, and identification evidence can be mistaken. If the death penalty is carried out, a miscarriage of justice can never be rectified.

Secondly, I have learned that the capacity of the individual for redemption and rehabilitation is extraordinary. I have had clients who have spent years on death row, who would have been hanged if the law had not been changed. Many are now on parole and have not re-offended. Some who are still in prison have been given weekend leave or have been employed outside the prison. Among my clients in prison I have met artists, musicians and counsellors. In their character they are not the same people who committed crimes of violence ten or twenty years ago. Their lives, which the court had ordered to be ended by the noose, have turned out to have real value.

I believe that the death penalty feeds that desire for retribution which has warped Jamaican society. Hanging legitimises the idea that it is all right to take life by way of revenge – which is precisely the mindset which we condemn when it leads to gang murders in the inner city or mob killings in the country villages. It is not a deterrent to murder, since some of the countries with the highest crime rates are also countries which retain the death penalty. Rather when the State kills, it teaches people that violence is the way to deal with injustice. It is the ultimate form of oppression to eliminate those who are perceived as the enemies of society. Jamaicans with their history of oppression should know better and should renounce this barbarity.

At the end of the day we must be guided by what is morally and spiritually right. It is paradoxical that Jamaican supporters of the death penalty quote the Book of Exodus - 'life for life, eye for eye, tooth for tooth' – when the Founder of Christianity in the Book of Matthew expressly went beyond that and exhorted His followers to show love to their enemies. It should be logical for Christian Jamaicans to abjure the deliberate taking of life, since it flouts the principles of Christianity itself. Given my own non-denominational spirituality, I simply say that I believe life to be sacred and beautiful, and that all human beings, including the most criminal, have a spark in them of the divine. It is against my deepest conscience that the State should ever put another to death, deliberately and with premeditation, and claim to be acting in my name and in the name of society. I look forward to the day when Jamaicans and other Caribbean peoples will renounce the death penalty entirely, recognising that there are other forms of punishment for crime which benefit society through the rehabilitation of the individual soul.

17

The CARIBBEAN COURT

B y a quirk of history, the highest court in the Jamaican legal system is not to be found in Jamaica, or anywhere in the Caribbean. It is the Judicial Committee of the Privy Council, composed of British judges, sitting in Downing Street in London. The Privy Council has its origins in the *Curia Regis*, the King's Council in feudal times. Its Judicial Committee, established in 1833, consists for the most part of the judges of the House of Lords, the highest court in Britain's legal system. Occasionally a senior judge from a Commonwealth country is invited to sit with them.

When Britain had an empire it made sense for the final court of appeal for its colonial subjects to be made up of judges from the imperial nation. The peoples over whom they exercised judicial power were also subject to the executive power of the British government. The existence of the Privy Council ensured that the same legal principles would be applied throughout the British empire. But as the peoples of the empire achieved independence, the role of the Privy Council in their systems was questioned and for the most part rejected. The independent states of the 'old Commonwealth' – Canada, Australia, New Zealand – retained the Privy Council for many years but in the end set up their own final courts. The new states of Asia and Africa opted for an independent final court from the moment of independence. By 2004 the only independent countries outside the Caribbean which still allowed appeals to the Privy Council were Mauritius in the Indian Ocean, and Kiribati and Tuvalu in the South Pacific.

The nations of the English-speaking Caribbean which became independent in the 1960s opted to retain the Privy Council. For Jamaica at least this was intended as a temporary measure, since the framers of the Jamaican Constitution treated the Privy Council differently from the courts below it. The Constitution enacted provisions for the Supreme Court and the Court of Appeal which were 'entrenched', meaning that it would require a two-thirds majority of both the House of Representatives and the Senate to abolish or to amend those provisions. Since the Constitution also provided for seven of the twenty senators to be nominated by the Leader of the Opposition, it would be impossible for a government to tamper with the constitutional arrangements for these courts, unless it had the support of the opposition party. The provisions for the Judicial Services Commission, which appoints all the judges of the Supreme Court except the Chief Justice, and all the judges of the Court of Appeal except the President, were similarly entrenched. This entrenchment provides a powerful guarantee of the independence of the judiciary from the executive.

By contrast the Constitution provided for a right of appeal to the Privy Council which was not entrenched. It could be abolished by a simple parliamentary majority. The framers of the Constitution clearly envisaged that the time would be coming when Jamaica would choose to dispense with appeals to the former colonial court.

A proposal for a Caribbean Court of Appeal was first made by the Commonwealth Caribbean Bar Associations in 1972. In 1987 the idea was considered by the Eighth Conference of Caribbean Heads of Government. The Attorneys-General of the member states were mandated to study the matter and make recommendations. After many meetings, drafts and redrafts, the Agreement establishing the Caribbean Court of Justice (CCJ) came into force in July 2003. The Court has an 'original jurisdiction' to deal with disputes concerning the Caribbean Community (CARICOM) Treaty, and an 'appellate jurisdiction' to act as the final court of appeal from the courts of member states. By the end of 2005 most Caribbean countries had accepted the original jurisdiction, but only Barbados and Guyana had signed up to the appellate jurisdiction.

I have myself supported the idea of a Caribbean final court of appeal, from the time I started practising law in Jamaica. I believe that the CCJ which is now in operation with seven judges appointed is the best option available to Jamaica for its final court of appeal. In reaching this conclusion I looked at the choices which Jamaica could make, which are: (a) not to have a second appeal court at all; (b) set up a Jamaican second appeal court; (c) carry on with the Privy Council; (d) take part in the CCJ.

I have no doubt that Jamaica needs a second appellate court above the Court of Appeal. Most developed societies have one. There are some issues which are so important that a single appeal may not do them justice. They may be constitutional issues, issues involving citizens against the Government, death penalty issues, or issues involving points of fundamental principle. The Jamaican Court of Appeal has made many good decisions. But it is very busy; it has limited research facilities; and it can be wrong. If one looks on the Privy Council website at the appeals from Jamaica which were decided over the seven years from 1999 to 2005, the record shows that out of 45 appeals, 23 were unsuccessful and 22 were successful, at least in part. The Court of Appeal's success rate is better in civil cases (22 out of 30 appeals were dismissed) than in criminal and constitutional cases (14 out of 15 appeals were upheld).

Some of the cases in which the Privy Council overturned the judgment of the Court of Appeal involved serious matters of principle, for example the case of Clinton Bernard, where the State was held to be liable when an off duty police officer used his police firearm to shoot a citizen without cause. In the criminal law, some notable injustices have been remedied by the Privy Council, such as the case of Mark Sangster and Randall Dixon, where the prosecution had failed to disclose a video recording of the crime, which was a robbery at a bank which had closed circuit TV cameras. It was only at the stage of the Privy Council appeal that the video came to light. The faces of the robbers could be clearly seen, and the prosecution had to accept that the faces of Sangster and Dixon were not in the video. In April 2006 the Privy Council quashed the conviction of Ricardo Williams, who had made a confession to murder when he was twelve years old. He had been kept in custody for a day without food or drink, and without being seen by a parent or any other adult. The trial judge and the Court of Appeal had seen nothing wrong with allowing his confession to go before the jury. The Privy Council ruled otherwise. By the time his appeal was heard he had reached the age of 24, and had spent half his life in custody.

I have referred to the intervention of the Privy Council in death penalty cases. The effect of its decisions has been to remove hundreds of prisoners from death row who would otherwise have been executed. The decisions have been criticised, but even the critics would not dispute that issues of great importance were raised which demonstrated the value of a second appellate court.

Some have suggested that the final court should be a purely Jamaican court. They argue that if the objection to the Privy Council is that it takes sovereignty away from Jamaica, then the same objection applies to the CCJ. So the answer is to keep the whole judicial process within Jamaica and not resort to foreign judges at all. The problem with this is that in a small country the number of fine legal minds is limited. The quality of the Court of Appeal would be diluted if its best judges had to be promoted to the final Court. Furthermore those judges would be sitting in judgment on fellow judges whom they knew very well. I doubt whether the judges in such a court would have, and be seen to have, enough independence of judgment to overrule their colleagues in matters of serious importance.

To me the CCJ offers greater independence and detachment, qualities which a final court must demonstrate if it is to command respect. The ceding of sovereignty to a multinational court does not worry me. Europe itself has shown that giving up sovereignty over matters of individual rights brings great benefits. The European Court of Human Rights has been hearing cases from Britain for decades, and the protection of rights has been stronger as a result.

A greater number of opponents of the CCJ have argued that the best final court is the one which we already have, the Privy Council. 'If it ain't broke don't fix it', is an argument which demands an answer. No lawyer who has appeared before the Privy Council can doubt the high quality of reasoning and the manifest impartiality which its judges display. In my young days as a barrister in England, the senior judges were seen as reactionaries; but today they are in the front line in the protection of fundamental rights against government attempts to whittle them down. Since there is no evidence that Britain, which pays the judges' salaries and the expenses of the court, is proposing to remove the Privy Council from Jamaica, why should Jamaica remove itself from the Privy Council?

My answer is that there is something seriously wrong, something undignified and demeaning, in the fact that the people of a sovereign nation have to seek justice from a court which sits in, comes from, and is paid by, a foreign country. When that country is the former colonial power whose judges are of a different race to the majority of Jamaicans, the indignity is worse. It fosters in the minds of Jamaican people the concept that when it comes to justice, White people do it better. As a short- term transitional arrangement, it worked. But it cannot be regarded as a long-term solution.

One consequence of the subordination of our legal system to the rulings of British judges is that Jamaican judges have no chance to shine at the highest level. The common law has been enriched over the last century by the judgments of judges throughout the English-speaking world. British judges now draw extensively on the Supreme Courts of India and Canada, the High Court of Australia and the South African Constitutional Court when considering issues which have universal significance. The judges of the Caribbean are hardly known outside their region. Yet the peoples of the Caribbean were forged out of a struggle for the achievement of basic human rights. Their jurists have a contribution to make to the advancement of human dignity under law. But their judgments cannot be final or authoritative, and as a result they contribute little or nothing to the development of human rights and justice internationally. It is the Privy Council which judges the judges of the Caribbean.

The attorneys of the Caribbean also suffer from a lack of confidence. While in theory any Jamaican attorney may argue a case before the Privy Council, few in fact do. Many of the cases are argued by British attorneys. But if Jamaica joined the CCJ it would be a tremendous incentive to our attorneys to excel. Access to the court would be much easier. Jamaican attorneys would have the right to file appeals directly before the court. If they felt strongly about an injustice that their client has suffered they would strive to remedy it before the Caribbean Court. They would act *pro bono* if necessary, which is very difficult before the Privy Council because of the air fares and other expenses in London.

But it is not mainly judges and lawyers whom a Caribbean court will benefit. The litigants will be able to access it at far less cost. At present a client who wants to pursue an appeal to the Privy Council has to be advised that funds are needed for retaining a London solicitor as well as the counsel who will argue the case. If Jamaican attorneys are retained they have to fly to London, which usually means at least a week's trip even if the case only lasts a day. As a result, most cases before the Privy Council are brought by the companies and institutions which can afford these costs, including the State; and by death row prisoners, who benefit from a *pro bono* scheme operated by English solicitors and barristers. Many appeals which could have been successful have been prevented by the barrier of cost.

The accessibility of the CCJ will also benefit the media and the Caribbean public. The press will be able to attend the court, so that instead of judgments being handed down from afar, the people will be able to follow the cases as they are argued. The treaty establishing the CCJ provides that while its seat is in Port of Spain, it may sit in the territory of any of the contracting parties as circumstances warrant. We may be able to recapture the excitement of the days when the public was passionately engaged in important court cases, attending the court and following the arguments through media reports. It is healthy for the rule of law when the public is engaged in the working of the legal system.

In principle I like the concept of a court which spans the nations of the Caribbean. There is a shared history and culture which is now underpinned by economic and social cooperation. The idea of courts crossing national boundaries in the Caribbean is not new. During the short lived Federation of the West Indies there was a West Indies Supreme Court which heard appeals from all the states of the Federation, and I am told that its reputation was excellent while it lasted. Six of the smaller islands of the Eastern Caribbean have shared sovereignty over legal matters through the Eastern Caribbean Supreme Court and Court of Appeal. Lawyers in those islands cross regularly from one country to another in the pursuit of justice.

Now there is a different form of collaboration between the nations of the Caribbean. The Caribbean Single Market and Economy (CSME) will soon be a reality, creating an economic union throughout the region. As has happened in Europe (where there are two supra-national courts, one dealing with human rights and one with European Union issues), a court for the Caribbean is again appropriate. The CCJ has the potential to be part of a new regional solidarity. It will be a court of our region, financed by our money, sitting where we can hear it.

We still have to scrutinise carefully the detailed conditions under which the court will function and its judges chosen. To me the essential ingredients of a final court of appeal are fourfold. First, its judges should be selected and should serve under conditions which ensure their independence and impartiality. Second, the financing of the court should be stable, sufficient and not open to manipulation by governments. Third, the judges must be judges of excellence, capable of safeguarding the rights of citizens under the law. Fourth, the status of the court must be so entrenched in the constitutions of participating states that a government which does not like its decisions cannot pull out of it at will.

I am very satisfied that the first and second ingredients are satisfied in regard to the CCJ. The judges, other than the President of the Court, are selected by a Regional Judicial and Legal Services Commission whose eleven members have been appointed or selected in a variety of ways over which governments have no control. The appointing bodies include Bar Associations, the Deans of Law Faculties, and the Secretary General of CARICOM. The Jamaican Bar Association must take a lot of credit for its recommendations which resulted in the Commission being a body which can be truly said to be broad based and non-political. The President is appointed by a qualified majority vote of three-quarters of the contracting parties, on the recommendation of the Commission. The judges hold office until the age of 72, and they can not be removed unless a tribunal has advised the Commission that a judge should be removed for inability or for misbehaviour. There is no basis for saying that these judges can be appointed or controlled by politicians.

The financing of the CCJ has been secured by the setting up of a Trust Fund in the sum of US$100 million. The sum has been raised by the President of the Caribbean Development Bank in international capital markets, with member states agreeing to repay the Bank in agreed proportions. The fund, whose income will provide for the salaries of judges and the facilities of the court, is administered by a Board of Trustees drawn mainly from the private sector and civil society. In this way the court will be protected from the financial uncertainties which have often beset other regional institutions when member countries have been slow in paying their dues. The Trust Fund is immune from any financial pressures which might be exerted by governments unwilling to pay for the court.

What about those qualities of excellence which the judges must display? Out of a maximum of ten judges, seven have been appointed so far. Two are judges of great experience: the President, Michael de la Bastide, Chief Justice of Trinidad and Tobago for seven years, and Desiree Bernard, a judge in Guyana since 1980 who rose to be Chief Justice and Chancellor of the Judiciary, which meant that she was the senior judge of appeal. Rolston Nelson has been six years in the Court of Appeal of Trinidad and Tobago, and Adrian Saunders was a judge of the Eastern Caribbean Supreme Court for six years and of the Eastern Caribbean Court of Appeal for two years. These four would seem to have a bedrock of experience as judges of appeal in the region. Of course questions have been asked: why is there no one of Indian descent? Why is there no Jamaican? The answer is that the court is not selected on the basis of national or racial quotas, and the Commission has, I hope, selected the best minds out of those who applied.

The other three appointees are outside the mould of judges with experience of high judicial office. David Hayton is an English professor, a leading expert in the law of trusts, estates and land law, who has served for two years as an acting judge of the Bahamas Supreme Court. Duke Pollard has never been a practising lawyer or judge; he is an international jurist who was the principal consultant for CARICOM in the drafting of the CCJ treaty and the development of the court. Jacob Wit is a judge from the Netherlands with considerable experience in the courts of the Netherlands Antilles, territories whose legal system is very different from ours. It all makes for a fascinating mix, and the different backgrounds of these judges may well contribute positively to the new court.

The CCJ treaty states that the court when it sits in its original jurisdiction, dealing with disputes over the Chaguaramas Treaty, shall have its own chairman, and be composed of at least three judges who must possess "the expertise necessary for the court to adjudicate the matter". So only judges with appropriate expertise will sit on original jurisdiction cases. But any of the judges may sit on appellate jurisdiction cases. The judicial qualities which are appropriate for adjudicating a dispute over international trade are different from those needed to interpret the fundamental rights clauses in a Constitution, or to settle difficult points of criminal or civil law. So I have a concern as to whether it was wise to combine the two jurisdictions within the same court.

The fourth ingredient, that the court should be entrenched in the constitutions of its member states, is the one which has given trouble. The Treaty did not require entrenchment; it left each participating state to decide how to incorporate the CCJ in its constitution. It provided that a contracting party may withdraw from the Treaty by giving three years' notice in writing. If notice is given, the withdrawal takes effect after five years. So it is not easy for a country to pull out, but it is possible. A government which disliked the judgments which were coming from the Court could give notice of withdrawal, which would tend to discredit the standing of the Court in that country. The purpose of entrenchment is to remove the judicial arm of government from being undermined by political threats to its stability.

The Jamaican Government was keen to join the new court and de-link from the Privy Council as soon as possible, even though the Opposition Jamaica Labour Party (JLP) was unwilling. So in 2004 it put forward three bills in Parliament, which would have given legal effect to the CCJ Treaty and substituted the CCJ for the Privy Council as the final court of appeal. It claimed that these bills could be passed by a simple parliamentary majority. It argued that since the section of the Constitution which provided for appeals to the Privy Council was not entrenched, Parliament had the right to amend those sections and to replace the Privy Council with the CCJ, and the amendment would not need to be entrenched.

While the Bill was still going through Parliament, the Government was challenged by the JLP and by the Independent Jamaican Council for Human Rights, who brought constitutional motions in the Supreme Court. Their argument was that if a new appellate court was to be put in place over the Supreme Court and the Court of Appeal, such a court would have to be as entrenched as those courts are. The challengers accepted that the government could abolish appeals to the Privy Council by a simple majority. But the imposition of a new court required the full treatment of an entrenched provision, starting with a two-thirds majority in the House of Representatives which the governing party in 2004 did not possess.

I have been known in Jamaica as a supporter of the CCJ, and have been more outspoken on the subject than most of my colleagues at the Bar. But I also believe in the need for entrenchment. The courts are the protectors of the rule of law, if necessary against the ambitions of the executive. Even in Britain the government of Tony Blair has been attacking the judiciary and seeking to influence their decisions on the detention of suspected terrorists. In Trinidad and Tobago one of the main arguments for the CCJ is the displeasure of some politicians with the Privy Council's rulings on death penalty issues. Politicians are fully capable of putting pressure on judges if they think it can work. There is a real danger that judges, if not fully independent and secure, might be pressured in a crisis to rule in favour of a government which is threatening to dispense with their services. It does not happen with the Supreme Court or the Court of Appeal in Jamaica, because those courts are entrenched. But it could have happened with the CCJ if the bills proposed in 2004 had come into force.

The Jamaican courts dismissed the constitutional motions. The Supreme Court took a procedural objection, saying that the bills could not be challenged until they were enacted. The Court of Appeal did consider the merits of the challenge, but ruled against the claimants. Its reason was that since the only amendment being made by the bills to the Constitution was to alter the unentrenched section dealing with the Privy Council, no question of entrenchment arose. Undaunted, the team of attorneys led by Dr Lloyd Barnett took the case to the Privy Council. Photographs were taken in the antechamber of the Privy Council before the attorneys went in to face their Lordships. The Government team were all wearing wigs, while Dr Barnett's team were all wigless. They set a fine precedent, not only in the matter of dress, but in winning the appeal.

The Privy Council overturned the judgment of the Court of Appeal and ruled that the bills, which by then had become Acts of Parliament, were unconstitutional. The judges said that the question must be approached as one of substance and not of form. In substance, the new legislation weakened the independence of the judiciary. They concluded:

> An important function of a Constitution is to give protection against governmental misbehaviour, and the three Acts give rise to a risk which did not exist in the same way before. The (Privy Council) is driven to conclude that the three Acts, taken together, do have the effect of undermining the protection given to the Jamaican people by entrenched provisions of Chapter

VII of the Constitution. From this it follows that the procedure appropriate for amendment of an entrenched provision should have been followed.

The decision of the Privy Council was attacked by some in Jamaica and outside as a colonial interference. I do not agree. My belief is that the judges of the Privy Council would be very happy to lose the jurisdiction over the affairs of the Caribbean which they now enjoy. The United Kingdom is in the process of establishing a Supreme Court in place of the House of Lords, and the priorities of the judges must be to maintain and improve the quality of justice in their home country. When I have been in front of the judges of the Privy Council, I sometimes sense behind the courtesy a sense of impatience. The decision in the CCJ case was based on sound legal principles and not on a desire to obstruct Jamaica's wish to leave the fold. It just had to be done in the proper way.

The decision has created an impasse which may take time to resolve. At present the Government can only move forward if it has the support of the JLP. That party has indicated that they would not give such support without a referendum. The ruling People's National Party (PNP) believes that a referendum could turn into a vote of no confidence which it might lose. So we stay for the moment with the Privy Council. Personally I am well pleased with this, since visits to London help me to keep in touch with my family and friends, and with the chambers of which I am still the head. But as a matter of principle, I implore the leadership of the PNP and JLP to settle their differences and agree to set up the CCJ as an entrenched court. If the price of agreement is to be a referendum, I am very ready to go out and argue that Jamaica should join the CCJ. Indeed I would welcome the chance to do this, for the more the people are involved in and informed about the issue, the better.

If the argument goes to the people, one objection will be that the existing judicial structures are so shaky that we should not be spending money on a new one. It is an argument born of an understandable cynicism and despair. I have argued earlier that while there is much to be worried about, the defects in Jamaica's system sometimes obscure its virtues. I do not think that it is a matter of alternatives – either improve the existing system or join the CCJ. We should do both. Indeed I would hope that the judges of the CCJ would be vigilant and concerned to expose defects in our system if they come to light in cases before them. Jamaican judges have been heard to scoff at the criticisms which are made by the Privy Council. They might be more respectful of the oversight of Caribbean judges.

Like many of my progressive colleagues at the Jamaican Bar, I sometimes have my worries. Do the senior judges of the Caribbean have the same empathy with human rights issues as the senior judges in Britain are now showing? Will some of the landmark decisions in death penalty cases be rolled back? Will the CCJ be dominated by conservatives? Will the judges have access to all the relevant cases in different parts of the world? In short, will the new court be as good as the Privy Council? Will it administer justice in a way which gives confidence both to business interests and to citizens?

We cannot be sure. Such doubts are often expressed when people who have been looked after by others start to do things for themselves. Even at the time of Jamaica's independence there were fears that Jamaicans would not run the country as effectively as the colonial ruler had done. Such doubts should not stop us from doing the right thing, which is that the peoples of the Caribbean should take responsibility for their own system of justice and stop relying on British judges. Such doubts should rather be a spur to all of us who work in the system to play our part in making it excellent.

A special responsibility will fall to attorneys to make creative use of the new court. We must choose winnable cases and present compelling arguments with which to win them. We will have to argue cases ourselves instead of using British barristers to argue them for us. The quality of the judgments which the CCJ will hand down will depend to a great extent on the quality of the research and eloquence which we put in to our written submissions and our oral presentations.

I have come to practise law in the Caribbean because I want to make a difference to the quality of justice in the region. The CCJ enlarges the possibilities of justice. More cases can be taken for more clients at less cost. Instead of being content with a safety net inherited from colonial days, we lawyers should embrace the new court. We can make it a springboard which helps our people to obtain justice. Over time the new court should take its place among other respected courts in the Commonwealth. In the field of justice, as in so many other fields, it is time for the Caribbean to excel.

Part Three

Reconciliation

18

The BLOODY
SUNDAY INQUIRY

I n January 1998 Prime Minister Tony Blair announced the setting up
of a public inquiry into the events of 'Bloody Sunday', 30th January
1972, when thirteen civilians were killed by British soldiers at the
end of a civil rights march in Derry, Northern Ireland. Thirteen
others were injured, of whom one died from his injuries months later. I
remembered the event well. It was a defining moment in the history of
the conflict in Northern Ireland. The shooting of the young men was seen
by Irish Catholics as a brutal response to a peaceful march. Thousands of
people came to the conclusion that peaceful agitation for human rights
in Northern Ireland was useless. The ranks of the Irish Republican Army
were swelled with recruits over the following months. The Bloody Sunday
shootings shattered the possibilities of peace and compromise in Northern
Ireland. In trying to describe the impact of Bloody Sunday to Jamaicans, I
have compared it to the Sharpeville massacre in South Africa in 1961.

There had already been one public inquiry, conducted by Lord
Widgery, then Lord Chief Justice of England and Wales, in the months
which followed Bloody Sunday. Widgery had accepted the Army version
of events, namely that the soldiers had been fired on by gunmen and had
fired back at people who they believed to be carrying guns or nail bombs.
The furthest he would go in criticism of the soldiers was to say that in
one part of the scene where four men had been killed, in and around a
little square known as Glenfada Park North, the firing 'bordered on the
reckless'. He had refused to enter into any inquiry into the responsibility
of British politicians, and had made no criticism of the commanders on
the ground. He had ignored a mass of statements taken from civilian

witnesses by the Northern Ireland Civil Rights Association, which had organised the march. His exoneration of the army created as much anger as the events themselves.

I had been on marches in London in protest at the killings, and I had spoken at one of the rallies which were held in Derry each year on the Bloody Sunday anniversary. I had listened to James Wray, the father of one of the deceased Jim Wray, who came to London and spoke with fierce emotion about the events and the subsequent cover-up. I had a close connection with Derry going back to 1969, including my own unofficial inquiry into the deaths of Seamus Cusack and Desmond Beatty at the hands of British soldiers in 1971. All these memories came back to me when in September 1998 I got a call to ask if I would represent the family of Jim Wray before the new inquiry. I was told that the inquiry was expected to last two years. In fact it occupied me for the greater part of the next six.

It was a major disruption for me and my family. Tina and I rented a small house in London which became our main residence, from which I flew every week to Derry and she went to study at the London College of Fashion and Goldsmiths College. At the same time the practice in Jamaica could not be abandoned, and I flew the Atlantic almost every month to see my clients and appear in court. It was an exhilarating period of my life, and I did not ever regret that I had agreed to represent the Wray family in this historic inquiry.

James Wray senior had died before the inquiry was announced. The most articulate voice of the family was now his son Liam. Liam Wray was angry, passionate, and extremely well informed about the facts of Bloody Sunday. He read every document and kept us on our toes from start to finish. A quieter but no less powerful voice was Margaret Wray, who had been very close to her brother Jim. As I got to know her over the years, I felt that her sense of grief and outrage over his death had stayed at the centre of her soul. Family conferences also included brothers John, Raymond and Alex. They were all much more than clients, more like a team of allies working with their lawyers in a common determination to see justice done.

At first the family had intended to boycott the inquiry, as James Wray had done in 1972. He had made a brief and very dignified appearance on the first day of the Widgery Inquiry, and had said bluntly that he believed Lord Widgery, as a former Brigadier, was not a suitable person to investigate the conduct of the British army. He said that he was in favour of an independent inquiry, but would take no further part in this one. The Wray family was alone in taking this line. When the new inquiry was set up the family had similar doubts about its independence. In the end they decided that they would be involved provided they could have their own legal team.

The legal team with me at the beginning was Derry solicitor Greg McCartney and Belfast barrister Barry Macdonald. Greg was a tough operator who expected the very best from his barristers. He read the thousands of statements and documents which the inquiry had gathered, and he could pull a cross-reference out of his mind with uncanny skill. He never stopped teasing me with the fact that he had applied twenty years before to be a pupil in my chambers in Wellington Street and we had turned him down. We were wrong – he would have made a tenacious and highly effective barrister. He had the advantage of knowing many of the Derry witnesses and was able to brief us as to who was reliable.

Barry Macdonald had been Wellington Street's first pupil in 1974, and then went back to his native Belfast, where he had built a strong practice. Two years into the inquiry, he succeeded in a long held ambition to be appointed Queen's Counsel. He had to fight a litigation in order to achieve this, since the rules provided that a QC had to swear an oath of allegiance to the Queen, something which Barry was not prepared to do. He succeeded in proving that the rule was discriminatory and ought to be discarded. He then told me that he was not prepared to continue for years as a junior counsel before the inquiry when he could be building his practice as a leader.

To fill Barry's place I called my old friend Richard Harvey in New York. He accepted with eagerness, and there began one of the most fruitful collaborations which I have ever had in my professional life. Richard had been a radical barrister in London in the 1970s, and had moved to New York, married African-American Marlene Archer, and had joined the practice of Lennox Hinds, a leading Black attorney in Harlem. He had been active in organising protests and missions relating to human rights abuses in Northern Ireland, and knew many of the leaders on the Republican side. He had no difficulty in seeing the need to scrutinise the British Government's role in the Bloody Sunday events. He was a good archivist and researcher, and spent many hours in the Public Record Office extracting references to documents which the government had not disclosed. We worked brilliantly together, with Richard's radical militancy sometimes needing to be tempered by my sense of how best to persuade the judges. When the four principal players – Liam, Greg, Richard and I – held meetings, it was like a quartet of well-tuned different instruments playing together to create harmony.

We linked up closely with two other Derry solicitors, Paddy McDermott and Desmond Doherty. Behind their Irish good cheer lay a remarkable commitment to the cause of Derry people which was their cause too. The teamwork was oiled by weekly gatherings at the Clarendon public house near our hotel, where the solicitors and a variety of Derry friends would come to meet us. At first these evenings felt like a test to see whether the English barristers could take the rounds of Guinness or Irish whiskey which were bought for us, each full glass appearing long before the previous one was empty. But there was a deeper meaning to the boozing. It brought us closer to the Derry experience.

The inquiry was conducted in front of three judges. Lord Saville, a British law lord, was in the chair. Mr John Toohey, former judge of the Australian High Court, and Mr William Hoyt, former chief justice of the province of New Brunswick in Canada, sat with him. I knew that Mr Toohey had an impressive record, and I had read his judgment in the *Mabo* case, in which indigenous Australians had for the first time been granted judicial recognition of their rights to tribal lands. He displayed a keen analytical brain during the inquiry. As for Lord Saville, I had appeared before him when he was a judge of the Court of Appeal, and I had not enjoyed the experience. I had been representing a Trinidadian limbo dancer who had been severely beaten up by the police after giving a performance. We had achieved a partial victory at his trial before a jury in the High Court, but the damages awarded had been less than the offer which the police had made, so that he was penalised by having to pay costs and came away with nothing. I felt his trial had been unfair because some old criminal convictions for minor offences had been put before the jury, even though an Act of Parliament said that such convictions should not be mentioned in a civil case unless it was in the interests of justice. Lord Justice Saville decided the appeal against my client by posing to me what he thought was an unanswerable dilemma: "Lord Gifford, if your client's convictions were insignificant, then they made no difference to the jury's decision. If they were significant, then it was just that the jury should know about them." I felt that this approach was theoretically clever but showed little understanding of how ordinary jurors make decisions, especially about Black people.

When I met the Wray family for the first time I spoke about my memories of their father, my connections with Derry, and my knowledge of the judges. My reservations about Lord Saville, although based only on a single experience, helped to reassure the family (who were sceptical about the ability of any British judge to conduct a proper inquiry) that I was not someone who stood in awe of a judge of the House of Lords. I promised that I would work in close consultation with them and make all possible efforts to ensure that the inquiry reached the whole truth, including the truth about the role of the British Government which their father, instinctively, had believed to be at the heart of the tragedy.

The statistics of the Bloody Sunday Inquiry are awesome. There were nine preliminary hearings and 435 main hearings. Oral evidence was given by 922 witnesses, and 1,555 further witnesses gave statements. The opening statement by the Inquiry Counsel Christopher Clarke lasted 42 days. The costs of the inquiry had reached £163 million by the end of October 2005.

Much criticism has focused on the fees paid to lawyers, which had reached about £87 million out of the total spend. The fees paid to barristers and solicitors from the public purse have been published from time to time, most recently in February 2006. The biggest earners were Christopher Clarke, senior counsel to the Tribunal, and Edwin Glasgow, who led the soldiers' legal team. Both had earned over £4 million from the inquiry, and in my opinion they deserved it. For both of them it was an intensely demanding full-time employment, with large amounts of overtime, for over six years. My own earnings were £718,830, or about £120,000 per year over the six years of the inquiry's life. Most of the QCs acting for the families had earnings at around the same level; the soldiers' barristers earned far more. Barristers pay out about a quarter of their fees in chambers expenses, and I in addition had to pay for several dozen transatlantic flights to Jamaica. I feel no shame in having earned this money for carrying out a highly responsible job.

The wider criticism of the inquiry is that it was unnecessary to spend so much time and money. I totally disagree. The Widgery Inquiry had been a disaster because it heard from only a fraction of the relevant witnesses. Clearly the Saville Inquiry had to hear from all who could contribute evidence. Thousands of people had been on the march on Bloody Sunday, and hundreds had witnessed one or more of the fatal shootings. Dozens of journalists and photographers had been at the scene. Hundreds of soldiers and police had been deployed. The role of the IRA had to be investigated. The responsibility of military commanders, intelligence officers, civil servants and politicians had to be analysed. Lord Saville and his colleagues were absolutely right in deciding that nothing less than a comprehensive public investigation would do.

Those who question the cost of the Bloody Sunday Inquiry forget the enormous hidden benefits of the process which took place. Accepting the demand for an inquiry, which was made with increasing urgency as more and more new evidence came to light, was an integral part of the broader peace process in Northern Ireland. Without the setting up of the inquiry in January 1998, the Good Friday Agreement in April 1998 might never have been possible. Without the inquiry, the demand for it would have intensified, threatening the peace which has been maintained over the years. Without the inquiry the hurt of the families and the society of which they are part would have been untreated. There are, of course, thousands of other victims and grieving relatives who have suffered from the conflict in Northern Ireland, and there is a case for other inquiries, or for a broader truth and reconciliation commission. But Bloody Sunday was exceptional, both for its context (a massive and peaceful civil rights march) and its impact (bitter alienation among Northern Ireland Catholics). The least that the British government could do, by way of reparation for its past misdeeds in Northern Ireland, was to uncover the full truth of Bloody Sunday, cost what it may. Tony Blair is to be commended for his grasping this during the first year of his tenure as prime minister.

The first test which the inquiry faced was an application by the majority of the soldiers, including those who had fired the fatal shots, that they should remain anonymous, identified only by letters and numbers. They claimed that their lives would be in danger if they were named and if their faces were shown on public screens. We argued that it would weaken the credibility of the inquiry if these most important witnesses were able to hide under a cloak of anonymity. The inquiry was a public inquiry, and secret evidence as to identity should only be allowed if security concerns demanded it. The evidence from the security services indicated that the risk to the soldiers was considered to be 'moderate'. In reality the names of many of the soldiers were already known, as were the names of their commanders, and none of them had come to any harm. We were in a period of peace, and the likelihood of anyone connected with the inquiry being attacked was fanciful. As the years of the inquiry passed, our confidence proved justified. So far as I am aware, there was never the remotest security threat to the inquiry or any of its participants.

We argued also that publicity would assist the central objective of the inquiry, which was to discover the truth about Bloody Sunday. When justice is done in public, anyone can read about it or follow it in the media. If members of the public see the name or face of a person whom they know or have spoken to, giving evidence, they may recall that he told a different story to them. Or they may know something else which affects his credibility. The consequences of publicity are impossible to foretell, and justice done in public is more likely to produce the truth.

The Tribunal at first came up with a compromise solution. It ruled that the surnames of the soldiers would be made public but not the first names. The soldiers challenged the decision in the High Court in London, and won. The High Court judges found that there were a number of errors in the Tribunal's approach, and ordered it to think again. It held further hearings, and ordered that the full names of the soldiers who had fired shots on Bloody Sunday should be given. It concluded that "the danger to the soldiers who fired live rounds on Bloody Sunday does not outweigh or qualify our duty to conduct a public open inquiry." The Tribunal did not accept our argument about publicity assisting the search for the truth, but relied rather on the importance of public confidence. Another application to the High Court followed, and the soldiers won again, and also in the Court of Appeal. The essence of the Court of Appeal's decision was that the right to life of the soldiers, to which they were entitled under the European Convention, was at issue. The reasons given by the Tribunal about the need to carry confidence with the public could not prevail over the soldiers' right to life.

In this confrontation over anonymity, the Tribunal revealed a positive quality which it continued to display throughout the inquiry process. Lord Saville and his colleagues never wavered in their determination to ensure that the search for the truth should be open and transparent. Through the use of advanced technology they made sure that every document could be read on the Internet and seen on a screen when it was being referred to during the hearings. They did their utmost to ensure that the public relations aspects of the inquiry were well handled. Even so, their decisions on anonymity were flawed. They failed to appreciate that openness to the public was not just a matter of public relations but also a matter of the public helping them to discover the truth. It would have been more difficult for the courts in England to overrule the anonymity decision if it had been based on this wider understanding of the value of publicity.

Protection of the soldiers again became an issue half way through the inquiry, when the soldiers applied to be excused from coming to Derry to give their evidence. Once again they claimed that their lives would be in danger. I was angry with this application, and publicly accused the soldiers of cowardice. I thought that the former members of the Paratroop Regiment, which prided itself on its bravery, should have the moral courage to come back to the city where they had caused so much suffering, and give an account of their actions to the citizens of that city. By then it was clear that the people of Derry were committed to supporting the inquiry, and the idea of a soldier being harmed was fanciful. The Tribunal convened a meeting of security personnel and was persuaded that arrangements could be made to protect soldier witnesses, as had been done in Belfast on many occasions, even at the height of the conflict. True to its mission, the Tribunal was determined that the people of Derry should be able to participate fully in this important section of the hearings. It issued a ruling that the soldiers should give evidence in Derry.

Once again the High Court in England intervened. Once again the right to life of the soldiers was invoked. Since the evidence showed that the soldiers would be marginally safer in London than in Derry, their interests prevailed over the interests of the people of Derry. The High Court ruled that the soldiers were not obliged to run that marginal risk, and other arrangements would have to be made. The people of Derry must have reflected that however independent and international the Tribunal claimed to be, the real power lay, as it always did, in London.

At this point the Tribunal delivered a bombshell. It proposed that when the soldiers gave their evidence, they should be in a suitable location in London, and the Tribunal and all the lawyers should stay in the Guildhall in Derry and receive the evidence by video link. The technology would be so advanced that the soldiers could be cross-examined as effectively as if they were in the same room. Our clients were appalled. If there was one thing which they had been waiting for, it was to see the confrontation between their barrister and the soldiers who had been responsible for the killing of Jim Wray. However brilliant the technology might be, for the soldiers to be in a different place would let them off the hook. Since Lord Saville was keen about technology (he would often be seen showing off the inquiry's advanced technical equipment), I was concerned that it would be difficult to change his view.

We needed to respond quickly and effectively. Richard had recruited the voluntary help of Canadian attorney Gina Fiorillo, who had spent some time in Derry assisting us with research. At the time of the Tribunal's letter about the video link, I was in Jamaica, Richard was on holiday (with his laptop) in the Canary Islands, and Gina was in Vancouver. With the ability to link together through emails and the Internet, these geographical separations did not matter a jot. Gina and Richard discovered material on video linkage from Australia, the United States, Canada and the International Criminal Tribunal on Yugoslavia. The consensus from the cases and reports which we found was that while video linkage was recognised as a convenient way of arranging for testimony from witnesses who could not easily come to court, it was not the best method in cases where the credibility and honesty of the witness were in issue. On the basis of this research I wrote an opinion and emailed it to Greg for submission to the inquiry.

The Tribunal agreed with what we said, and so the whole apparatus of the inquiry moved to Central Hall in London, where the evidence of the soldiers, the senior officers, and the British politicians and civil servants was heard. Arrangements were made for the relatives of the victims to stay in London if they wished. The Guildhall in Derry remained open so that members of the public could watch the London proceedings on a screen. Thus at great cost steps were taken which maintained the integrity of the inquiry in spite of the ruling – an unnecessary and wrong-headed ruling, in my view – which the soldiers had obtained.

The first two years of the inquiry's hearings consisted mainly of the evidence of civilian eye-witnesses to the civil rights march and its bloody aftermath. Many of the images are well known. Over ten thousand people were marching to protest against internment without trial, which the British had re-introduced into Northern Ireland the previous August. Over 500 people were still interned. Allegations of the inhumane treatment of internees had come to light, which were later to be upheld by the European Court of Human Rights. The march was born out the legitimate anger of thousands of people at these abuses of fundamental human rights. It was peaceful and good-humoured in an afternoon of winter sunshine. When it reached the city centre it was blocked by an army barricade. The organisers tried to shepherd the marchers to a meeting place in the Catholic community of the Bogside. Some young men confronted the barricade, throwing whatever missiles they could find. The army responded with water cannon and tear gas, and most of the young men began to disperse into the Bogside. Until then it had been a classic Derry riot of the kind that had happened often before.

Suddenly a convoy of armoured cars drove at speed past the barricades and down Rossville Street, the main entry into the Bogside. The retreating marchers scattered in panic before them. Soldiers of the Parachute Regiment, one of the toughest units of the British Army, leapt out of the armoured cars, chasing the retreating marchers. A few dozen people stopped at a barrier of rubble across Rossville Street, and some young men hurled stones towards the soldiers. The soldiers opened fire down Rossville Street towards the barrier, and into the car park of the Rossville Flats, a high rise block to the east of the street. Six young men - Michael Kelly, William Nash, John Young, Michael McDaid, Hugh Gilmore and Kevin McElhinney - were killed in the area of the rubble barrier and one, Jack Duddy, in the car park. Father Daly was close to Jack Duddy when he fell and tried to get him to safety, a brave action which was immortalised by television and became one of the defining pictures of Bloody Sunday.

Thirty or forty people sheltered from the onslaught behind the gable wall of Glenfada Park North, a small square on the west of Rossville Street. Some of them helped to carry the body of Michael Kelly to safety across the square. Soon after they did so, a small squad of paratroopers entered the square, and as men ran from the gable wall across the square, the soldiers opened fire. When they had finished, the dead bodies of Jim Wray and William McKinney were lying in the square, a few feet from an exit in the corner. The body of Joe Mahon, severely injured and pretending to be dead, was beside them. The dead bodies of Gerard Donaghy and Gerard McKinney were lying in Abbey Park, just the other side of the corner exit. Three other men were injured as they ran through the square.

The final horror occurred when one of the soldiers who had come through the square to the area of the gable, fired his rifle to the back of the Rossville Flats and killed two more men, Patrick Doherty and Barney McGuigan. Barney McGuigan, a much loved man in the community, had stepped out from the flats waving a handkerchief to help Patrick Doherty, when his eye and skull were shattered by the soldier's bullet. The people who had remained at the gable end were all arrested, but no charges were pursued against them.

Jim Wray appeared on some of the photographs taken during the march. While the stoning of the barricades was going on, he was seen in a photograph holding up the banner of the Northern Ireland Civil Rights Association. In another photo he was sitting in the roadway in a gesture of passive resistance. Moments before his death he was pictured in Glenfada Park North, helping to escort the people who were carrying the body of Michael Kelly. Every image of him was peaceful.

His death was seen by a number of witnesses. People who were sheltering at the gable wall saw three men who made a run for it across the square and fell in quick succession. One of them was Jim Wray. Other witnesses who were sheltering at the corner exit looked back and saw Jim on the ground, trying to raise himself with his arms. Then they heard more shooting, and Jim collapsed, never to rise again. The shooting of Jim Wray had this extra twist of cruelty: having been felled as he ran across the square, he had been executed as he lay wounded on the ground.

The only person watching from inside the square was the injured Joe Mahon. In dramatic and emotional testimony he described Jim's final moments of life. After describing a soldier who was shooting from the hip, he said that this soldier walked towards the body of Jim Wray, a few yards from where he lay. "The soldier then pointed the rifle at Jim Wray's back and fired two shots into his back at point blank range. I could see Jim Wray's coat move twice. I then saw the soldier walk into the alley way. I then heard more shots." The further shots marked the deaths of Gerard Donaghy and Gerard McKinney in Abbey Park.

Jim Wray had received two bullets in the right side of his back which passed through his body and exited. Was he standing or lying down when these wounds were inflicted? Much might turn on the opinion of the experts retained to advise the inquiry. They stated that both wounds could have been caused either when he was upright and leaning forward, or on the ground. One of the exit wounds had a feature which suggested that the body may have been pressed against a hard surface, but this was not conclusive. At one time it seemed that the expert evidence could not help one way or the other.

However James Wray senior, and after his death Liam, had carefully over the years preserved the jacket which Jim had worn on Bloody Sunday. I had assigned the treatment of the expert evidence to Richard, and he asked the Tribunal to allow the experts to look at the holes in the jacket and to try whatever experiments might be needed to explain the configuration of the holes. The experiments were revealing. In his evidence one of the experts, Kevin O'Callaghan, concluded that it was more likely that the deceased was on the ground with the jacket crumpled, rather than running, when the second shot hit him. When one matched the scientific findings with the evidence of the eyewitnesses, the conclusion that Jim had been deliberately shot when lying helpless on the ground, was, as we argued to the Tribunal at the end of the inquiry, overwhelming.

The soldiers who first entered Glenfada Park North were known as Corporal E, Lance-Corporal F, Private G and Private H. In statements made at the time each of these soldiers claimed to have opened fire soon after he entered the square. Lance Corporal F said he fired two aimed shots at a man who "lit something which I saw fizzle and spark and who raised his arm as if to throw some form of bomb". Private G said that he fired three shots at one of two men who were holding "what appeared to be small rifles". Corporal E said he fired two shots at a man who threw two petrol bombs. Private H said he had fired two shots at a youth with a nail bomb, and then claimed to have put no less than 19 more shots through an upper floor window in the square, where a gunman appeared and kept on reappearing.

These explanations were totally inconsistent with each other and with the civilian evidence. We considered them to be a tissue of lies, a shameless attempt to justify criminal acts of shooting by bogus claims of self-defence. No nailbombs, or petrol bombs, or rifles, were ever found in Glenfada Park or seen by any other witnesses at the time of these events. No explosions were heard apart from the gunfire of the soldiers. The occupant of the house where Private H had fired his '19 shots' had testified to the Widgery Inquiry that only one shot had been fired through her window. Private G's rifle was proved by ballistic evidence to have been the weapon which fired the bullet which ended up in Gerard Donaghy in Abbey Park, on the other side of the Glenfada Park North, a place where G himself never admitted having been to at all. The impression I had from reading the statements was that any stories would do, however absurd and contradictory, so long as they offered an excuse for every shot which was fired.

Since the evidence of the four soldiers was so riddled with falsehood, our job in representing the family of Jim Wray was not easy. We had to try and identify who it was who fired the shot which brought him down and the shot which entered his body as he lay on the ground. To make things more difficult both Corporal E and Private G had died before the inquiry started. Lance Corporal F claimed to have no memory of the events at all, and Private H stuck to his bizarre story of the 19 shots through the window.

Private 027 was a soldier from the same platoon who was following closely on the heels of the first four. He had not been a witness at the Widgery Inquiry, but in 1975, after leaving the Army, he had given a remarkable account of his life as a member of the Parachute Regiment in Northern Ireland. He described the contempt which his fellow soldiers had for the Irish, and the spirit of gung-ho daring which inspired the regiment. In a detailed account of Bloody Sunday he described how in the briefing the day before his lieutenant had given the strong impression that he was expecting some 'kills'. He described what he saw when he entered Glenfada Park North (the soldiers' code letters have been substituted for the actual names which he used):

> E, H, G and F and myself then leapt the wall, turned right and ran down Kells Walk into Glenfada Park, a small triangular car park within the complex of flats. A group of 40 civilians were there running in an effort to get away. H fired from the hip at a range of 20 yards. The bullet passed through one man and into another and they both fell, one dead and one wounded. He then moved forward and fired again, killing the wounded man. They lay sprawled together half on the pavement and half in the gutter. E shot another man at the entrance of the Park who also fell on the pavement. A fourth man was killed by either G or F. I must point out that this whole incident in Glenfada

Park occurred in fleeting seconds and I can no longer recall the order of fire or who fell first but I do remember that when we first appeared, darkened faces, sweat and aggression, brandishing rifles, the crowd stopped immediately in their tracks, turned to face us and raised their hands. This is the way they were standing when they were shot.

If truthful and accurate, this account was a confirmation from within the ranks of the soldiers that a man – clearly Jim Wray – had been first wounded and then shot again on the ground. Private 027 was clearly going to be a key witness. The document in which his account appeared was typewritten – apparently a transcript of something written by 027 himself and sent to a journalist called Sean McShane whom he met in New York. The plan had been for McShane to publish a book of 027's experiences, but this never materialised. The document resurfaced in 1998 when it was sent to the Irish television company RTE. It became one of the major pieces of new evidence which was used to support the demand for the inquiry.

Private 027 had made a statement to the military police soon after Bloody Sunday, in which he said that he had followed the four soldiers into Glenfada Park. Before catching them up he heard shots, and when he entered the Park he claimed to have seen soldier E shoot a man who attempted to throw a petrol bomb. He told the Tribunal that this was a lie spoken as a result of "the pressures inherent in the situation". Later he was seen by the army personnel who were taking statements for the Widgery Inquiry. He said that once he started to talk about soldiers firing at unarmed civilians, the investigators broke off the interview. One said: "We can't have that, can we Private? That makes it sound as if shots were being fired into the crowd." Private 027 was not called as a witness before Widgery.

When the Saville Inquiry was set up Private 027 felt his life to be in danger. He was a key witness who had turned against his former colleagues, and threats had been directed at him. He insisted on negotiating the terms on which he was prepared to give evidence, including a guarantee of anonymity and the payment of an allowance and other benefits designed to secure his protection. In the written statement which he made to the inquiry he described the general scene in Glenfada Park in words which fully supported the civilian witnesses. As he entered he heard "some 10 or 15 rounds fired in a series of rapid, staccato shots, which came in a burst. They were followed by some more intermittent firing". He continued:

> As I came on the scene there was at least one body down. I saw a crowd of about 40 shocked and terrified people along the south side of the car park,

trying to get away. They were in the process of exiting the south west corner of the car park, when, in the presence of the shattering noise of the SLRs (the soldiers' self-loading rifles) they became submissive and acquiescent. Some froze in a static huddle. I saw no civilians with weapons, neither could I see or hear any explosive devices during the entire situation. I was not personally at risk from anything that I could see and it never entered my head to fire my weapon.

Beyond this 027 could remember nothing. He said he had a 'memory gap' of what then happened in Glenfada Park. The soldiers' lawyers suggested that he had been lying in the 1975 document and had nothing to say which could be relied on. I was less sure. The events in the Park could have been so dreadful that he had blocked them from his consciousness over the years. Before discounting his evidence, as some of my colleagues representing the families were inclined to do, I wanted to examine everything about him. He had, after all, had the courage to speak out against his colleagues. He had been subjected to threats which may have come from those who wanted to silence him. He had been genuinely appalled by his experiences as a 'peace-keeper' in Northern Ireland. He deserved to be treated with respect.

It emerged that his account in 1975 was based on a diary which he kept in a field notebook during the time of his service in Ireland. This diary was real. A soldier who slept in the bunk below him for four months confirmed that 027 was accustomed to make diary notes in his bunk at night in 'a jotter or notebook'. The field notebook was still in existence in 1998, when his 1975 document came to light and he was interviewed by the media. A journalist working for Channel 4, Lena Ferguson, had captured some pages of it on film, including a page with a map of Glenfada Park. She had taken full notes of an interview with 027 during which he had been reading from the field notebook. But infuriatingly, 027 had flushed the notebook down a toilet in the Channel 4 building, in what he described as a state of anxiety about the danger of keeping the document. Its contents could only be gleaned from Lena Ferguson's notes. In relation to Glenfada Park the notes read:

> G – shot at a bloke in a crowd of 40 –
> Trying to get away
> Bullet passes through one and out another
> 3rd man by H in leg – he then went and
> finished him off. (Thinks it was leg)

E also fired and hit.

H further 15 rounds –   behind car

After events of Glenfada Park

> also at people
>
> crawling along pavement

For Richard and myself, trying to piece together how Jim Wray was killed, the 027 material was tantalising. He had seen it happen but now claimed that he had no memory of what he saw. He had written notes about it within days of the event in the field notebook, but years later he flushed the notebook down a toilet. He had directly accused H of murder in the 1975 account, and in the notebook, but he was not able to give sworn evidence against H. In spite of the question marks and concerns, his evidence provided powerful confirmation of the basic facts to which Joe Mahon and others had testified, that Jim Wray had been deliberately 'finished off' as he lay wounded across the kerb.

Who did it? The notes made by 027 suggested that H was the guilty soldier, H who had fired so many shots which could not be explained. But the evidence of Joe Mahon pointed more to G, the soldier whose bullet was found in the body of Gerard Donaghy in Abbey Park. He described how the soldier who shot Jim went into the alley towards Abbey Park, came back, took off his helmet and revealed a shock of fair hair - a description which fitted G not H.

G was dead, so that only H was available to be cross-examined. I established that he and G were working as a pair, in a 'brick with E and F'. The evidence showed that E and F went down the east side of Glenfada Park, and G went down the west side towards the alley. H accepted that it would be 'quite logical' that he followed G. I suggested to H that he fired into a crowd of civilians in the alley, treating them all as the enemy and firing regardless. He denied this. He said that he fired at 'a bomber'. He agreed that he 'worked round' the walls of the square towards the alley. He denied being the soldier that people had seen wearing a gas mask, advancing across the square and firing from the hip, though he agreed that he had on a gas mask. He denied the suggestion in 027's notes that he was the one who finished off the man who was wounded. In the end I suggested that he was either the person who shot Jim Wray or he was right beside G and saw him do it. He denied any knowledge of this. After drawing attention to his evidence about the 19 shots through the window, I accused him of firing "22 shots and every one of them illegal, some of them fatal and murderous". The last question and answer was:

Q. You and E and G and F were not just acting as a brick that day, I suggest, soldier H, you were acting as a death squad; were you not?

A. No sir.

In dealing with the other surviving soldier from the group, soldier F, I had used a more graphic metaphor. F was a soldier who was responsible for deaths in a number of different sectors. 027 described him and G as "self-sufficient and a law unto themselves…cunning and cute". He was one of the four who fired the first shots which brought Jim Wray to the ground. My cross-examination ended with this exchange:

Q. What was your platoon tasked to do on that occasion?

A. The task I think was, um, was to arrest rioters.

Q. It was to go into the no-go areas was it not?

A. That is correct.

Q. It was also to get some kills.

A. No.

Q. No?

A. I do not agree, no.

Q. I suggest that you personally relished the prospect of going into the no-go areas and getting to grips with the people of the Bogside?

A. No.

Q. I suggest that you were sent in like a school of piranha fish into a public swimming pool to create mayhem?

A. I do not agree.

Q. And you drew blood wherever you went?

A. I do not agree.

Cross-examining witnesses like soldiers H and F was not easy. I was sure that they committed outrageous acts of murder, but I knew that they would deny everything. I was asking questions after most of the barristers representing the other families had had their turn. I wanted my clients to know that I was aware of their pain, their outrage pent up over the years. The questions needed to reflect what they had for so long wanted to ask. I planned every question in advance. I marshalled all the evidence which contradicted their lying stories, so that anyone hearing or reading their testimony would be able to make the comparison.

As I write this chapter the Bloody Sunday Inquiry has not yet issued its report. The judges have a massive task. I hope that they uphold our submissions as to the circumstances of the death of Jim Wray. But the Inquiry has already achieved much of its purpose. As with the Truth and Reconciliation Commission in South Africa, the process is as important as the report which comes at the end of the process. I have expressed my reservations about Lord Saville, and I am not able to say in advance that I will accept his report when it comes out. But I have certainly admired the patience which he has shown, and the openness and thoroughness of the process over which he presided, and this in itself has had positive consequences

In October 2003 soon after soldiers F and H had concluded their evidence, I received a letter from Margaret Wray. She said:

> Congratulations and sincere thanks for a job magnificently done. I know it wasn't an easy or comfortable time for you or myself. This inquiry has been long, hard and drawn-out, and very stressful for everyone. I know that sometimes I tried your patience. I was afraid we would lose track of what we were about and who this inquiry was about. I knew my motives were pure and simple, to prove Jim was innocent and he was murdered. When we first met you gave me a commitment to prove this to the best of your ability and to use those two words as much as possible. I put my trust and faith in you and you did not break that trust or faith. I find it very hard to find adequate words to express my feelings of gratitude and thanks to you. All I can say is that since last Tuesday I have found an inner peace. In my heart and mind I have finally left Jim to rest in peace. I no longer have pain when I think about him. Thank you.

A barrister could never wish for a more wonderful letter of thanks. The letter is a tribute not only to me and my team, but to the inquiry process which Tony Blair initiated, and to which Lord Saville and his colleagues will have dedicated almost a decade of their lives.

19

THE CASE *against* EDWARD HEATH

When he appeared before Lord Widgery's Tribunal in 1972, Jim Wray's father had said that "the British Army, through policy laid down by the British Government, is responsible for this situation. I would say that the British Government should be under investigation equally with the British Army at this Tribunal." James Wray considered that the British Army would never have undertaken such a mission, entering the Bogside with guns blazing, causing 26 casualties, all in the presence of thousands of civil rights marchers, without approval from the highest echelons of the Government. Lord Widgery dismissed him with contempt, stating that "I will have enough to inquire into without inquiring into the British Government as well." James Wray must then have understood that the legal establishment, in the person of the Lord Chief Justice, was protecting the political establishment, led by Prime Minister Edward Heath. He would not have been surprised to read the minute of a meeting held between Heath and Widgery on 31st January 1972, the day after Bloody Sunday, in which Heath said that a speedy outcome of Widgery's Inquiry was needed, and reminded the judge that "We were in Northern Ireland fighting not only a military war but a propaganda war."

Our instructions from the Wray family were to probe as deeply as we could into the evidence which might suggest that Heath and other ministers knew about the plans for Bloody Sunday and approved them. Tony Blair had promised that all relevant documents from the period would be provided, and as the first government papers began to come through to us, it became clear that this was a totally legitimate field of inquiry. There had been a meeting of the Cabinet committee which dealt with Northern Ireland (known as the GEN 47, chaired by the Prime Minister) on the Thursday before Bloody Sunday. Lord Carver, the Chief of the General Staff, had reported to that meeting about the Army's plans for the day. His report had been approved. And on the same evening, the Prime Minister of Northern Ireland, Brian Faulkner, had had a meeting with Edward Heath at Downing Street, when the forthcoming Derry march had been mentioned. To be sure, the minutes of these meetings did not say in terms that casualties were expected, much less authorised. But at the least they showed that Heath was being kept informed at the highest level.

Was Heath party to a deliberate plan to confront the civil rights marchers with lethal force? On the one hand one could not conceive of the Army carrying out such a confrontation without political approval. On the other hand Edward Heath's witness statement, as presented to the inquiry, declared that he was taken by surprise by what happened, and had no idea, and no intention, that people would be killed. It was our duty to our clients, and to all those who wanted to know the truth about Bloody Sunday, to assist the Tribunal to get at the truth. More than any of the other families' representatives, we made it our task to make the case against Heath. Not because of political prejudice, but because as more and more material came to light, it became more and more clear that Heath was taking an intense personal interest in, and responsibility for, the affairs of Northern Ireland, during the months and weeks leading up to Bloody Sunday. An advocate before a public inquiry is not entitled to go off into wild speculation. But he or she is duty bound to advance arguments which fairly arise on the evidence, and which the clients believe to be true. That was the case with the arguments which we made that Heath had a personal responsibility for the tragedy. It is no light matter to accuse a former Prime Minister of complicity in murder; so we approached our task with the utmost seriousness of purpose.

When Christopher Clarke made his opening statement to the Tribunal, he made light of the suggestion that the British Government approved a plan to use the march to provoke a confrontation with the IRA or to draw it out in some fashion. He said:

> Such a plan would require a number of very senior personnel from the Prime Minister and Chief of the General Staff downwards to be involved, or if not involved, to be deceived or at best left in ignorance, and could not be carried out at all without giving the necessary instructions to the troops…. In the high level documentation that followed Bloody Sunday no indication is to be

found, or has yet been found, of the existence, fulfilment or non-fulfilment of any such plan.

I was angry at this comment. It seemed that the inquiry was once again getting the British Government off the hook before the evidence was heard. In my opening statement on behalf of the Wray family, I said:

> Sir, as we understand that passage, Mr Clarke was pointing the Tribunal, albeit tentatively and provisionally, towards a view that because no ulterior plan is referred to in the secret documents which have been disclosed, there was therefore no ulterior plan. Sir, we simply do not agree that such a provisional view should be formed, and particularly not at this early stage of the Inquiry. We submit that it is far too early to make such a comment on an issue of such fundamental importance. We say that on the contrary there is a body of evidence already available which does point to the formulation and implementation of a plan, a plan to kill young people in Derry and to teach Derry Catholics a lesson, not a plan to draw out the IRA.

I then drew attention to pieces of evidence which had by then come to light. First, the Commander of Land Forces in Northern Ireland, General Ford, had on 7th January 1972, only three weeks before Bloody Sunday, written a memorandum to his superiors stating his view that "The minimum force necessary to achieve a restoration of law and order in Northern Ireland is to shoot selected ringleaders amongst the Derry Young Hooligans after clear warnings had been issued." So the shooting of rioters was being openly espoused in the high echelons of the military. General Ford came to Derry on Bloody Sunday to be an observer of the events. I asked: "Is it not reasonable to infer that the killing may have been deliberately planned in order to fulfil the stated and desired objective?"

Secondly, I referred to the statement of Private 027 that in the pre-operation briefing: "I do remember the remarks revolving around the possibility of getting some kills the following day." His 1975 statement had been even more explicit: "When our Lieutenant said, 'Let's teach these buggers a lesson, we want some kills tomorrow', to the mentality of the blokes to whom he was speaking this was tantamount to an order." So contrary to Mr Clarke's statement, there was evidence that the 'necessary instructions' may indeed have been given to the troops.

Thirdly I reviewed three crucial meetings which had taken place on 27th January 1972, the Thursday before Bloody Sunday. At 10.30 a.m. the Joint Security Committee met in Belfast, bringing together senior Northern Ireland politicians, the General Officer Commanding (GOC) General Tuzo, the Chief Constable and various security advisers. The minute noted that the civil rights march would be blocked, and "the operation might well develop into rioting and even a shooting war". Why would there be a 'shooting war', if no aggressive action was planned by the Army?

At the same time a meeting of the GEN 47 was going on in London, chaired by Edward Heath and attended by the Home Secretary Reginald Maudling, the Foreign Secretary Sir Alec Douglas-Home, the Defence Secretary Lord Carrington, the Chief of the General Staff General Carver, and a number of other Ministers and advisers. This was a meeting of the highest officials of the British Government. It received a detailed report from General Carver, who said that between 8,000 and 12,000 people were expected to take part. The march would be stopped on the borders of the Roman Catholic areas of Derry. The Prime Minister commented, according to the minute, that "Instances of confrontation between the Army and the civil population were inevitable." The meeting agreed that the marchers "must be prevented from coming out of the Bogside and Creggan areas".

At 5.45 p.m. Brian Faulkner, the Prime Minister of Northern Ireland, came to 10 Downing Street to meet with Edward Heath. It had not been scheduled in advance, and the two men had not met since the previous October. There was a 'note for the record' prepared by the Cabinet Secretary Lord Armstrong. Mr Faulkner was recorded as saying that "It was important to make clear that those parading were not genuine 'civil righters' but 'civil disobedients'." He said that "The civil disobedience parades in the coming weekend in Derry would be difficult."

These three meetings show that the forthcoming civil rights march was high on the agenda of the two prime ministers and their most senior advisers. They knew that the numbers would be massive. They knew that the march would be blocked by the Army. They knew that there would be 'confrontation' and even 'a shooting war'. They approved the Army's plans, at least in general terms. The minutes did not, of course, record that any of the meetings had agreed that a regiment of paratroopers would invade the Bogside and open fire. But did the minutes reflect the real content of the discussions held and the agreements reached?

It was significant that James Callaghan, then a spokesman for the Opposition who was later prime minister, had said in April 1972, "Very heavy pressure was being brought to bear upon the army commanders to step up their attitude." When asked by the Inquiry, he could not remember what information he relied on for this statement; and he added: "I am sure that such information would never have been committed to paper but would have passed by word of mouth." In other words, in the higher reaches of Government, not everything which is said is recorded on paper.

General Carver (who became Lord Carver) himself appeared to have had no doubt that a firm stand had been taken by the British Government. In an interview in 1998 he referred to the rioting in Derry as a major problem, with hooligans pelting the army with bricks. He added: "And of course there were immense protests from the Protestant people about what was going on. I mean, it was agreed in the British Government, I mean, it was agreed that something had got to be done." Unfortunately Lord Carver died before being able to give evidence to the Tribunal as to what it was that was agreed by the British Government. Was it simply a plan to block the march and arrest people? Or was it a plan to invade the Bogside and shoot people?

One thing was startlingly clear. Not one person at any of these meetings showed the least bit of sympathy for the civil rights marchers, the least bit of understanding that they had a legitimate grievance, or the least bit of care lest innocent people might be harmed. The marchers were seen as troublemakers and lawbreakers. The Government of Northern Ireland had issued a ban on all marches. The ban violated the right of peaceful assembly guaranteed by the European Convention on Human Rights; but in those days the Convention was less well understood than it is today. So the marchers could be treated as criminals, arrested and prosecuted. To many who attended the meetings the marchers were not only criminals but their enemy. A military report which had been made to General Carver and others on 24th January 1972 quoted General Tuzo as saying that there was spreading hostility to the Army and "behind it all stands NICRA, the active ally of the IRA". So the senior military regarded the organisers of the march as terrorists.

These were the considerations which I laid before the Tribunal in my opening statement in November 2000. It was over two years before the key politicians and civil servants gave evidence. Edward Heath came to the Tribunal in January 2003. In those years Richard Harvey and I did our utmost to prise out from the authorities the further documents which we believed must still exist. Through visits to the Public Records Office Richard came to know what kinds of documents are normally to be found. He found briefing papers passing between senior civil servants and ministers. He found that handwritten minutes of important meetings often survived and were kept in the records. But for January 1972 there was little to be found, because it had all been gathered in for the inquiry. We submitted a series of memoranda to the inquiry, demanding that more effort be made to extract relevant documents from the various departments whose ministers had been involved in the meetings. We said that if nothing else were disclosed, we would have to conclude that there was deliberate and wilful obstruction at some level of government.

The pressure brought results. Every month brought some new additions to the 'G Bundle', the files of political and military documents which grew over the years from two to six in number. Whether the government disclosed everything which should have been disclosed, I do not know. But some remarkable documents came to light, and they made one think that there must have been more. For instance a hand written note of the GEN 47 meeting on 27th January 1972 had been made by one of the civil servants who attended. It records Edward Heath as saying: "Approve CGS'S (Chief of General Staff's) dispositions; and get publicity directed so far as possible to way in which NICRA (the Northern Ireland Civil Rights Association) being taken over by IRA and hooligans." This showed that the smear against NICRA, which the military briefing had recorded on 24th January, had been accepted as fact by the Prime Minister by the 27th – something which was never reflected in the official minute. But why were there no other such notes? Where were the hand-written notes of the crucial meeting between Prime Ministers Heath and Faulkner the same evening?

The briefings which Sir Burke Trend, one of Heath's most respected advisers, had written to him were also part of the late disclosures. On 26th January 1972 Sir Burke had referred to the anti-internment marches which had been happening across Northern Ireland throughout the month. He suggested to the Prime Minister that the soldiers of the Parachute Regiment had been "unnecessarily rough" in dealing with a civil rights demonstration the previous weekend; and continued:

> Overshadowing this question, however, is the graver issue of the attitude to be adopted by the security forces if the renewed ban on marches is openly defied. Are we able – and prepared – to deal with that situation? Perhaps the question should be explored urgently with Mr Faulkner during his visit to London.

On reading this briefing I felt that we were getting tantalisingly near the awful truth. The marches had been continuing throughout the month. Catholics were defying the ban. Protestants were expecting the British Army to "deal with that situation". A huge march was to take place the following Sunday in Derry. The issue would be on the agenda when Mr Faulkner came to meet Mr Heath. Now he was faced with the crunch question: are we able and prepared? And what did his shrewd Cabinet Secretary mean by "dealing with the situation"? At the least this material showed that Mr Heath was fully in the picture. At worst it meant that he was ready to assure Mr Faulkner that the British Government would use military might to show that illegal marching would not be tolerated.

As we discussed these revelations with the Wray family, we could sense their emotions. Just as their late father believed, the British Government had been directly involved in the preparations for Bloody Sunday. It was not merely an Army manoeuvre gone wrong. The Prime Minister himself had believed that the marchers were a menace which had to be dealt with. If only he had issued a note of caution; if only he had said 'Wait, the majority of these thousands of people are ordinary peaceful citizens, and the Army must make sure that they are not put in danger' – then the paratroopers would have been kept in the background and the day would have ended without loss of life. Such thoughts were far from the Prime Minister's mind.

We knew that Sir Edward Heath and Lord Carrington would deny any suggestion of complicity or negligence. The thrust of their written evidence was that the handling of the march was a matter for the Army units on the ground. All they had done was to approve the general dispositions. They had not expected any trouble. The way to cross-examine them was to confront them with the contemporary documents, and hope that the Tribunal and the broader public, comparing the documents with their bland disavowals, would appreciate that their responsibility for the killings on Bloody Sunday was real.

In the year 2003 I had the pleasure of questioning two former prime ministers. In Jamaica I cross-examined Edward Seaga, who had uttered a libel against a client of mine. In London I questioned Edward Heath. He was much the harder nut of the two. He gave evidence for twelve days, half a day at a time. I rose to my feet on the last day. Nervously I waited for my turn as he was questioned first by Christopher Clarke, then by the barristers for the other families. Michael Lavery QC, on behalf of the majority of the families, took four days in which he launched a general attack on Heath's contempt for the Catholics of Northern Ireland. Sir Edward, although plainly infirm in body at the age of 86, was mentally alert and showed a wily skill in dealing with unpleasant questions.

The thrust of the questions put by Lavery was that the Government had violated the rights of the deceased and wounded by neglect. He asked Sir Edward whether he really knew what was going on in Northern Ireland, and whether the Government really cared. At the end of his long innings he asked: "Do you think, Sir Edward, that if you had involved yourself a bit more closely in what the Army were planning to do on Bloody Sunday, things might have been different?" Sir Edward was answered that he was involving himself as Prime Minister to the right extent, and that "power had been passed over to those who were more closely involved'. In other words it was an operational matter which he left to the Army commanders.

This approach was the opposite of that which Richard and I had decided was called for by the evidence. Michael Mansfield and his team, who acted for another group of families, shared our view. We considered that the evidence showed such a close and intense personal involvement on the part of Heath, that he must have approved an Army operation in response to the march which exposed unarmed civilians to death and injury. We did not claim that Heath ordered the shooting of 26 unarmed civilians. But we believed him to have had a personal role in agreeing to a strategy which clearly carried that risk.

Our position was put in a series of propositions formulated by Mansfield and read out to Sir Edward: (1) That the NICRA march was regarded by the Army as entailing a real and inevitable risk of a shooting war with IRA gunmen. (2) That the march was to be used as an opportunity to mount a specific and sizeable arrest operation by armed troops. (3) That therefore there was a serious foreseeable risk that unarmed civilians would be shot. (4) That such casualties had to be accepted as the price to be paid in the context of a war on IRA gunmen. (5) That the responsibility for those casualties could be attributed to the organisers of the illegal march. (6) That approval for this operation which embraced that possibility must have been communicated to General Carver, either in an unrecorded private meeting or in the GEN 47 for which there are incomplete records. Sir Edward responded that he rejected the propositions.

Lord Saville allowed these allegations to be put to Sir Edward and other witnesses, having insisted, correctly, that we formulate them in writing in advance. But he seemed reluctant to understand what our case really was. There had been a telling moment during my questioning of Lord Carrington, who had given evidence in December 2002. After going through evidence that the Army's tolerance of the earlier civil rights marches had alienated Protestant opinion, I suggested to Lord Carrington that the firm action of the Army on Bloody Sunday was designed to improve the prospects of a political solution. Lord Saville intervened:

> Well…the blunt way of putting it, Lord Gifford, is that the design of the British Government was to shoot people on the streets of Derry in the hope and expectation that it would aid the political process; what is your comment to that?
>
> Carrington: It did not seem likely
>
> Gifford: I am saying to you, and I want my allegation to be firmly known: that it was the design of the British Government to cause risk, clear danger to Catholic lives in order to appease public opinion.
>
> Carrington: I have made it fairly clear that it is an accusation which really does not make sense.

Lord Saville had distorted the case, making it appear extreme and ridiculous. I had corrected him. But his approach gave me no confidence that the senior ministers of the Government would attract any criticism from the Tribunal when it came to publish its conclusions.

The basis of the case which we made against Prime Minister Heath can be understood by looking at the pieces of evidence which led us to argue that he bore a serious personal responsibility for the tragedy. I will set them out so that others can judge whether we were right.

(1) The background to the march was the decision taken in August 1971 to introduce internment without trial in Northern Ireland. This decision was taken against military advice because Mr Faulkner had made a personal appeal to Mr Heath. Thus a severe violation of human rights was approved in order to placate Mr Faulkner and his Unionist supporters.

(2) Mr Heath and Mr Faulkner met again in October 1971. They considered that "a solution to the security problem was the key to progress elsewhere".

(3) Mr Heath, who was simultaneously negotiating Britain's entry into the Common Market, said at this time that the crisis in Northern Ireland "continued to overshadow the work of the Government in many fields and threatened to jeopardise the success of economic and defence policies and the approach to Europe". This was a sign of the supreme importance of Northern Ireland to the Government's general strategies.

(4) Between October 1971 and January 1972 the GEN 47 Cabinet Committee met 19 times. Mr Heath never missed a meeting.

(5) According to Lord Carver's statement to the inquiry, Mr Heath "was influenced by his military background and wanted to solve problems by the use of military means".

(6) In late September 1971 Mr Heath ordered from the Ministry of Defence a "fully documented and argued appreciation, including an assessment of what measures the Army would propose if they were instructed that the primary objective was to bring terrorism to an end at the earliest possible moment, without regard to the inconveniences caused to the civilian population". Here clearly was a strong military mind at work.

(7) In October 1971 Mr Heath said to the GEN 47 that: "The first priority should be the defeat of the gunmen using military means and that in achieving this we should have to accept whatever political penalties were inevitable."

(8) By December 1971 the military command was reporting positive developments in two of its three operational areas, Belfast and the border, but not in Derry "where a major military operation… could have widespread political consequences". The problem was that areas of Derry had become 'no go areas'. The Army wanted to mount a major operation "which would involve, at some stage, shooting unarmed civilians". But General Carver appreciated that to carry out such an operation would wreck any chance of a political settlement.

(9) Mr Heath visited Northern Ireland just before Christmas to boost the morale of the troops. His visit included Derry, and he told the Tribunal that "no other area in Northern Ireland was comparable". He was briefed that the IRA were strong in the nationalist Bogside and Creggan areas.

(10) Cabinet briefing papers in December and January show that the Government faced a dilemma. If they allowed the no go areas to remain, there was little hope of any Unionist support for a political initiative. But if a military operation was mounted to occupy the no go areas it would be likely to alienate the Catholics and involve civilian casualties.

(11) Civil rights marches organised by NICRA were held on Christmas Day 1971 and thereafter every week in different parts of Northern Ireland. The response from the Army was relatively low key, and Unionist politicians were expressing anger at the failure of the authorities to support the ban on marching.

(12) On 7th January 1972 Mr Heath sent a note through his Private Secretary referring to the bringing of prosecutions against

identified leaders of the marches: "The Prime Minister considers it very important that this should be done, and be seen to be done as speedily as possible. He would be grateful for a report on progress." The note is clear evidence of Mr Heath's hands-on approach and of his antipathy to the marchers.

(13) On 11th January 1972 Cabinet Secretary Burke Trend sent a brief to Mr Heath, in which he drew attention to the "relatively gentle" handling of the marches and added: "If we are putting our money on Mr Faulkner's survival, we cannot afford to expose him indefinitely to the accusation that he is using kid gloves to deal with provocation and intimidation." So Mr Heath was being advised that the way in which marches were being handled by the Army had direct political side-effects.

(14) General Ford's memorandum, containing the view that selected ringleaders of the Derry hooligans should be shot, had been sent to General Tuzo. The memorandum referred to the march being planned for Derry, where Ford anticipated "some form of battle". General Tuzo reported to the Joint Security Committee on 13th January 1972, chaired by Mr Faulkner, that "certain measures were in mind with a view to putting down the troublesome hooligan element". General Tuzo died before the inquiry was able to take a statement from him, so there was no evidence before the inquiry as to what he did when he received the memorandum. While there is no direct evidence that it reached London, some of the ideas contained in it certainly did.

(15) By mid-January the civil rights marches were causing grave concern. The Government's Security Adviser in Northern Ireland, Mr William Stout, described the processions as being "organised by Civil Rights and other 'front' organisations of the IRA". He recommended that directions to the police and Army should be revised, and recognised that "a generally firmer line will precipitate violence in what might otherwise be a non-violent situation". Evidently the 'kid gloves' were now to be taken off.

(16) On the weekend of 22nd/23rd January 1972 there were four marches and demonstrations in different parts of Northern Ireland. This prompted a lead story in the *Times* on 24th January 1972 to the effect that "Loyalist societies" were threatening to defy the ban on marches. Dr Ian Paisley called for the "political handcuffs" to be taken off the security forces.

(17) At top-level meetings about the forthcoming Derry march the organisers were accused, falsely, of being connected to the IRA. General Tuzo on 24th January said, "Behind it all stands NICRA, the active ally of the IRA." Mr Heath himself, as we have seen, spoke on 27th January of the "way in which NICRA being taken over by IRA and hooligans".

(18) Proposals for a political initiative were reaching maturity, and were discussed at the GEN 47 on 27th January 1972. The essence of them was that Roman Catholics should be brought into a significant role in the Government of Northern Ireland. The problem was whether the Protestant leadership could be persuaded to agree.

(19) On 26th January 1972 a senior official at the Ministry of Defence referred to the danger of the Protestant community being "highly critical if there are not immediate indications that at least some of the marchers will be prosecuted". He reported that General Tuzo had it in mind "to attempt to arrest a fair number of such hooligans and to arrange for a special court sitting on Monday morning".

(20) At the Joint Security Committee meeting in Belfast on 27th January 1972 General Tuzo referred to the "more serious difficulties" presented by the Derry march, and reported that the blocking operation by the Army might develop into rioting "and even a shooting war". No one seems to have questioned whether a shooting war could be avoided.

(21) At the GEN 47 meeting in London there was discussion of there being 8,000 – 12,000 marchers; that the march would be prevented from coming out of the Creggan and Bogside; that 20 companies of troops would be deployed; and that there would be arrests and court proceedings. The meeting approved 'the dispositions' which General Carver had described. The meeting must have appreciated that a confrontation between 20 military companies and up to 12,000 civilian marchers was fraught with danger to innocent lives. But no note of caution was recorded.

(22) Top military personnel expected bloodshed to occur. Lord Carver said in his written statement to the inquiry: "My first reaction was to heave a sigh of relief that so few had been killed." His military assistant Sir David Ramsbotham said in evidence that "everyone knew that there was a risk" of bloodshed if there was any engagement with the IRA. He added that: "I am quite certain that General Carver

would have alerted the Prime Minister as to the possibility." A senior officer at the Ministry of Defence, Colonel Dalziell-Payne, referred in a briefing on 27th January 1972 to "stronger military measures" which were to be taken at the weekend; his brief was written to anticipate "the problems we may face on Monday 31 Jan 72 if events on Sunday prove our worst fears".

(23) On the evening of 28th January 1972 the Prime Minister's Press Secretary sent out a chilling message to Mr Faulkner asking him to put out a public statement stating that "all responsible citizens of Londonderry should keep off the streets" and that "the security forces will take the measures which the tactical situation requires". He said that the purpose of the message would be to prepare public opinion for "violent scenes on TV" following the march.

(24) In the light of all this evidence the assertion by Sir Edward in evidence to the Tribunal that "most people believed that we could have a quiet Sunday" was simply incredible.

(25) In the evening of 27th January 1972 Mr Heath and Mr Faulkner met and discussed the Derry march among other topics. Mr Faulkner described the marchers as "civil disobedients". In his pre-meeting briefing from Sir Burke Trend Mr Heath was invited to discuss the question: are we able – and prepared – to deal with the situation of open defiance of the ban on marches? The inference to be drawn is that there must have been such a discussion, and if there was, the attitude of both prime ministers was that it was necessary for the Army to be tough – to take the kid gloves off.

(26) Lord Kilclooney, then Mr John Taylor and one of Mr Faulkner's ministers, told the Tribunal that the purpose of Mr Faulkner's going to London was "presumably to acquaint the Prime Minister as to how serious the situation was that was developing in Londonderry".

(27) On the night of 30th January Mr Lynch, the Taoiseach (Prime Minister) of the Republic of Ireland telephoned Mr Heath to protest about the killings in Derry. The conversation was recorded. Mr Heath expressed no surprise or shock, or regret. He said that the march was against the law: "The people who deliberately organised this march in circumstances which we all know, in which the IRA were bound to intervene, carry a heavy responsibility for any damage which ensued. It was against the law and should never have been countenanced by anyone".

(28) On 3ʳᵈ February 1972 there was another meeting between Mr Heath and Mr Faulkner. Mr Faulkner spoke of "a new solidarity" on the Unionist side following the events of Bloody Sunday, and said that in the longer term it might be that the events "would be seen to have cleared the air". Mr Heath asked "whether the grave nature of the events in Londonderry would assist a settlement". It would seem that both men were still hoping that the actions of the Army could have had useful political consequences.

It was the gathering of all these strands of evidence which made us confident that we had a strong case to put to Sir Edward Heath when my turn came to question him. Michael Mansfield went before me and covered some of the ground with great skill. He confronted Sir Edward with his words to Mr Lynch "in which the IRA were bound to intervene". "They have only one meaning, I suggest to you: that you were telling Mr Lynch, on the evening of the 30ᵗʰ, that you had anticipated that this march was bound to attract the intervention of the IRA; that is what you were saying, were you not?" This question brought one of Sir Edward's least convincing answers: "(Pause) Yes, I was telling him that I had recognised it then but in the afternoon I had not recognised that."

I was the sixth barrister to question Sir Edward on the twelfth day of his evidence. My questions were carefully prepared. I had to avoid repeating any of the questions which had already been asked, since Lord Saville had imposed a strict rule against repetitive questioning. Michael had concentrated mainly on the contradictions between what was said after Bloody Sunday and Sir Edward's evidence. So I went through all the material prior to Bloody Sunday which revealed Sir Edward's close involvement; his interest in a military solution; and his awareness that trouble was likely to break out. I got him to agree that he regarded the civil rights marchers as law breakers against whom the law should be enforced with rigour. He agreed that by mid-January when the 'kid gloves' briefing was written, it was "time to carry out the law". But when it came to the meetings on 27ᵗʰ January 1972, he was adamant that he wanted to avoid trouble. I asked: "You were accepting inevitable incidents of confrontation in the context of a march of thousands of people?" He answered: "No... we were doing our utmost to prevent it happening." Dealing with the difficulties of the march mentioned by Mr Faulkner, he said: "That was Mr Faulkner's affair, not mine." Asked whether he agreed with Mr Faulker's categorisation of the marchers as 'civil disobedients', he said: "Yes, but we made a special attempt on that

Sunday to ensure that they would not cause trouble and we could then have a quiet day."

I then said: "I am going to be suggesting that neither you as Prime Minister nor any of the forces of the Army, made any special attempt to ensure people had a quiet time. Can you point to anything to justify what you say, that you made an attempt to have a quiet time?" He simply retorted: "I am telling you, you are quite wrong." I referred to his relationship with Mr Faulkner, whom he had described as his 'political friend': "I suggest you trusted yet again, perhaps for the last time, your political friend, Mr Brian Faulkner, and agreed and approved that this tough line should be taken in order, as a calculated decision, in order to allay Unionist anger which would otherwise endanger the political initiative." He said that I was completely wrong. I ended by asking: "Was it not intended to help a political settlement by satisfying the Unionist side, that this robust approach to the march was authorised by you?" He answered: "No, and there is not one scrap of evidence you can produce that that was the case."

I have laid out the evidence that we produced. I believe that we did our duty to the Wray family. We called the prime minister of the day to account, which is what Jim Wray's father wanted. Edward Heath has now passed on, having stubbornly declared to the Tribunal that he bore no responsibility for the deaths and injuries which his troops had caused. Those who survive can read the material and make their own judgments.

Edward Heath was one of many leaders who were called to account during the course of the inquiry. Other politicians in Britain and Northern Ireland; senior advisers who usually stay behind the scenes; intelligence chiefs whose existence is normally never revealed; generals and brigadiers and colonels who have never before had to face a hostile non-military questioner – all these were called to bear witness before Lord Saville and his colleagues. Some appeared to be deeply resentful that their judgment, and often their very integrity, was questioned. To me it was a fascinating, often chilling insight into aspects of the British military and political establishment.

All this was necessary in order to answer the question: why did these 13 men die and why were 13 others injured? To me the inquiry process has already provided the answer. They died because of the prejudice of the British. They died because the march which they took part in was seen as a menace to law and order rather than a legitimate expression of a serious grievance. They died because the hardline Unionists who ran Northern Ireland wanted the Army to take off the 'kid gloves' and teach these troublesome Catholics a lesson. They died because it was convenient for the British Government to go along with what the Unionists wanted. They died because generals and the soldiers under them wanted to show that they controlled things in Derry. They died because the politicians in London did not care to take any steps to prevent them from dying. They died because soldiers who were not led by principled commanders could and did turn into ruthless murderers. They died because their human right to life was not considered to be worth protecting.

I felt immensely privileged to have been a part of the process which wrestled with these truths. I am deeply grateful to the Wray family who retained me and the legal team who worked so hard alongside me.

20

THE CASE *for* REPARATIONS

In 1992, when I was building my Jamaican practice, I received a request from Dudley Thompson who was then Jamaican High Commissioner to Nigeria. He asked me if I would prepare a paper to be delivered to the First Pan African Conference on Reparations, to be held in Abuja, the capital of Nigeria. He wanted me to research the legal basis of the concept that African peoples should receive reparations for the damage done by the transatlantic slave trade and the institution of slavery in the Americas. It was an awesome request. In essence he wanted me to write a legal opinion for the benefit of Africans and their descendants in the African diaspora – hundreds of millions of people spread over the continents of African, North and South America, the Caribbean and Europe – as to whether they had grounds to make a claim against the nations of Europe and the United States which had been enriched by the profits which they gained from trading in and owning slaves.

The Conference was to bring together some of the most remarkable people I have known. Dudley Thompson, the veteran of the Jomo Kenyatta trial, had become a friend since the time that I first met him after my visit to Grenada in 1983. He had defended me when I was excluded from the Grenada Bar. His remarkable life included service in the Royal Air Force during the Second World War and practising law in colonial Kenya and Tanganyika. He became Minister of Security and later of Foreign Affairs in the Michael Manley administration in the 1970s. Throughout his life he had been an ardent Pan-Africanist, and he had attended the Fifth Pan-African Congress in Manchester in 1945. When Manley was re-elected as Prime Minister in 1989, he appointed Dudley as Jamaica's diplomatic representative to the continent of Africa. There could be no more fitting appointment. From his High Commission in Lagos he acted as, in effect, the ambassador of the whole Caribbean to the whole of Africa. Then in his mid-seventies, he took on the task with incredible energy. So when I received his request, I knew that it was something to be taken very seriously.

I had learnt about the issue of reparations from another remarkable man who also had become my friend, Bernie Grant, the Member of Parliament for Tottenham in North London. We had become close during the time of the Broadwater Farm Inquiry which I had chaired in 1985-86. He was the most radical and outspoken of the four Black MPs elected in 1987. One of his initiatives was to found the African Reparations Movement in Britain. He had explained to me how there could be no real equality between Black and White people in Britain until Britain faced up to its infamous role in the transatlantic slave trade and was prepared to negotiate some form of reparation with Black people. When I moved to Jamaica the issue arose again, as a Committee on Reparations had also been formed in Jamaica in 1991 under the leadership of George Nelson. I had been invited to some of its meetings, and had been asked to do some work on the legal issues, even before Dudley Thompson had contacted me.

The catalyst for awakening the concept of reparations in Africa itself was supplied by another larger-than-life individual, Chief Moshood ('M. K.O.') Abiola of Nigeria. He was a multimillionaire businessman who at the beginning of 1993 had been selected as one of the two candidates to be president of Nigeria. Nigeria was then under the control of the Armed Forces Ruling Council which had seized power in 1985. The head of state was General Ibrahim Babangida who had agreed to restore democracy through elections to be held in June 1993.

Chief Abiola had for some years been pushing the case for reparations. He was chairman of the Group of Eminent Persons on Reparations to Africa and Africans in the Diaspora, which had been set up by the Organisation of African Unity by a resolution passed in June 1991. He had led a delegation to Gorée Island in Senegal, the point of no return for millions of the African captives shipped across the Atlantic Ocean. Dudley Thompson was part of that delegation and had been appointed rapporteur of the Group of Eminent Persons.

Chief Abiola had the reputation of being a capitalist who retained a deep sense of honour and generosity. He had made a lot of money, but also used his money in the education and upliftment of his people. The cause of reparations was his supreme act of philanthropy. He spent large amounts of his own fortune in promoting the cause. The Pan-African Conference was largely financed by him. I met him first in Jamaica when he visited on a mission to promote the conference. He arrived in his personal Boeing 707 jet, but was very late. He had been delayed by the United States authorities who could not believe that a Black African was the owner of such a plane. He spoke with contemptuous wit about his experience that morning in Washington. "Next time", he had told the Americans, "I shall bring my 747." His message to Jamaicans was encapsulated in a quote from a speech he made in 1992: "While we demand reparations in order to enforce justice, to feed the poor, to teach the illiterate and to house the homeless, this crusade is also important because only reparations can heal our land, comfort our souls and restore our self-respect."

Other members of the Group of Eminent Persons included Professors Ali Mazrui of Kenya and Ade Ajayi of Nigeria; Congressman Ronald Dellums of the United States; Dr M'Bow, the former director of UNESCO; the international singer Miriam Makeba; and Graca Machel whom I knew and greatly admired from my links with Mozambique. These were the people who were organising the conference to be held in Abuja, Nigeria, on 27th to 29th April 1993. I took it as an exceptional honour that this Group had asked me, a White British lawyer, to prepare a paper on the legal aspects of the issue.

At the back of my mind there was also the knowledge that my own family had played a role in the destruction of Africa. The third Lord Gifford had been a senior officer in the force led by Sir Garnet Wolseley which had waged the Ashanti Campaign in Ghana in 1873-4. In 1991 I had been visiting Ghana at the invitation of President Rawlings, to take part in the process of drafting a democratic constitution for Ghana. I had visited Cape Coast Castle, where in the museum I had seen an engraving which depicted Lord Gifford subduing an Ashanti village. Later in the visit I went to Kumasi, capital of the Ashanti people, and had an audience with the Asantehema, the Queen Mother of the Ashantis. I made an apology for the crimes committed by my ancestor against the Ashanti people, and said that I came to Kumasi with a quite different spirit. She thanked me and said that "the Ashanti bear no personal grudge against the British." It was my small personal act of reparation.

I was not an expert in international law, so I took time on a visit to London to read some of the leading text books. I found that the concept of reparation was well established in international law. The Permanent Court of International Justice had defined the principle in 1928 in the Chorzow Factory case between Germany and Poland. "Reparation must, as far as possible, wipe out all the consequences of the illegal act and re-establish the situation which would, in all probability, have existed if that act had not been committed." Restitution in kind, and payment of compensation, were the main forms of reparation imposed by international law.

I recognised that there were formidable questions which any serious proponent of the claim for reparations had to answer. Was the slave trade contrary to international law? Were there any relevant precedents? Did it all happen too long ago? Who would be entitled to make the claim? Who would the claim be made against? What would be the components of the claim? And in what court or tribunal could it be made? These are basic questions which arise in the daily life of an advocate. But in the context of a slave trade covering several centuries and continents, affecting tens of millions of Africans and African descendants, it was a challenge to try to answer them.

I started the paper with some biographical facts about my involvement in the struggles against colonialism and racism. I said that to me as a lawyer it was essential to locate the claim for reparations within a framework of law and justice. It should not be merely an appeal to the conscience of the White world. I noted that blatant racist advertising in Britain had not been stopped until laws were passed which forbade it. Apartheid in South Africa began to crumble as it became regarded as a crime against humanity and a threat to peace, so that international sanctions could be imposed. These examples showed that the demand for justice and legality is an essential element in the struggle for a just cause.

I continued with words which I stand by today: "So it is with the claim for Reparations. Indeed, once you accept, as I do, the truth of three propositions:

(a) that the mass kidnap and enslavement of Africans was the most wicked criminal enterprise in recorded human history;
(b) that no compensation was ever paid by any of the perpetrators to any of the sufferers; and
(c) that the consequences of the crime continue to be massive, both in terms of the enrichment of the descendants of the perpetrators, and in terms of the impoverishment of Africans and the descendants of Africans; then the justice of the claim for Reparations is proved beyond reasonable doubt."

To answer the crucial questions, I developed the three propositions into seven. The first was that **the enslavement of Africans was a crime against humanity.** I cited the Charter of the Nuremberg War Crimes Tribunal, which defined crimes against humanity as: "Murder, extermination, enslavement, deportation and other inhumane acts committed against any civilian population… whether or not in violation of the domestic law where perpetrated." I referred to the Genocide Convention, which did not create a new international crime but gave it new and more effective legal form. It recognised genocide as a crime against international law, and defined genocide as being "acts committed with intent to destroy, in whole or in part, a national, ethnical, racial or religious group as such". The invasion of African territories, the mass capture of Africans, the horrors of the middle passage, the sale and use of Africans as worse than beasts, the extermination of family life, culture and language, were violations of these international laws.

I have never accepted the argument that because the slave trade was legal under the British laws of the time, it could not have been a crime against international law. The Nuremberg Charter dealt with that argument, which might have been used in the context of laws passed by the elected Nazi Government in Germany, in the last part of the definition quoted above. As international law experts have written, acts which are so reprehensible as to offend the conscience of mankind, directed against civilian populations, are crimes in international law and always have been. The criterion is the conscience of decent human beings (who in Britain were indeed outraged by the slave trade) not the standards of those who perpetrated and condoned the crimes.

Nor am I impressed with the comment that African societies themselves permitted slavery, or that many Africans helped the slave traders by capturing and selling the people who were transported. The peculiar cruelties of the transatlantic trade, and the subsequent conditions of slavery in the Americas, were infinitely worse than the indigenous African practices of enslaving prisoners of war or criminals. Africans did not treat each other as racially inferior, subhuman beings. Africans did not imprison each other in stinking dungeons or crowd them into the holds of ships with less space than pigs in a sty. Africans did not work slaves to death because it was cheaper to replace them than to keep them alive. Every book you can read about the transatlantic slave trade will confirm to you that its barbarities were not paralleled in history until Nazi Germany imposed its 'final solution' on the Jews.

As for the culpability of the African slave dealers, it is a sad but inevitable fact that every large scale criminal enterprise will attract collaborators. Some are seduced by greed, some are coerced by intimidation.

The participation of Africans in the capture of their fellow Africans does not, to my mind, detract from the culpability of those who promoted and organised the trade. It was Europeans who created the transatlantic slave trade. It was Europeans who demanded an ever-increasing pool of slave labour to work in their plantations. It was Europeans who were determined to enrich themselves without regard to the suffering of those who created their wealth. It was Europeans who created the market for the trafficking in people on a massive scale – between 12 and 25 million captives snatched from their homes and families.

In my assessment the transatlantic slave trade, and the institution of slavery in the Americas, were the ultimate crimes against humanity, because they depended on the denial of human status, on racial grounds, to a vast section of humanity.

My second proposition was that **international law recognises that those who commit crimes against humanity must make reparation.** I noted some of the modern examples of reparation. The Federal Republic of Germany had reached agreement for the payment of reparations to Israel, following a claim by Israel for the cost of resettling half a million Jews who had fled from Nazi controlled countries. Austria also agreed to make reparation payments to holocaust survivors. The governments which made the payments were not the perpetrators of the crimes, but they accepted responsibility for the crimes committed by their Nazi predecessors. Japan had made reparations payments to South Korea for acts committed during the occupation of Korea by Japan. The United States had passed the Civil Liberties Act in 1988, giving reparations to Japanese Americans who had been interned during the Second World War. The Act expressed an acknowledgment of the "fundamental injustice" which the internees had suffered, apologised on behalf of the US, and provided restitution to those individuals of Japanese ancestry who were interned.

I also drew attention to the steps taken to recognise the rights to restitution of indigenous peoples in different parts of the world, whose land had been plundered and whose people had been killed or degraded. In the United States, Canada, New Zealand and Australia, there have been settlements of various kinds, including recognition of rights over land and financial payments. While these have been inadequate gestures, they recognised that the surviving generations of indigenous peoples had the right to a measure of reparation for the crimes committed against their ancestors.

I continued with a third proposition which attacked the argument that it all happened too long ago. **There is no legal barrier to prevent those who suffer the consequences of crimes against humanity from**

claiming reparations, even though the crimes were committed against their ancestors. I argued that in law, the descendants who still suffer from the consequences of the crime have the right to restitution as much as the immediate victims. Under the British Foreign Compensation Act, which provided for reparations for those whose property had been sequestrated in Egypt, a person who is the owner *or the successor in title to the owner* could make a claim. The descendants of those whose property, including works of art, was seized by the Nazis, have successfully made claims for the restoration of the property.

To found a claim which is legally supportable, African claimants would have to show that they, the descendants of the transported captives, continue to suffer the consequences of the crime. I believe that the evidence of this is overwhelming. I wrote in the paper:

> On the African continent, flourishing civilisations were destroyed; ordered systems of government were broken up; millions of citizens were forcibly removed; and a pattern of poverty and underdevelopment directly resulted, which now affects nearly every resident of Africa. In the Americas, the slavery system gave rise to poverty, landlessness, underdevelopment, as well as to the crushing of culture and languages, the loss of identity, the inculcation of inferiority among Black people, and the indoctrination of Whites into a racist mindset – all of which continue to this day to affect the prospects and quality of Black people's lives in the Caribbean, USA, Canada and Europe.

There is no limitation period in international law. The countries which were damaged by the international slave trade, in Africa and the Americas, had no means of pressing a claim, because slavery was accompanied with colonialism which continued into the second half of the twentieth century. Only then could any former colony speak with independence on behalf of its people. In 1993 I said: "Indeed I would argue that now, as never before, is the right time for this claim to be made, as African leaders are speaking with a new confidence and operating new democratic structures." I was thinking particularly of the two wealthiest countries of Africa, Nigeria and South Africa, both of which were then on the verge of a transformation to democracy.

The claim would be brought on behalf of all Africans, in Africa and the Diaspora, who suffer the consequences of the crime, through the agency of an appropriate representative. With this proposition I was sailing into uncharted waters. Hundreds of millions of people in different parts of the world had an interest in the issue of reparations. Some minds are so daunted by the practical problems that they conclude that the claim

249

is unrealistic. But, I wrote: "Difficulties of scale or procedures should not be obstacles to justice. The unwillingness of the White world to consider the claim is not a reason for giving it up, but rather a spur to mobilising awareness and support around the issues." Governments in Africa and the Caribbean should neither be excluded from nor have sole control over the prosecution of the claim. Many who still suffer the consequences of slavery, in the United States and Britain for example, had no government which could speak to them. So some form of appropriate, representative and trustworthy body would be required.

The claim would be brought against the governments of those countries which promoted and were enriched by the African slave trade and the institution of slavery. I concentrated on governments because they fostered the trade and allowed it to continue; because they represent the countries which were enriched by the trade; and because they would be responsible for the international conventions and agreements which a reparations package would require. I thought that trying to identify and make claims against individual companies, or the descendants of plantation owners or slave traders, would create many problems in international law. But in the case of works of art, stolen from Africa and held in individual collections, the principle of restitution demanded that they should be returned to the people from whose shores they were taken.

The components of the claim would be assessed and formulated in each region affected by the institution of slavery. With this proposition I was suggesting that the concept of reparations would cover a wide spectrum of demands. The damage could be classified and researched under different headings. There was economic damage, cultural damage, social damage, psychological damage. Another approach would be to look at the extent of the enrichment of the various slave-trading and slave-owning nations. Recognising that I did not know the answers to the difficult questions which were raised, I sketched the broad elements of a package which might include: an apology by the governments of the slave trading nations to Africans world wide; the cancellation of debt; programmes of development in the inner cities where African descendants suffer still from the racism inculcated in the days of slavery; the rebuilding of the infrastructure of the African continent, once a land of well developed trading networks; facilitation of the return to Africa of those, including Rastafarians, who long to go to the continent from which their ancestors were taken. I suggested that the very process of formulating and negotiating the claim would be "an educative process through which the horrors of the past will be re-examined".

The claim, if not settled by agreement, would be determined by a special international tribunal recognised by all parties. I noted that there was no court which would be competent to hear the claim for reparations. In cases where reparations had been paid in the past, once the legitimacy of the claim was accepted, the necessary mechanisms were established. A commission was set up to consider claims for reparations for American property confiscated in Iran. With the claim of the Japanese Americans, an Act of Congress was passed. The payment of reparations by Germany to Israel came about by voluntary agreement. I concluded that: "The international recognition of the justice of the claim is a condition precedent to the setting up of any machinery." In accepting the absence of any presently existing judicial body, I was recognising that the reparations claim, while based on legal principle, could only be realised by political agitation and moral persuasion.

The atmosphere at the conference in Abuja was dynamic. There were delegates from many parts of Africa, the United States, the Caribbean, Brazil and Britain. President Babangida's message, read by his vice president, opened the conference. He spoke of the independence and civil rights struggles and continued:

> The reparations movement seeks to preserve and forward the gains of these earlier struggles, to make Africa progress into the next century and beyond, and to make our continent and its scattered people one and whole again. Reparations combine morality with logic and historical necessity by claiming the right of the injured to compensation. If history demonstrates that Africans have been injured by slavery and colonialism, and if morality demands that injury be compensated, then the logic of the reparations movement is established alongside its morality.

He warned the conference against seeing reparations as seeking revenge or proceeding in anger and ill-will. The reparations movement had no element of racism, but called upon men and women of all races to help put an end to the hatred and contempt that divided the human race over the past six hundred years.

It was heady stuff. Chief Abiola, chairing the conference with panache, pledged that if he was elected president in June, he would take the case for reparations to the United Nations. "Our legs have been broken by

slavery and colonialism, and we must insist that these legs be mended."
He concluded that the claim for reparations was not about vengeance;
rather, it is about justice. "It is justice we demand; by the grace of God, it
is justice we will get." There were messages from the presidents of Senegal
and Cuba. The Secretary General of the Organisation of African Unity,
Salim Ahmed Salim from Tanzania, said that this was a crusade which went
beyond financial considerations. "It will be the overwhelming mobilisation
in pursuit of justice, time and space and for the dignity of man."

Dudley Thompson gave a speech which vibrated with his passionate
Pan-Africanism. He quoted from Dr W.E.B Dubois' speech to the First Pan-
African Congress, held in Paris in 1919: "The problem of the 20th century
is the problem of the colour line." He acknowledged the Black leaders
who had inspired him: Marcus Garvey, Kwame Nkrumah, Jomo Kenyatta,
George Padmore, Toussaint L'Ouverture, Franz Fanon, Martin Luther
King, Nelson Mandela. In his person, and through his achievements,
Dudley symbolised the re-uniting of African peoples. Pan-Africanism, he
said, was not a plea for charity. "It is the burden of this Conference to show
that the reparations aspect of Pan-Africanism rests on a basic philosophy
as old as justice itself; it rests not only on an unassailable moral ground,
but on ancient and modern precedents." He quoted from Dr King's dream
that "one day the sons of former slaves and the sons of former slave owners
will be able to sit down together at the table of brotherhood".

I befriended one of the delegates from Brazil, and helped her to
translate her message from Portuguese, learning at the same time
how Afro-Brazilians suffered from "an ideology of the desirability of
whiteness", which had led to "the negation of our racial identity". I listened
to Dr Ronald Walters of Howard University, who led the USA delegation,
who spoke of the struggle for reparations as "yet another chapter in the
decolonisation of the African mind." My own paper was well received
by the delegates, but not I think by the European diplomatic observers,
who clamoured to have copies. I remembered a recent exchange with a
leading Foreign Office diplomat, Sir Anthony Goodenough, whom I had
first met when he was high commissioner to Ghana. On hearing that I
was preparing a paper on Reparations, he had reacted with consternation,
and told me, only half in jest, that the British government should get
reparations for their role in suppressing the slave trade after the Abolition
Act had been passed.

I believe that what disturbs the British profoundly about the concept
of reparations is that it changes the whole basis of the dialogue between
Black and White, North and South, Europeans and Africans. Instead

of African pleas for aid to be dispensed by a benevolent and kindly Europe, the Abuja conference demanded justice from a Europe which had committed crimes. British imperial history has often been characterised by hypocritical assertions of moral superiority by the colonisers. They went into Africa on a 'civilising mission' and committed barbarities. They brought 'Christian values' to the Caribbean and allowed slaves to be whipped and worked to death. They portrayed emancipation in 1838 as a gift from Britannia to grateful slaves, forgetting that it was only through slave rebellions in the Caribbean and popular demonstrations in Britain that the ending of slavery was finally conceded by a ruling class which had resisted the demands for it during the previous forty years. They paid £20 million in compensation to the slave owners (roughly 40% of Britain's national budget at the time), and not a penny to the slaves.

The Abuja declaration, passed at the end of the Conference, challenged this version of history. It declared that the damage sustained by African peoples was "not a thing of the past, but is painfully manifest in the damaged lives of contemporary Africans from Harlem to Harare, in the damaged economies of the Black world from Guinea to Guyana, from Somalia to Suriname". It drew attention to the historic precedents of reparations paid to Jews and Japanese Americans. It observed that compensation for injustice could be paid both in capital transfer and in other forms of restitution. It declared the delegates' conviction that the claim for reparations was well grounded in international law, and urged the OAU to set up a legal committee on the issue. In a generous recognition of the unity of Africans, it exhorted African states to grant entrance of right to all persons of African descent, and the right to obtain residence. It urged those countries which were enriched by slavery to give total relief from foreign debt. It called for a permanent African seat on the Security Council of the United Nations. It emphasised that "what matters is not the guilt but the *responsibility* of those states and nations whose economic evolution once depended on slave labour and colonialism." It called for the return to Africa of stolen artifacts and traditional treasures. It recommended the setting up of national reparations committees in Africa and the Diaspora. Finally, it called upon the international community "to recognise that there is a unique and unprecedented moral debt owed to the African peoples which has yet to be paid – the debt of compensation to the Africans as the most humiliated and exploited people of the last four hundred years".

I wish that I could say that the Abuja conference led to the case for reparations being speedily put on the world agenda, as the framers of the Abuja Declaration had intended. In fact the exhilaration of Abuja was followed within two months by the disaster of the aborted Nigerian elections. Everything looked set for the return of democracy in Nigeria. The run-off was between two presidential candidates who were both representative of business interests. Between the two, Chief Abiola appeared the more popular. But after the elections were held on 12th June 1993, the government refused to publish the results. They were leaked on 18th June by the Campaign for Democracy. Chief Abiola had comfortably defeated his rival industrialist, winning 19 out of 30 states. On 23rd June President Babangida announced that the elections had been annulled. The National Electoral Commission was suspended and no further challenges were allowed through the courts of law. President Babangida stepped down in favour of an interim Head of Government, but the real power was with General Sani Abacha, Minister of Defence, who in November 1993 took power and reinstated military rule.

Chief Abiola, who declared himself to be the lawful president, went into hiding and was arrested in June 1994. He remained in prison in humiliating solitary confinement during the whole of General Abacha's military rule, until the general died in May 1998. A month later Chief Abiola also died, still in prison.

The aborting of the election and the imprisonment of Chief Abiola dealt a bitter blow to the campaign for reparations. He was the continent's most vocal spokesman on the issue, and as President of Nigeria he would have had the authority to raise it internationally. Working with Dudley Thompson as Jamaican ambassador, he would have brought together African and Caribbean nations and the broader African diaspora. The campaign would have had resources behind it; after he had gone there was no one able and willing to fund meetings or publications or other initiatives. It was a tragedy for the wider interests of Africa, since I believe that Chief Abiola had the moral stature and political support which would have changed the standing of Nigeria in the world.

As I watched these events unfold, I wondered why they had happened. I never heard of any convincing reason for the annulment of the elections. It was an extreme action which shattered Nigeria's image in the world. It seemed so unnecessary and wrong. I suspected, and still suspect, that a part was played by Britain and the United States, between them the biggest outside influences on Nigeria. The coming to power of Chief Abiola was threatening to them, not because of anything in his economic or social programmes, but because of his dominant and determined role in the movement for reparations. The demand for justice which he had proclaimed from the podium at Abuja would have vibrated ominously through the Foreign and Commonwealth Office and the State Department. Had they persuaded General Babangida, in spite of his enthusiastic message to the Conference, that Chief Abiola would not be an acceptable President of Nigeria?

It would be another eight years before the issue of reparations would be mentioned at an international conference in Africa. If the motive for the removal of Chief Abiola had been to set back the cause of reparations, those who planned it had succeeded, at least for a limited time.

21

REPARATIONS REVISITED

I came back from Abuja to Jamaica. My paper, "The Legal Basis of the Claim for Reparations", was published on five successive Sundays in the *Gleaner*, and I earned a reputation for being a reparations advocate. Jamaicans seemed puzzled by my position. Most people, I suspect, felt it to be a lost cause, and saw it as one of my likeable eccentricities that I espoused such an anti-British position. Some radical activists showed resentment at the fact that I, a White European, had become a reparations expert.

The most supportive Jamaican was Jah Lloyd, a Rastafarian who had been advocating reparations for many years. He was an irrepressible personality, always coming to me with schemes which were usually sound in theory but fizzled in practice. Some of his ideas were based on his belief in 'Theocracy Government', which essentially meant the restoration of the Ethiopian monarchy and its extension to Jamaica. On that we agreed to differ, but there was much else we could share. Jah Lloyd understood that reparation was not the same thing as repatriation, and we both agreed that repatriation should be part of any reparations package. Jah Lloyd welcomed my paper without reservation, and we remained close until he was finally able to make a journey to his beloved Ethiopia. He fell ill in Addis Ababa and died on African soil.

The Jamaica Committee on Reparations was revived and I went to some of its meetings. One evening I was challenged by Ibo Cooper, the musician. He berated me for confining my advocacy of reparations to audiences in Africa and the Caribbean. He said that if I really believed in it, I should be speaking to my own people in Britain who most needed persuading. I mulled over this conversation for a long time, and saw that he had a point. I had a ready-made platform in the heart of Britain's Parliament, and it was time that I used it.

Since setting up a residence in Jamaica I had been an absentee member of the House of Lords. I had made only one speech there, protesting about the treatment of Jamaicans at Gatwick Airport. But I was still a member with full rights, including the right to initiate debates. I knew that by putting down a question on the House of Lords order paper, I would be able to get a hearing in a matter of months. So in the Parliamentary Report for 14th March 1996, it is printed that at 9.18 p.m. "Lord Gifford rose to ask Her Majesty's Government whether they will make appropriate reparations to African nations and to the descendants of Africans for the damage caused by the slave trade and the practice of slavery." In the gallery were friends who included Bernie Grant MP and the Jamaican historian Richard Hart, and High Commissioners from Africa and the Caribbean. I had invited them to give me moral support in what I knew to be unfriendly territory.

I summarised the horrors of the transatlantic slave trade and the consequences which continue to flow from it: poverty, landlessness, the new shackles of debt, and the persistence of the philosophy of racial superiority which "continues to poison our society today". I referred to the historic precedents, and added a new one which I had just learned about. In November 1995 the Queen had personally signed the Waikato-Raupatu Claims Settlement Bill in New Zealand. Through this bill the New Zealand Government apologised for the seizure of Maori lands by British settlers in 1863, and paid substantial compensation in land and in money to the Maori people. The presence of the Queen symbolised the recognition of an ancient grievance. It was a telling example of how, over a century after the illegal act, effective reparation can be made.

I went through some of the elements of an appropriate reparations package: an apology at the highest level; the cancellation of debt; the return of treasures and works of art; programmes of development in Africa and the Caribbean; and promoting equal rights and justice within the countries of the West. I ended with a plea that all of us would be healed if we moved in this direction:

> As we move to the next millennium, none of us can deny that there is a growing divide between North and South, between Black and White, across frontiers and within frontiers. It is in the interest of all of us to recognise that the reasons for that divide lie in a shameful past. If we realise that, we will be on the way to doing something to repair the wrong which was done, even

though it may cost heavily in terms of pride and revenue. The steps to be taken will bring a happier world for all our children.

Immediately a conservative Lord, Lord Burnham, intervened with a question: "My Lords, before the noble Lord sits down, can he tell the House which country first stopped the slave trade?" I saw the old trick. To offset my condemnation of Britain for the crimes of slavery, he wanted me to praise Britain for ending the crime. I was not quite sure of the answer to the question, so I answered guardedly:

> My Lords, after carrying it on and profiting massively from it, the slave trade was stopped by the nations of Europe. I pay tribute to the ancestor of the noble Lord, Lord Wilberforce, who played a leading part in stopping the trade. However, no compensation was paid when it was stopped and the unredressed grievance remains with us today.

Richard Hart in the gallery managed to pass down a note. It corrected the assumption behind Lord Burnham's question. At a later stage in the debate, when another Lord, Viscount Falkland, was trumpeting the achievements of the British abolitionists, I intervened to say: "My Lords, the noble Viscount is interesting and erudite in his history, but I am sure that he will accept that it was the Danes who were the first European nation to abolish the slave trade. We followed them six years later." I was glad that I had not fallen into the trap which Lord Burnham had set for me.

My reference to Wilberforce was a courteous recognition of the presence in the House of the present Lord Wilberforce, an eminent law lord, descendant of William Wilberforce MP. As president of Anti-Slavery International, which campaigns against modern slavery, he made a speech in the debate. He was not satisfied with the legal case for reparations. He said that in the cases which I had cited the guilty party was clear – the German state in the case of the Jews. And there were "identifiable victims of the wrong and direct and assessable consequences". He did not find those conditions satisfied in the case of the African slave trade. However, he accepted that there was a moral responsibility to mitigate the consequences of slavery. He referred to the low prices for commodities and the burden of debt, "which is itself a form of slavery". He ended by saying: "The case now is not one of guilt but of morality."

Not all the speeches reached the same lofty tone. Lord Willoughby de Broke thought that reparations "breed envy and distrust and stir up hatred". But he thanked me for initiating the debate, "because looking at the clock, I find I have missed the train home and I shall claim appropriate reparations by way of an overnight allowance". The Viscount of Falkland, who had worked in East Africa, said: "The African people are immensely forgiving. To encourage the kind of attitude of fervent desire for reparation suggested here would go against the grain, certainly among Africans, because it is not in their nature." Lord Gisborough said: "Almost every country was responsible for slavery in those days, including the French, the Spanish and the Blacks themselves." Declaring the idea of reparations to be absurd, he asked, "Where would it stop?"

The strongest speech in my support came from Lord Judd, speaking for the Labour opposition. As Frank Judd MP, he had been a member of the Committee for Freedom in Mozambique, Angola and Guiné which I had chaired in the early 1970s. He was kind enough to say that I spoke in the tradition of Thomas Clarkson and William Wilberforce. He said that it was not only slavery but colonialism which had brought a tragic aftermath. He traced the connection between Belgian colonial policies and the genocide in Rwanda. Then he spoke eloquently about the costs of structural adjustment in Africa. He described how the burdens of debt were crippling Uganda, Zambia, Tanzania and other countries. He described as "unproductive madness" how billions of pounds of development aid were diverted into servicing multilateral debt.

Lord Chesham replied to the debate on behalf of the Conservative Government. Predictably, he said that while slavery was "a moral outrage", the Government did not accept that there was a case for reparations. But for the first time the Government of a former slave-trading nation was obliged to set out the reasons for being against reparations. He said that first, slavery was practised by Arabs and Africans as well as Europeans. Second, African leaders were active participants in the slave trade. Third, it was not the British Government which traded in slaves but individual traders and companies. Fourth, there was no evidence that the effects of slavery were still being felt by Africans now living in Africa and the Diaspora. Fifth, racism was not just a Black and White problem, but occurs between different ethnic groups all over the world. Sixth, it would be impossible to say which Africans should benefit from reparations.

Lord Chesham described the payment of reparations by Germany and Japan and Iraq as "a red herring". As for the Queen's apology to the Maoris, the situation was entirely different. "It was not a question of slavery but one of the possession of land resulting from war." I said to myself, so what? Both were crimes against international law, and the suffering caused by the slave trade was on a huger scale, requiring greater atonement.

Part of Lord Chesham's response was intended to push the blame for the slave trade onto other people. The Arabs and the Africans were involved. It was not the Government but the individual traders. Other ethnic groups practice racism. Lawyers call it the *tu quoque* (you too) defence. I was not impressed, especially since the early British slave trading ventures were conducted by the Royal African Company under a Charter signed by King Charles II in 1672. The trade was sanctioned by British law and tenaciously supported by the British Parliament, until its abolition in 1807. It was a distortion of history for Lord Chesham to say that "responsibility for British involvement in the transatlantic slave trade does not rest on the shoulders of the British government".

I was interested by Lord Chesham's fourth reason. He was, I believe, profoundly wrong to claim that there is no evidence of the slave trade having damaging effects on African people today. Living in Jamaica I see the evidence daily, in terms of poverty, underdevelopment, inequality of resources, family breakdown, and the frequency with which disputes are settled with violence. The persistence of racism and racial discrimination against Black people in the United States and Britain arises directly from the doctrines of racial superiority which were used to justify the trade. As to Africa, the slave trade robbed it of millions of its strongest people. Walter Rodney, in his classic work *How Europe Underdeveloped Africa* (1972), shows how the population of Africa stagnated between 1650 and 1850, while that of Europe and Asia grew almost threefold. To me there can be no doubt that the systematic squeezing of Africa for the extraction of profits for Europe, was the ruination of a continent that boasted some of the most civilised kingdoms of the world in the pre-slavery era.

However, the corollary of Lord Chesham's fourth reason was that if the evidence could be shown, at least a moral case could be made out. I have no doubt that those who run Britain are well aware of the moral strength behind the arguments for reparation. They know that the history of the British plantations in the Americas, and how they were supplied with labour, is shameful. They try to deny the connection because to admit it would logically entail measures of compensation being implemented. Lord Chesham's statement was a challenge to the proponents of reparation to gather the evidence and prove him wrong.

I found the debate to be very instructive. I was impressed by the approach of Lord Wilberforce, that the issue was moral rather than legal. Although I still consider that the case for reparations is based on the principles of international law, I do not argue that it is a kind of super-litigation which could be brought before some court at some time. Rather it is a question of facing up to a fundamental injustice which permanently affected the relationship between African and European people. The process of facing up to what was done in the past, and its consequences, will necessitate measures of atonement and reparation to level the playing field. I see it as a healing process, not a conflict.

In 2000 I was introduced to a particular reparations claim which fascinated me. It was being advanced by the Garifuna people. Who are they? you may ask. They are the descendants of the 'Black Caribs' who lived in the island of St Vincent in the Caribbean before the invasion of the British in the eighteenth century. They were probably a mix of native Caribs and free Africans. They refused to be enslaved or colonised. They occupied the mountainous areas of St Vincent and made it impossible for the British to control the island.

One person who knew their story was Richard Hart. He lent me a book, published in 1795 by a British planter, called "An Account of the Black Charaibs in the Island of St Vincent's". It describes the planters' attempts to subdue these rebellious people, who made agreements with both the British and the French, using one against the other for their own advantage. The author laid before the agent of the British Government the nub of the problem:

> Without interposition of the strong hand of Government, it is feared that the most healthy, rich and beautiful island of St Vincent's may, to all intents of national advantage, be lost to the crown of Great Britain. Mere regulations respecting the Charaibs can no longer be deemed effectual. Laws cannot reach them in their woods. The British planter can no more trust to professions. The nation can have no further confidence in treaty. Under all these circumstances and considerations, the Council and Assembly of St Vincent's in the instructions to their agent in London, declare the sole alternative to be – *That the British planters, or the Black Charaibs, must be removed from off the island of St. Vincent's.*

The British Government chose the alternative of removing the Black Caribs. It sent a large expeditionary force to St Vincent which rounded up 5,000 men, women and children and imprisoned them on a barren island, where many died of malnutrition and disease. In 1797 over 2,000 survivors were herded onto British ships and ferried over a thousand miles to an island off the coast of Honduras, where they were dumped and left to die.

The Garifuna (as the Black Caribs called themselves) did not die, but settled in Honduras and neighbouring countries. They faced discrimination wherever they went, but they survived, and so did their language. In 2000 they held the first World Garifuna Congress. Their paramount chief Dr Theodore Aranda invited me to deliver an address at the opening of the Congress, held in the town of Dangriga in the south of Belize. Several hundred Garifuna had gathered, some speaking Spanish (from Honduras, Guatemala, and Nicaragua) and some speaking English (from Belize, St Vincent and the United States). I attended a preliminary meeting of a group of delegates on the eve of the conference. Dr Aranda explained that as some spoke no English and others spoke no Spanish, they would be speaking Garifuna which they all understood.

The following morning, before the Congress, there was a Catholic service held in the Garifuna language. Children read from the Bible in Garifuna. They recited the Garifuna prayer to 'Bungiu Baba' (Lord God), which included a plea for God's help for reparation and development ('Luma aranderuni, Lumagien awanseruni'). The language had been preserved as a living tongue during over 200 years of exile in different countries.

I spoke about the international legal principle of reparation, and applied it to what was undoubtedly a criminal act committed by the British in 1797: the forcible removal and attempted destruction of an entire people. I said that a united and sustained effort would be needed to obtain justice from Britain. Public opinion in Britain had to be informed, since few people knew of the Garifuna. There was a dissenting tradition in Britain, people and organisations which would be most supportive if they only knew the story. I quoted the famous Bob Marley song: "Get Up, Stand Up, Stand Up For Your Rights." I suggested that a Garifuna delegation should visit Britain, and I promised to help them with introductions. So far nothing has come of this; but I retain a sweet memory of this people who have refused over so long to give up their heritage and their language.

In 2001 the United Nations convened the World Conference against Racism, Racial Discrimination, Xenophobia and Related Intolerance. It was to be held in Durban, South Africa. In the preparations for the conference new life was breathed into the reparations issue. For how could the world discuss racism without mentioning the causes? Several African governments insisted that the past must be on the agenda. In a 'non-paper' prepared in advance of the conference by the group of African nations, some key themes were inserted into the conference draft resolutions:

- "Remembering the past, unequivocally condemning its major racist tragedies, and telling the truth about history are essential elements for international reconciliation."
- "An explicit apology should be extended by States which practised, benefited or unjustly enriched themselves from slavery and the slave trade."
- Those who benefited were urged "to assume full responsibility through, inter alia, enhanced remedial development policies, programmes and concrete measures".

This was a call for reparations in all but name.

The United States responded with a 'non-paper' of its own. "We would like the World Conference against Racism to focus on the current form and manifestations of racism as it was intended to do by the UN General Assembly, rather than to apportion blame for past injustices or seek to exact compensation for these acts." The US agreed that slavery and the slave trade "must be acknowledged, discussed, learned from and condemned", but "we simply do not believe that it is appropriate to address this history – and its many and vast aspects – through such measures as international compensatory measures". The US was "willing to join others in expressing regret for involvement in those historical practices", but "we are not willing to agree to anything that suggests present-day liability on the part of one state to another for that historical situation".

I had not been to South Africa since the historic democratic elections of 1994. Since then the work of the Truth and Reconciliation Commission (TRC) had begun and ended its work. I had followed the reports of the TRC with admiration. Under the chairmanship of Archbishop Tutu, it had shown the world that it was possible for gross injustices to be exposed and confronted. The new South Africa seemed to be the right place in which the world would meet and talk about the evil of racism. I had to be in Jamaica during the week before the Conference, and at the Bloody Sunday Inquiry in Northern Ireland the week after. But I could not resist taking the trip, from Kingston to London to Johannesburg to Durban, to be there for an all too short six days.

I discovered that the exciting part of the conference was taking place outside the conference hall, in the Forum of Non-Governmental Organisations which was based in a nearby cricket stadium. There was a buzz of activity as thousands of participants in different tents discussed the vast spectrum of topics to be addressed in the Conference. I raised my voice from the floor at a meeting on Reparations, and addressed a meeting which was organised by the International Association of Democratic Lawyers. I was touched when Congressman John Conyers, who year after year had tabled a motion in Congress calling for a Commission to study Reparations for African Americans, came to the meeting and praised my speech. Also at the meeting was South African law lecturer Max du Plessis who had written an academic paper on the issue of Reparations for Slavery and Colonialism. Quoting extensively on my paper and House of Lords speech, he concluded, like Lord Wilberforce, that legal claims would fail, but that the call for reparation, in some form, "surely has a legitimate moral grounding".

I was not part of the intense negotiating that took place behind the scenes on the wording of the Conference Final Declaration. I have heard that the Caribbean delegations, especially from Jamaica and Barbados, played a pivotal role. The United States had walked out of the Conference, expressing displeasure about the way in which two key issues – rights of Palestinians, and reparation – were being dealt with. But the European governments, led by the British and the French, were there to prevent anything too radical being included in the Declaration. The alliance of African and Caribbean delegations pushed for a clear statement that the transatlantic slave trade was a crime against humanity.

The Final Declaration stated that "we profoundly regret the massive human suffering" caused by slavery and the slave trade. It acknowledged that the slave trade and slavery "are a crime against humanity and should always have been so" (fudging the issue as to whether it was a crime against humanity at the time). It noted that "some States have taken the initiative to apologise, and have paid reparation, where appropriate, for grave and massive violations committed". Those who had not taken such initiatives were urged "to find appropriate ways to do so". It noted further: "We are aware of the moral obligation on the part of all concerned States and call upon these States to take appropriate and effective measures to halt and reverse the lasting consequences of those practices."

The Conference Declaration reeks of compromise and imprecise language. That was inevitable, given the conflicting interests of the different participants. What was important was that there was a successful attempt to face up to the connection between the horrors of the past and the racism and poverty of today. There was plenty in the Declaration, and its accompanying Programme of Action, for activists to work on. Much more was said on the subject of reparation than the former slave-owning states would have liked.

In Jamaica the conference brought to life the Jamaican Reparations Movement, now guided by the Rastafarian activist Barbara Blake Hannah who had been part of Jamaica's delegation to the conference. The problem in Jamaica is that while many people are sympathetic, few are prepared to give time or money to the work of an organisation. Musicians have put the theme of reparations into their songs, but attempts to organise a fund-raising concert have so far fallen flat. In a country where so many people are struggling to survive economically, they have little space or energy for voluntary effort. On the positive side, there is now a committee set up by the prime minister to work on the commemoration of the 200th Anniversary of the Abolition of the Slave Trade. In Jamaica there is no contradiction between the interests of government and the aspirations of the reparations movement. Officially the Government supports the call for reparations, but it seems constrained by its economic situation from speaking out too vocally on the issue.

In the wider Caribbean, Barbados in October 2002 hosted the Africa and African Descendants Conference against Racism. It was intended as a follow-up to the Durban Conference. Barbados, taking the lead in the Caribbean, had set up an official Commission for Pan African Affairs, which sponsored the conference. Unfortunately the conference split over a dispute as to whether White people should take part, and a vote was taken to exclude 'non-African-descended people'. The reparations claim is an issue in which all races have a part to play; yet I understand the anger which comes from bitter experience, and which exploded with this decision. Too often White people, in England especially, have insisted on leading struggles against racism and apartheid, pushing Black people to the sidelines when they should be in the lead. However there was no danger of this in the Reparations Conference. The campaign for Reparations has always been led by Black people, in Africa and elsewhere. The problem has been to get White people interested at all. The decision of the Conference was wrong, and the reports of it overshadowed the positive work which the Conference did.

In recent years the most spectacular gains of the movement for Reparations have been in the United States. The National Coalition of Blacks for Reparations in America (NCOBRA) has grown into a powerful movement. It has achieved important local successes. In January 2005 the bank J.P.Morgan Chase came under pressure from the City of Chicago to declare its historical links to slavery if it wished to do business with the city. It revealed that its predecessor banks in Louisiana had allowed 13,000 slaves to be used as collateral on loans. In 1,250 cases the borrowers defaulted and the collateral was seized by the bank. J.P.Morgan apologised and created a $5 million scholarship for African-American students in Louisiana. While the response of the company has been criticised as inadequate, the precedent is being followed in other cities in the US. American lawyers have also been in the forefront of the campaign, bringing a number of lawsuits against companies whose predecessors were involved in slavery. The suits have so far failed, on the basis that too long a time has passed; but they have proved to be an important focus for publicity and mobilisation.

During 2005 I was invited to speak at a conference on "Historic Injustices: Restitution and Reconciliation in International Perspective", at Brown University, the prestigious Ivy League college in Providence, Rhode Island. Providence had been a major slave trading port. The conference included an excellent presentation made by a local White activist whose family had been leading slave traders. She showed a moving film of the journey made by her and her relatives, back to the slave castles in Ghana where her family's slaves had been held captive. Another speaker was Dr Mongane Wally Serote, South African poet and freedom fighter, who had been Arts Minister in the first ANC government. I had known him in exile in London, and it was joyous to meet him again and to learn that he was now director of the Freedom Park in Pretoria, a project dedicated to the memory of all who died in South Africa's conflicts over the centuries.

I spoke of my audience with the Queen Mother of the Ashantis, and about the value of an apology. As I did so, I looked into the eyes of the President of Brown University, Professor Ruth Simmonds, the first Black head of an Ivy League university and one of the convenors of the conference. I said:

> Most White people find it impossible, either at a national or a personal level, to say, 'My people did your people a grievous wrong. I apologise, and I want to do what is necessary to remedy the damage which that wrong has caused.' Yet it would be such a healing thing to say. Both Black and White societies are sick from the consequences of slavery. Black societies around the world are economically sick, deprived of land, psychologically made to feel inferior. White societies are spiritually sick, deprived of soul, psychologically

266

infected with racial prejudice. I advocate the cause of reparations because a just society which faces the horrors of its past is a happier society for me as well as for you.

Speaking to the mainly White audience, I said: "I believe that White people should be responding positively to this movement in a spirit of brotherly love, and in recognition of the justice of the case for reparations. It is not a question of guilt, but of responsibility. You and I are not to blame for the institution of slavery, but we would be to blame if we did nothing to rectify the injustices which are still being suffered because of slavery. Reparation is about reconciliation, not about conflict. The conflict will happen if we refuse to listen to those who have a just cause."

That speech sums up what I feel about the reparations issue. I have not changed much from the position which I took in Abuja in 1993. I have moved more clearly into believing that the issue is about reconciliation between the race which was grossly abusive and the race which was grossly abused. The difficulty is that the abusing race will not recognise its own responsibility. I said at Brown University:

> The reluctance of White Europeans and White Americans to come to terms with the historic injustice of slavery is caused, I believe, by both the depth of the prejudice and the magnitude of the issues to be faced. The notions of White virtue are so ingrained that they cannot admit to the barbarities which their ancestors committed. If they respond at all to the claims of Black people for justice, it is by way of 'development aid' or 'anti-discrimination laws', which imply that their generosity is bestowing benefits on the poor suffering Blacks. It is easier to help victims than to pay compensation for past crimes.

That is the attitude which needs to be rejected as we approach a historic anniversary. In 2007 the 200th anniversary of the abolition of the slave trade will be commemorated. I fear that it will be used mainly to praise the British abolitionists. It is easier to take pride in having ended an evil than to express shame in having carried out that evil for centuries. I fear also that the sacrifice of the Caribbean peoples who rebelled, at huge cost to their lives, in Haiti and Jamaica and Barbados and Guyana and elsewhere will be overlooked.

And yet this anniversary could be the turning point. Already one pillar of the British establishment, the Church of England, has voted to apologise to the descendants of victims of the slave trade. Its General Synod recognised that a church organisation, the Society for the Propagation of the Gospel, had owned the Codrington Plantation in Barbados, where slaves had the word 'SOCIETY' branded on their backs with a red-hot iron. The Church had been compensated when its slaves were emancipated. Now the Archbishop of Canterbury shared in the apology for the evil which was done in the Church's name. The British Government should use the anniversary to make its own apology, and having done so, to sit down and discuss what should be done by way of amends.

The issue will not go away for as long as Black people are mistreated and White people feel racially superior. The French Government has made a grand gesture in naming May 10th as a national day of commemoration of the suffering of slaves. The British Government can do something less grandiose but more lasting, as well as more difficult. It can take a giant step towards reconciliation by expressing its apology for the appalling crimes which were committed in its name against the people of Africa, and its determination to make appropriate reparation.

22

LOOKING
forward

I have written about the reasons why I love my work in the law. Another reason which I now appreciate is that if you are an independent advocate, no one can retire you. At the age of 66 I look forward to many years of active practice in Jamaica and in Britain. I will not cut my links with either country, so transatlantic flights will continue to be part of my life. Flying from London to Kingston, I find that I can go into court the next day without any problem. Flying from Kingston to London, I need a clear day to beat the jet lag.

Jamaica continues to draw me because of its beauty and its climate and the spirit of its people. It draws me because my daughter Sheba is still at school in Kingston. It draws me because of the variety of the cases which come across my desk. When Jamaica joins the Caribbean Court of Justice there will be opportunities to cross the Caribbean and present cases to the court. Yet sometimes the frustrations of living in a third world economy overwhelm me. Justice is so slow. I feel sad when I have to explain to a client that it may take four years before his case will be tried. Especially where poor people have been wronged, their pain and their needs are so acute that the hope of eventual justice is of little comfort.

The problems of an economy which is overburdened with debt are seen in every aspect of the life of the country. While the rich live in beautiful houses, but behind burglar bars on every door and window, thousands of poor people are out of work, and many of them are drawn into crime as a way of earning quick money. Between the rich and the poor there is the mass of wage-carners for whom life is a daily struggle. I was in court recently in May Pen, which is connected to Kingston by a new twenty mile toll road. The clerk of the court apologised for being late because on his salary he could not afford to pay the toll.

The education system is under stress. Sheba goes to a good school, but there are 43 girls in her class and her access to laboratory equipment and computers is limited. Medical costs are prohibitive unless you are covered by an insurance scheme at work. The police are underpaid, and an unknown number of officers supplement their incomes with bribes. Buses are overcrowded. Roads are full of potholes. The stresses of daily life erupt too often into domestic violence. Jamaicans tell me that people do not smile as they used to.

So there are times when I am eager to be in Britain again. Britain draws me because my son Tom, my grandson Joseph and my daughter Polly are living there. It draws me because of the dynamic political life of London, its mix of nationalities and the variety of its entertainments. It draws me because I am head of a chambers of sixty barristers who have a commitment to justice and who miss my presence. And it draws me because of the fees which can be earned in solid pounds for work done on legal aid. As Sheba grows older I want to spread my time more equally between Britain and Jamaica.

The other place which does not stop calling to me is the continent of Africa. In 2005 I went back to my beloved Mozambique, for the first time in sixteen years. The country was celebrating thirty years of independence. I have described how its early promise had been smashed by the South African apartheid regime, which had trained terrorists to create chaos and bloodshed. It had been further ravaged by floods and drought and AIDS. It had to swallow the medicine of structural adjustment. The country was opened up to privatisation and foreign investment, and while some became rich the majority remained desperately poor, especially in the rural areas.

But as democracy took root in neighbouring South Africa, there were signs that Mozambique too was being reborn. Its membership of the Commonwealth, and its commitment to multiparty democracy, made it one of the preferred recipients of overseas aid. A new president had been elected, Armando Guebuza whom I had known as a young militant of FRELIMO when he came to speak at meetings organised by our committee. My friends in Mozambique were hoping that he would bring a new dynamism and commitment to poor people, in the manner of Samora Machel.

I was invited to be the guest of the Government at the anniversary celebrations. I booked a ticket with the help of my saved air miles, and flew via Johannesburg. As the plane flew in to Johannesburg airport, I realised that I had four hours to spare before my connexion to Maputo. I remembered my meeting with Wally Serote at Brown University, and I asked the first taxi driver I saw "how far is it to Pretoria?" It was less than an hour away, so I rang Wally and he laid on a young guide to take me around the Freedom Park. The first phase which had been completed was the Isivivane, meaning symbolic resting place. At the end of a walk uphill you see a circle of nine vast boulders. Each had come from a sacred place in the nine provinces of South Africa. There had been cleansing and healing ceremonies conducted by various faith based organisations, as each boulder was taken up and placed in the circle. A traditional healer Shirley Thebe described the meaning of the site: "It brings back home the spirits of those who were not accorded proper burials."

The completed project will include sculpture and other art forms, a museum, theatre and library. Its object is to continue the process of reconciliation. Its mission statement says:

> Freedom Park must stand as a monument to our new democracy founded on the values of human dignity, equality, human rights and freedom. A symbol of the tortuous journey to, and sacrifices made for freedom. A celebration of the achievement of the achievement of democracy and a beacon of hope and inspiration for the future.

Wally Serote has written: "This means facing our past, dealing with the pain, and 'treating' by cleansing the pain, to encourage healing, which of course takes a long time."

Standing in the middle of the stones I marvelled at the triumph of the new South Africa. Painfully, the ANC Government is not only dealing with the legacy of racial oppression, but also of gender oppression. In speaking of the new society, its leaders always describe it as non-racial, non-sexist, and democratic. Achieving the non-sexist ideal is a constant struggle, but uniquely in Africa, and as far as I know in the world, South Africans have articulated gender equality as a central aspect of their ideals. Freedom of sexual orientation is also enshrined in their Constitution. The eleven main languages of the country are all official languages. Four of them figure in the national anthem. The Constitutional Court, newly built on the site of the prison where both Mohandas Gandhi and Nelson Mandela were held, has delivered seminal judgments on human rights issues. South Africa already has so much to teach us.

I flew on to Maputo, where the independence parade was held, with thousands of Mozambicans processing through the streets, young and old, able-bodied and disabled. The images were positive, but of course they were not the whole story. A quick trip to meet the members of a neighbourhood court took me into slums as grim as anything in Kingston. I met up with Judge Sacramento, who took me to the impressive building where the Court of Appeal sat. I gave a talk to the students of the Legal and Judicial Training Institute, young people who were been trained to go into the provinces of Mozambique and to administer justice as magistrates and prosecutors. I heard from the British High Commissioner that British economic assistance was being channelled straight into budget support, a sign of Britain's trust in the integrity of Mozambique's government. I talked with President Guebuza. I renewed my faith in Mozambique which Eduardo Mondlane had first kindled in 1968.

I returned via London in time to watch the Live 8 concert in Hyde Park. The images of Africa which I then saw were of starving children and people on their knees. The performers were overwhelmingly White, and in the audience of 200,000 I could see only a tiny number of Black people. The message was that African children were dying and the good people of the West could save them by putting pressure on their governments. The causes of the disaster were said to be civil war, corruption and misgovernment. No presenter attributed any responsibility for Africa's problems to the policies of Western governments.

Yes, there is famine and civil war in parts of the African continent. But there are also many success stories. Mozambique, Namibia, Botswana, Tanzania, Ghana, Senegal, Mali and of course South Africa are some of the well-governed democracies where the dominant picture is far removed from the pathetic images on the screens in Hyde Park. I wish that Bob Geldof had shown less virtuous pity and more respectful solidarity, including having African artistes on the platform. Given the influence of Africans on the music of the West, and the objective of supporting Africa, to have a nearly all-White line-up was wrong.

But I do not dismiss the actions of the thousands who turned out to register their protest against the injustice of African poverty. They were showing the same sense of solidarity as the thousands in Britain 200 years ago who petitioned and campaigned to end the slave trade. It is not for the West to save Africa. Africans are capable of saving themselves. But if the leaders of the rich world, in response to the voice of the protestors, can remove the economic shackles in which they still keep Africa bound; if they can agree to pay back in a fraction of the wealth which they took from Africa, then African suffering will be reduced and its progress will be much accelerated. When that happens, the crowds in Hyde Park may understand that Africans can be role models and not just victims.

Tony Blair showed his compassion for Africa in a remarkable speech to the Labour Party Conference in October 2001. It was made a month after the World Conference against Racism had discussed reparations for the effects of slavery. He said: "The state of Africa is a scar on the conscience of the world. But if the world as a community focused on it, we could heal it. And if we don't, it will become deeper and angrier." He was right. Poverty breeds so many other evils. Because of poverty, people try to emigrate at whatever cost from Africa to Europe. Because of poverty, HIV/AIDS increases its toll on the peoples of Africa and they cannot be treated. Because of poverty, democracy becomes more fragile and civil war more likely. In spite of Blair's eloquence, the world community has not focused on Africa. Whether one argues from the perspective of reparation for past wrongs, or of moral obligation to the less fortunate, or of simple self-interest, the cause of African economic freedom is indeed our cause.

Looking back over forty years I see both huge advances and huge reverses in the promotion of human rights. Fascist regimes in Spain and Portugal and Greece are distant history. The communist dictatorships of the Soviet Union and Eastern Europe have fallen. Apartheid ended in South Africa with only limited loss of life. Throughout South and Central America, the hideous bloc of military juntas, supported by the United States, are no more. Instead there are popular democracies in many South American countries which are trying to find new means of using resources for the benefit of the masses.

Yet the extension of political rights in many parts of the world has been accompanied by a reduction of economic rights and a hideous growth in absolute poverty. In the slums of the vast cities of South America and Asia the lives of the underclass seem to be without hope. In the Caribbean region, Haiti continues to suffer, as it has for two centuries, for its effrontery in rebelling against European domination. President Aristide, when Haiti celebrated 200 years of independence, dared to demand back the equivalent of the 90 million gold francs which it was forced to pay to France in 1825 by way of 'reparation' for the lost 'property' (slaves) of the French settlers. He said that "poverty today is the result of a 200-year plot". His demand on France was made in January 2004. Two months later he had been ousted by the United States and forced into exile.

In Britain the growth in human rights consciousness in the legal profession and generally in the county has been exciting. Yet it has become as necessary as ever to fight against encroachments on personal freedoms. Internment without trial, introduced and then discredited in Northern Ireland in the 1970s, resurfaced in 2001 when the Anti-Terrorism, Crime and Security Act allowed the detention of nine Muslims indefinitely and without being charged, on the grounds that there was a situation in the aftermath of the September 11th attacks which "threatened the life of the nation". The House of Lords declared the measure to be incompatible with the Human Rights Act. Lord Hoffman said: "The real threat to the life of the nation, in the sense of a people living in accordance with its traditional laws and political values, comes not from terrorism but from laws such as these."

We are living with the consequences of the invasion of Iraq, a flagrant illegal act committed in the name of the American and British peoples. The invasion had no justification in international law. The people and their representatives were lied to, through bogus claims that Iraq possessed weapons of mass destruction. Bush and Blair have unleashed death and destruction and civil war. They have replaced the dictatorship of Saddam Hussein with the dictatorship of anarchy. The regime of Saddam would have ended in time, as all tyrannies have ended, through the actions of the Iraqi people. What Bush and Blair have created is a nightmare without end. Just as Bloody Sunday caused the ranks of the IRA to swell, so their invasion of Iraq has created al-Qa'ida networks in Iraq and elsewhere, including Britain, which were never there before. They justify the hellish prisons in Guantanamo Bay and other secret places where the rule of law does not reach. They have forfeited any claim to moral leadership in the world.

Osama bin Laden and his fellow conspirators of al-Qa'ida are criminals, using Islamic pretexts to justify their crimes and plots. I took part in the extradition hearing relating to two men who were accused of being involved in the bombings of the US Embassies in Nairobi and Dar-es-Salaam in 1998, and I read translations of al-Qa'ida communiqués. I was shocked at the ferocity with which all Americans, civilian or military, were targeted. But the way to deal with criminals is through sound criminal investigation, good intelligence, surveillance when necessary, and the patient police work through which crimes are prevented and detected. Good intelligence means working with British Muslims, not provoking them to anger and extremism through attacks on Muslim countries and bans on Muslim associations. When Blair proclaimed after the attacks in

London of 7th June 2005, that "the rules of the game have changed", he was expressing a sinister and authoritarian Anglo-American policy which has already perverted constitutional rights in the United States. Human rights advocates must resist it with all their eloquence and skill.

These are some of the challenges which face the passionate advocates of today. Some of the locations of human rights abuse have changed, but the principles for which we stand and the ways in which we uphold them have not. There is work to be done internationally, linking with brother and sister lawyers across the world. There is work to be done inside the country where you work, whether Britain or Jamaica or anywhere else. In Britain the Haldane Society of Socialist Lawyers has sprung to life under the leadership of Michael Mansfield and Richard Harvey. The Bar Human Rights Committee is active, and the Association of Human Rights Lawyers, with Lord Lester as its President, was recently launched with hundreds of founder members. There is so much scope for legal activism.

Human rights advocacy is not just about campaigns on the big issues. As I have tried to show, it is an attitude of mind and spirit which is put to use in the smallest case in the civil or criminal courts. Human rights are not just at risk through the policies of governments, but in the petty daily abuses of immigration officers, police officers, prison officers, town hall officials, human resource executives, and other public and private holders of office who have the power to wreck people's lives. The globalisation of the world means that poverty and acute need are not simply third world phenomena, but there are hundreds of thousands of exploited people, often immigrants or refugees, within the prosperous economies of Europe and the United States. They are equal before the law, and if you can vindicate their legal rights, your life will be enriched as well as theirs.

The work of each radical lawyer is a small stream which feeds the river of justice. It was flowing before we were born and it will continue to flow after we die. For myself, I am fortunate to have been part of the river and to have met some of those who have contributed copiously to it. One of them, Ian Ramsay, little known outside Jamaica and the Caribbean, was not just a superb and passionate advocate but also a mentor of young lawyers. He died before he could pass on any written account of his remarkable legal practice. I told him before he died that he had inspired me to write down my thoughts and experiences. That is why this book is dedicated to his memory.

Our work is full of intellectual and emotional demands. We witness a lot of human suffering, and some of it we cannot change. We strain to find the legal arguments through which justice can be done. In the middle of all the stress it is important for us to find our own inner balance. A stressed out lawyer will in the end be no good for his or her clients. Since 1997 I have found Tina, the person who balances my life. This book is also dedicated to her. She is even more passionate about injustice than I am, and she has put her own life on the line for the cause of freedom in Haiti. She is a creative artist who has surrounded me with beauty in my home and my office. She is a healer who knows the value of rest and calm in my energetic life. She is a spiritual person who often has to instruct her agnostic and down-to-earth husband that if we have faith in our own divine selves, we can go beyond today's anxieties and achieve miracles. With her beside me, I can look forward with eagerness to another decade or two of participation as an advocate in the noble profession of law.

Index of Case References

Readers who have access to law reports may wish to know the references to cases mentioned in this book which are reported:

p.40: The judge's decision to view Banaba Island is reported as *Tito v Waddell* [1975] 3 All ER 997. His final decision in favour of the islanders is at [1977] 3 All ER 129

p.45 Pat Arrowsmith unsuccessfully appealed against her conviction but her sentence was reduced: *R v Arrowsmith* [1975] 1 All ER 463

p.50 The appeals of the Garden House students are reported as *R v Caird and others* (1970) 54 Cr. App. R 499

p.54 Lord Denning's observations are from the Court of Appeal judgment in *Hunter v Chief Constable of West Midlands* reported at [1980] 2 All ER 227. The House of Lords upheld his judgment: [1981] 3 All ER 727

p.54 The unsuccessful appeal of the Birmingham Six is partly reported as *R v Callaghan and others* (1989) 88 Cr. App. R 40

p.144 The case of John Franklin is reported as *Vincent v R* [1993] 1 WLR 862

p.156 Huntley's case is reported as *Huntley v Attorney General of Jamaica* [1995] 1 All ER 308. For the Pratt and Morgan case see p.211 below.

p.164 The Bank's appeal and all other recent Privy Council cases can be found on the Privy Council website (www.privy-council.org.uk) by going to the relevant year and case number: in this case *National Commercial Bank (Jamaica) Limited v Raymond Hew and others* [2003] UKPC 51

p.164-6 *Gleaner Company Limited and another v Eric Anthony Abrahams*

[2003] UKPC 55; (2003) 63 WIR 157

p.166 *Clinton Bernard v Attorney General of Jamaica* [2004] UKPC 47; also reported at [2005] IRLR 398 and (2004) 65 WIR 245

p.169-70 *Kavanagh v Hiscock and another* [1974] 2 All ER 177

p.174-77 The full title of the Grand Lido case is *Village Resorts Limited v Industrial Disputes Tribunal and Uton Green (representing the Grand Lido Negril Staff Association)*. Its reference is Supreme Court Civil Appeal No. 66/97, decided on 30th June 1998. Unfortunately it is not in any published report – the Jamaica Law Reports have not been published for any year after 1997.

p.177 The decision in the Pinochet case relating to Lord Hoffmann's bias is *R v Bow Street Metropolitan Stipendiary Magistrate, ex parte Pinochet Ugarte (No. 2)* [1999] 1 All ER 577

p.178-80 *Jamaica Flour Mills Limited v Industrial Disputes Tribunal and National Workers Union* [2005] UKPC 16

p.181 The case on the implied duty of trust and confidence is *Malik v Bank of Credit and Commerce International SA* [1997] 3 All ER 1

p.191 The gay rights case in the European Court of Human Rights is reported as *Dudgeon v UK* (1981) 4 EHRR 149 or can be found via the European Court's website.

p.193 *Pratt v Attorney General of Jamaica* [1993] 4 All ER 769

p.194 *Lewis and others v Attorney General of Jamaica* [2000] UKPC 35, (2000)

277

57 WIR 275
p.195   *Lambert Watson v R* [2004] UKPC 34;
         (2004) 64 WIR 241
p.196   *State v Makwanyane* 1995 (3) SA 391
p.200   The cases referred to are *R v Mark*
         Sangster and Randal Dixon [2002]
         UKPC 58; (2002) 61 WIR 383; and *R*
         v Ricardo Williams [2006] UKPC 21
p.205-07 The challenge to the legislation
         setting up the CCJ was the case
         of *Independent Jamaican Council for*

Human Rights and others v Hon.
Syringa Marshall-Burnett and
Attorney General of Jamaica [2005]
UKPC 3; (2005) 65 WIR 268
p.215-17 The judgment of the Court
         of Appeal in the case about
         anonymity is reported as *R v Lord*
         Saville of Newdigate, ex parte A
         [1999] 4 All ER 860
p.245-46 *Chorzow Factory Case* (Germany v
         Poland) (1928) PCIJ Sr. A, No. 17

Index

Acknowledgements

The people who have most shaped this book are the human rights lawyers in many parts of the world who have been my guides, and the clients whose experiences of injustice I have tried to articulate. In the preparation of the book I thank Dudley Thompson, Polly Gaster, Maurice Saunders and Richard Harvey for their constructive criticisms; my family – especially Tom, Polly and Tamara – for their constant support; and Tina for her loving wisdom.

Anthony Gifford QC, a barrister in England and an attorney-at-law in Jamaica, has been involved throughout his legal career in seeking justice for those whose rights have been abused.

His publications include *Where's the Justice? A Manifesto for Law Reform* (1986); *South Africa's Record of International Terrorism* (1981); *The Broadwater Farm Inquiry: the Report of the Independent Inquiry into Disturbances at the Broadwater Farm Estate, Tottenham* (1986); *Broadwater Farm Revisited* (1989); *Loosen the Shackles: the Report of the Inquiry into Race Relations in Liverpool* (1989); as well as numerous articles in newspapers and legal journals.